Bless you, Carrie.

Thank you for the thrilling update on Abba's love in the Holy Land, and your undying pursuit of servanthood and He who created you!

Be filled with glory of the Living God with strength and courage.

Glenisaah Stauffer
Alberta, Canada
April 24, 2013

I always enjoy reading your adventures and the spiritual, emotional essence that embodies all your activities. I admire your love for the land and know that if you could, you'd stay forever.

Shana Tova. Hatzlacha in all your endeavors.

Much love,

Perrie Nordlicht
New York, USA
September 22, 2014

Carrie of Canada, welcome home with a warm embrace!

Thanks again for sharing this one last adventure in the land, your home away from home. You are so good at chronicling your experience, you make your readers feel like they are right there with you.

Thanks, Carrie. Blessings and shalom.

Jackie Clarke
Ontario, Canada
September 29, 2014

Hello, Carrie!

You had the warm welcome from family and friends (and strangers, I am assuming) when you got back from Israel—and I am not surprised, because you are that kind of person who attracts people who want to support the kind of work, adventure, writing, filming and experiences you did in Israel! You did amazing things, had amazing adventures, and touched many people's lives (including mine).

A big hug!

Marilyn Brown
California, USA
December 25, 2014

A Taste of Israeli Life

Walking into Deeper Identity with the Jewish Nation

Carrie Taylor Goldberg

WESTBOW
PRESS®
A DIVISION OF THOMAS NELSON
& ZONDERVAN

This book is a work of non-fiction. Unless otherwise noted, the author
and the publisher make no explicit guarantees as to the accuracy of
the information contained in this book and in some cases, names of
people and places have been altered to protect their privacy.

Views expressed in this book do not represent any public or private organizations
with which the author may at any time be affiliated. Rather, they reflect a
personal and progressive cross-cultural and spiritual learning journey.

WestBow Press books may be ordered through booksellers or by contacting:

WestBow Press
A Division of Thomas Nelson & Zondervan
1663 Liberty Drive
Bloomington, IN 47403
www.westbowpress.com
844-714-3454

Because of the dynamic nature of the Internet, any web addresses or
links contained in this book may have changed since publication and may
no longer be valid. The views expressed in this work are solely those
of the author and do not necessarily reflect the views of the publisher,
and the publisher hereby disclaims any responsibility for them.

To inquire about the book, or to request the author to speak to your community group,
please contact: TaylorGoldberg@writeme.com

Carrie Taylor Goldberg, Photographer

ISBN: 978-1-6642-3193-1 (sc)
ISBN: 978-1-6642-3195-5 (hc)
ISBN: 978-1-6642-3194-8 (e)

Library of Congress Control Number: 2021908189

Print information available on the last page.

WestBow Press rev. date: 06/23/2021

Contents

Preface

The number 18 (chai) in Hebrew signifies life. This book was conceived before I even considered writing one. Years ago, I recall someone predicting I would write a book one day. It began with my simple e-updates from my journey in the Land of Israel. Family and friends had requested I keep them posted on what was happening with me there.

To my surprise, more and more people gave unsolicited feedback on what I thought were my basic writing skills; the common response was the feeling that they were right there with me. For some, it was their first taste of Israel; for others, it was a chance to revisit familiar places through my eyes. Now that I am back in Canada, adapting excerpts of my writings into book chapters, I hope to retain that sense the reader had of being there with me.

So come, jump into the pages and explore the land and the people I so love and appreciate. Am I biased? Yes, and I make no apology. This nation is my nation, and these people are my people. I will be quick to defend against any who would attack out of sheer, senseless hatred. I invite you to approach with humility, to open your hearts without agenda and to learn from the ones whom God appointed to be a light unto the nations.

Acknowledgments

This book is dedicated to my dad, who told me there's no such thing as *can't*. Also to my nana, who assured me she always loved me no matter what. They both went on to Shamayim in the course of writing these pages.

Grandad was my first known relative to visit the Land of Israel before me. Nana told me that when he returned from there in the 1930s, he believed in the one true God. My paternal grandma was an example of selfless generosity, like those who later helped fund my publishing costs.

Mom observed how happy and healthy I was while in the land. Her eagerness to receive a first copy of this book motivates me to keep going. Throughout my journey, my aunt Sylvia and uncle Bob instilled in me a sense of family.

I regard as mentors friends Cheryl, Tish and Carol, who listened and encouraged me along the way. My longest friendships with Shelley, Sharon, Angie and Linda have taught me confidence from their examples of steadfastness.

Several other friends, some authors ahead of me, inspired me to share my writings in larger circles. I extend much gratitude to those like Donna, who introduced and welcomed me to Israel, and who like Ruth of the Bible was eager to learn alongside me. I deeply value each family member and friend.

Thank you to my employer for allowing me time off work to explore this fascinating culture, and to the volunteer organizations that provided me opportunities to be of service. I appreciate my publisher's patience as I come to terms with submitting a less-than-perfect manuscript.

The birth of this book was put on hold to make wedding preparations in Canada, and now it resumes as I have settled with my husband in the United States. Mutual Israeli friend Hannah introduced us, becoming our matchmaker. My husband, William, has a wonderful servant heart and keeps supporting me to see this final edit through to completion.

Special tribute goes to the Toronto Jewish community for their warm and extraordinary hospitality during my transition to married life. Dear Dolores recently came to rest her weary body in the earth of beloved Israel. Thank you to our new neighbours in the American Midwest who welcomed me. Deep appreciation goes to our Israeli friends and to the many people along my path who are interwoven in the stories of this book.

Above all, the greatest thanks goes to our Creator and Redeemer, the God of Israel.

Introduction: Five Senses

Tasting and Touching the Sights, Sounds, Scents

What is it to taste something? To taste a culture? It is more than simply touching from the outside, making a connection externally with one's eyes and ears and sense of smell. I did that as a tourist, and there's nothing wrong with that. But after having observed from without, I wanted to enter within. Tasting involves the other senses initially; the sight and aroma create desire. Then by choosing to open one's mouth, one gets a sense of the texture and may then proceed to chew for a while, listening to one's own ruminations. Having absorbed the taste and savoured it, eventually I swallowed and ingested some of Israeli culture into my very being.

I explored the land, engaging all my senses.

Taste

Shuv v'shuv (again and again), Israel is referred to in the Bible as the land of milk and honey. Well, I can't say I saw a lot of cows or bees, but the *chalav* (milk) and *gvina* (cheese) sure tasted creamier, and the honey was richer than the North American variety. Oh, and the *glida* (ice cream)—now that's a real treat! Spilling over the containers like frozen molten lava, in a wide array of colours and exotic flavours, it practically beckons to you to partake.

Although burger joints are increasing in popularity, shawarma is the more typical Israeli *basar* (meat) fast food. Stuffed into pita bread is shaved roasted chicken, turkey or lamb. If you are vegetarian, if your budget is lower or if you simply prefer, falafel is the Israeli "hot dog." Deep-fried chickpea balls are also stuffed into pita, with your choice of added vegetation (I highly recommend fried eggplant, topped with chips) and toppings of hummus (made of chickpeas) and tehina (made of sesame seed). My personal favourite is from a kiosk in Jaffa that's been in operation since the 1950s.

Bread from the earth? Not directly, though it is a land of miracles. This fresh, tasty staple food requires our partnership with God: He causes the wheat and barley (and other grains) to grow, as His people plant and tend to the soil. He measures out the sun and rain, and we reap the harvest. The most memorable samples for me were the humongous challah loaves being passed around a Jerusalem rabbi's Shabbat tables. Each loaf was about two feet long and six inches wide. After the blessings over wine and bread, hungry guests looked forward to that first bite of fluffy, tender baked dough dipped in a tad of salt.

Though occasionally I visited a grocery store and bought an imported product familiar to my North American culture, I usually preferred to eat as the locals do. Salad is more common for breakfast than cereal. Besides, a mid-sized box of my favourite sold for the equivalent of $8–10 Canadian! Or, if you're a busy person on the go, you may grab a *bureka* (cheese or potato filled) or some other nutrient-less pastry at one of the many store displays lining a street, or inside a bus station.

At many army bases, standard fare went like this: tomatoes and cucumber (comes in assorted cuts), sliced bread with liquid white cheese slapped on top and bashed hard-boiled eggs. The beverage of soldiers (besides that world-famous cola) is *shoko*, consumed by biting off a corner of a small plastic bag and sucking back the cool, sweet chocolate contents. Such was part of the three-week breakfast and supper menu at one of my assigned locations.

Now for more variety, and a good bargain, either the Carmel market in Jaffa, or the Mahane Yehuda *shuk* in Jerusalem were the places to go. These massive indoor and outdoor venues are resplendent with produce of the land that fills the globe with her fruit (cf. Isaiah 27:6 NIV). Everything seems to taste better, sweeter and juicier here. Take for example the small green Jaffa oranges, the mouth-watering mangos and the creamy, tangy guava juice. I likened my previous experiences with guava outside of Israel to eating melted metal with sugar added! But one weekend at a kibbutz, I tried this bumpy, green, pear-shaped fruit and discovered I liked the Israeli version. Since childhood I have enjoyed pomegranates, but never so much as that sweet, juicy one I picked off a tree on another kibbutz. Likewise, I savoured the flavour I scooped out of a passion fruit that had fallen from the tree outside a place I lived. Locally grown Jericho bananas make our imports taste bland by comparison. It's really amazing how anything grows in a land where there's barely any rain, yet in Israel you find even supersized veggies, such as radishes the size of baseballs and carrots too big for that cartoon rabbit's mouth!

Touch

Back in 2007, I recall the uncontainable excitement over the plane landing, as well as my feet touching ground upon exiting the airport. I was actually here, the faraway land previously only known in others' pictures and in the words of the Bible. Now I had opportunity over the ensuing couple of weeks to walk through history myself.

The past here is inextricably linked to the future. I climbed the steep side of the Mount of Olives, standing atop where the prophet Zechariah (chapter 14) proclaimed that Hashem Himself would plant His feet in the end of days, during the Messianic era. At last the world would realize there is alone one God over all the earth, and that He is King. From this famed mount is a stunning panoramic view overlooking Jerusalem and the surrounding Judean Hills.

Down below, upon entering the walled Old City, my sandals occasionally slid, and I caught my footing on the narrow cart ramps and uneven, age-worn stone slabs that lined the narrow streets. I remember the first time some Canadian friends and I explored on our own. The main corridors were packed with people buying or selling all kinds of wares. I was unable to see over the middle of the backs of strangers in front of me, and suddenly I was walloped in the shoulder by an old wooden cart of goods some vendor was pushing through. Minutes later I felt nudged again, this time by a donkey's head! I began to catch on and kept on the alert for other oncoming traffic, ready to dart out of the way—if only there were space to do so! Eventually my friends and I neared an exit point, ancient Damascus Gate (aka Shar Shechem, as I later discovered when a border guard didn't know where the other gate was). Just as we were approaching the light, another cart shot out and struck my friend, knocking her off balance. We shouted, another vendor shouted, and my friend was spared from being run over. Someone had reached out to steady her and left a flour handprint on her black clothing. Such was our first experience of the most ancient part of the city.

Over in Jerusalem's downtown core, I've had occasional collisions with shin-high cement obstacles protruding from sidewalks, which are a particular hazard for first-time tourists focused on gazing around at sights, not looking down where they walk.

A far more pliable but still painful point of contact is the prickly sabra fruit. I carefully reached over with index finger and thumb to pluck one by the ends off a cactus plant. Despite best efforts to cut open the juicy, sweet, bumpy core, it is virtually impossible to enjoy without a few of its whiskers implanted in your lips and fingers, but it is well worth the treat. The sabra is also a term of endearment for native-born Israelis. If you lived with constant hostility toward you as they do, you might be a bit prickly in reaction at times too. But the real jewel is inside, the tender hearts of the local people.

In contrast to the inside of a sabra, around the Tel Aviv area and farther south in the desert is dry, cracked earth, soil that, in response to its people's long-awaited return, amazingly produces multiple crops. You mean the ground recognizes its inhabitants? In some mysterious way, yes! According to Scripture, such was prophesied (cf. Ezekiel 36:8–12 NASB). The once barren land became fertile again, especially after 1948.

Considering all the time I spent in Israel, I rarely saw rain. In fact, the next morn after an unusual overnight downpour on our base, I actually took a picture of a puddle! But for my first time there during the winter rainy season (February 2013), we were scooping up floodwaters away from our barrack doorways, stepping across on raft-like pallets! Then in December of that year, I experienced my first major snowstorm in Jerusalem. By Western Canada standards, it would have been a common winter day, busy as usual. Not so in the world's capital city. Virtually everything came to a standstill, leaving vehicles abandoned in the streets. Government offices and most businesses were closed. The odd small store remained open, such as a coffee shop on Ben Yehuda Street, which had an Israeli-style snowman (cucumbers for eyes and ears) welcoming customers, cup of coffee in hand. Outside our window, soldiers laughed as they playfully tossed snowballs at one another.

On Yom Ha'atzmaut, Israeli Independence Day, which occurs between April and May, other fluffy white stuff could be found on the streets and covering pedestrians. This substance came from spray cans, a fun custom to celebrate national freedom, along with inflatable rubber hammers with which you bop people you know … or don't know. Barbecues and fireworks are also popular. That eve in 2013, a friend and I made our way through the crowds pouring down Jaffa Road, singing and dancing. My friend was also my spotter as I manoeuvred a large video camera, avoiding oncoming trains and the less lethal but potentially damaging whipped cream from landing on the expensive borrowed equipment. That's the stuff of which memories are made.

After approaching the bumpy, waxy Kotel (ancient western retaining wall of the Second Temple) and placing my hands where millions before over the centuries have leaned and davened, pouring out their hearts to God—even wailing—there I too connected with the God of the universe. Most Shabbat morns in Jerusalem, and during major *chaggim* (holy days), I would come there to read the Scriptures and reflect.

A perhaps less spiritual of favourite spots in Israel for me were the beaches of Tel Aviv-Yafo. Yet here I could look out at the expanse of the Mediterranean and remember how small I am, how big God is, and how much wiser it is to trust Him. I soak in the warmth of the sun, at around 30 degrees Celsius much of the year, and roll my bare feet through the thousands of grains of sand. The misnamed Dead Sea, known to locals as the Salt Sea, is full of life-enhancing minerals which leave your skin feeling silky smooth on emerging from floating in the buoyant water. It's very peaceful there.

Everywhere I go in Israel, I want to be tactile, cherishing God's handiwork, holding and smelling the flowers on the ground, on bushes and on trees. Such spectacular colour is bursting from blossoms of unusual shapes. To think the Creator of the universe took the time to make such tiny, detailed specimens for our and His pleasure!

Sights

My first time in Israel, I was especially astounded at the mushrooming date palms, tall and majestic, swaying in the breeze. Rows lined the precisely flowered grounds outside the wall-sized airport window on arrival. My first memorable close-up was of the one on hospital property, bearing a bunch of bright, orange-coloured dates. Then there were the more reddish clusters visible at eye range from atop the rampart walk, the ancient walls around the Old City Jerusalem. A word of caution about getting too close: beware the bark—it bites! Some palms are clothed in what looks like a bushy beard, but others contain sharp thorns. I learned from experience!

I nicknamed this often-told tale after a popular 1950s TV series about American army life. We volunteers were on a field trip in Jaffa with the Israeli army. I noticed a piece of bark on the ground and considered playing a harmless practical joke on one of my buddies. When I picked up the piece and discovered it was heavier than expected, I ditched my idea and the bark, but it bounced back off the ground and bit me in the left shin! It actually resembled a snake bite, with two tiny holes side by side about half a centimetre apart. Knowing I'd left my first aid kit back on the base, I thought, *No big deal. I'll deal with it later that evening.*

When tweezers were not able to reach it, a fellow volunteer offered me use of her sewing needle, and my barracks mate loaned me her lighter to sterilize the tool. Concerned about later infection, another team member offered me some of his aftershave lotion. Still, the tiny object in my shin resisted coming out. I did have international medical coverage, but I didn't like the inconvenience of needing to be transported off base to wait in a hospital line for something so minor. Therefore, I took more drastic measure upon myself. Out came the foldable camping knife a friend had given me back in Canada, a reward for my wilderness survival skills. The army buddy (on whom I'd considered playing the practical joke) came out with a halogen head lamp, ready for surgery. I stretched out my leg on the army cot outside in our sand pit while another fellow on our team had his phone video ready for action. Hands-free with the head lamp, my army buddy held my skin taunt while I carefully made a tiny incision, connecting the dots. If the imbedded object was perpendicular to my shin bone, I could slide it out sideways, I reasoned. Still no success.

The concerned volunteer with the antiseptic lotion convinced me it was time to tell our *madrichot*, the soldier guides in charge of our group. One of them suggested I see the base doctor, who would be on site in the morning. Pulled briefly out of work duty, I accompanied a madricha to the medical unit, where I waited in line with the soldiers. When my turn came, the madricha explained in Hebrew what had happened, the doctor responded in Hebrew, and the madricha gave me a summary in English. Basically, the doctor felt that if—after all we had tried—the object did not come out of my leg, it was best to leave it, to let it eventually come out on its own … which I understood she estimated to be within twenty hours! How she may have arrived at that calculation, I don't know. Well, she was a bit off in her timing. After applying more disinfectant, bandaging my shin, and my later rubbing on Vitamin E oil to deter a scar from forming, about six weeks later back in Canada, I noticed a black point. I pressed on the sides of my shin, and it slowly emerged: about a centimetre-long thorn, which I packaged and labelled as a "souvenir" of the land! So that's the account of my sitcom episode. Don't try this at home.

Moving beyond that visual, I want to share some other images of the land. Another weekend off from the army base, I was amazed I could look so far across this tiny but vast land, across Mitzpe Ramon Crater in the Negev, which is Israel's version of the Grand Canyon. It's really something to see sun and shadow dance across the red and brown earth formations. Even from a friend's backyard in the Judean Hills, the green speckled wadi with dried-up creek bed was a sight to behold. Farther north, after hiking nine kilometres uphill, I was rewarded with the view from on top of Mount Hermon. Actually, the rest of the way to the top was only by ski lift, which runs even when there is no snow. From this point, the mountain ranges of Syria are visible, and the civil bloodshed is shielded from sight.

Going back south in the Galil region is the small but grand green Mount Tabor, considered to be the sight of transfiguration, where Moses and Elijah encountered Salvation (ישׁוע). Many receive and believe this radiant and later resurrected Yeshua to be our sinless sacrifice on a tree, providing the only way to forgiveness through blood atonement. Heading west from here toward Haifa is a spectacular pastel patchwork of fields below Mount Carmel, criss-crossed by branches in the foreground, the site where Elijah challenged false prophets of Baal to prove who is the one true God.

Besides the mounts and valleys, Israel has much varied terrain. There's the mighty Jordan River, initially spurned by Syrian commander Naaman when instructed to dip and therein obtain healing from leprosy (see 2 Kings 5, especially verses 10–12 NIV). The core wider area, the immersion site, was tranquil with green-hued water and foliage overhanging, as was the spot close to the Jordanian border, believed to be from where Joshua led the people into the Promised Land. But other stretches of the river were less impressive, appearing no different than a gentle river or creek in some other country.

Winding like a river are roads traversing diverse landscape: wooded green areas in the north (with mint blue rushing Dan River), desert dunes in the south coming to a point (as an ice cream cone) to the famed Red Sea, portal of Israelite deliverance. Modern asphalt highways run through with green signs in Hebrew, Arabic and English. In residential and industrial areas, curbs were painted to signify parking codes (red/white: not there; yellow/red: public transit; blue/white: fair game, not free). Unlike the ticket patrols lurking in Toronto, your chances of getting fined seem far less in Israeli cities. In fact, in some places you find cars parked on sidewalks, leaving the roads to pedestrians to share with moving vehicles!

In Jerusalem and Jaffa, there are an abundance of blue plaques to stop and read on various buildings, citing what historic event occurred there. Often these were memorial sites, signifying how people lost their lives through senseless hatred. Consider the multiple explosions on Ben Yehuda Street. Even the plain-looking regions hold historic significance, such as the weedy Elah Valley, where David slew Goliath. Quaint Old Jaffa, with its winding stone passages and history of over 4,000 years, is known for its port from where Jonah tried fleeing from God, a large whale monument there to remember his change of will. I loved to watch the sun set over the silhouettes of this ancient treasure of a city.

The more modern Tel Aviv Central Bus Station, with its main entrance turnstile, was a regular meeting spot inside amongst split-level shops and services. Over in Jerusalem is their bus depot with a huge, glass-front clock—perhaps a reminder this city is central to history, where time will be wound up, ushering in a new eternal era.

Like Paris, Tel Aviv is a city where people cherish their dogs. They are found walking the boulevards and playing on the beach. One woman even lifted her little pooch up to take a few laps from a public drinking fountain. Like Toronto or New York, cities that never sleep, one can see rundown areas around clubs, with drugs and poverty (yet not to the same extent; rarely did I see people very drunk in public). Occasionally eyes are drawn by sudden shouts, and one spots a poor soul with some variation of "Jerusalem Syndrome," coined to describe people deluded into thinking they walked straight out of the Bible as one of its characters, such as Moses, Elijah, or Jesus.

To gain grounding, some recommend getting away from Jerusalem every so often. One calming place is the sometimes tumultuous Kinneret, an inspiration of romantic poems. Alongside this Galil lake is buried one of Israel's most famous poetesses: Rachel, nearby famous folksinger and composer of "Jerusalem of Gold," Naomi Shemer.

Ah, Jerusalem. My favourite places: hiking atop Mount Zeitim (Olives), reading on Shabbat morn by Hakotel (Western Wall), hanging out with friends on Ben Yehuda Street, strolling along the historic train track promenade (with archived photos and stories from the British mandate period), and residing within stretches of cookie-cutter *olim* apartments built for the 1950s influx. Representatives from all nations are here, in fulfilment of prophecy making aliyah (especially in these days of resurgence of vicious anti-Semitism). Ammunition Hill and Lion's Gate are associated with the Six-Day War and reunification of the city.

Sounds

Sounds, or the absence of sound, can be pleasurable or disconcerting. I experienced mostly the former during my time in Israel. While standing on the shore, I was mesmerized by foamy white Mediterranean waves crashing under moonlight. By day, familiar were the steady pings and pongs of avid beach players with their rackets. Not far from the beach on many an occasion, my army buddies and I heard red alert sirens and exploding rockets in the skies above us. That was the summer of 2014, when an unprecedented number of assaults came our way from the Gaza Strip. In contrast to this was awakening to the soothing cooing of doves, those winged symbols of peace.

I stood outside our rabbi's place, socializing with other guests until the door opened Friday nights, and that hubbub of expectant mix of languages was a highlight of my week. That, and being greeted with a warm, genuine welcome from the rabbi saying, "Your presence enhances our Shabbat." Inside, between blessings and teachings and courses of scrumptious food, were not always harmonious voices joyfully making a noise there. Yet even those were welcome sounds.

During my first annual civic parade of nations participation in Jerusalem, I felt the warmth of welcome as local gals formed a circle and sang to us "Hava Nagila." At different intervals, flutes and drums of bar mitzvah processions can be heard around the Jewish Quarter of the Old City. Over in another culture, five times daily a mosque calls to prayer, reverberating throughout the atmosphere. Sometimes it sounded almost beautiful, and other times it felt quite eerie. Once I stumbled upon a large gathering across from Damascus Gate, a robed man calling out as followers all bowed down. Also outside Damascus Gate, frequently I was accosted by taxi drivers spotting me from a distance, walking with my backpack: "Lady! Taxi?" I would reply, "La shukran (no, thank you)." Those Arabic words came in very handy!

On other loudspeakers, affixed to the Western Wall complex, resounded during Pesach and Sukkot the priestly (Aaronic) blessing as expectant crowds filled the Kotel plaza, arriving in the early morn. These words, I could be confident, declared life to all who would receive. Such life was lived out in the talking and laughter of patrons along Ben Yehuda Street, especially after Shabbat. That revived ancient language of Ivrit, spoken with beloved Israeli accent: *zero* (meaning: that's it)!

Scents

While walking through the Old City's narrow streets, I thought how in our high-tech world, we can reproduce sights and sounds and share these with family and friends back home. Apart from bringing back souvenirs, we cannot replicate the texture or taste or smell of what is experienced in Jerusalem. Take for instance that mix of spices and incense wafting into your nostrils as you walk through the cobblestone streets inside the gates. How may one describe the smell and taste of za'atar? The combo of aromas of the artistically sculpted spice pyramids? The pots full of different colours and textures side by side?

For North American coffee fans, the usual fare of Turkish coffee may not be so appealing, especially the part of straining it through your teeth. It doesn't seem to have the same caffeine kick. Nonetheless, it is standard army fare, for which to be thankful. It does smell much better than it tastes, so use it for aromatherapy, if you will. Nana tea, made of fresh spearmint leaves, is another favourite custom of hospitality, spanning both Arab and Jewish Israeli cultures.

But undoubtedly, beyond description are the myriad of flowers found across the land. The scents are out of this world. The one that enlivens my senses most, which is like honey dripping off lilies, is the distinctive tiny white jasmine. I could sniff that all day.

Before embarking on stories of my first trip to Israel, here is a preview glimpse of my progressive journeys.

The doors opened, and I stepped into the streets of Jerusalem. The *rakevet* (light rail train) rolled down Jaffa Road, the main artery of the city. I got off by King George Street and cut through an alley over to the famous Ben Yehuda Street, otherwise known to locals as the *midrachov*. This pedestrian thoroughfare is one of my favourite places to hang out. There is a relaxed atmosphere, a mixture of tourists and citizens, who mingle at the numerous souvenir shops and outdoor cafes. Street musicians add to the rich ambience. One innovative Israeli donned a white flowing robe and found fortune atop a severely pruned tree trunk (wounded in last December's snowstorm). From his perch, he played his flute, the tunes drawing passersby to look up and linger. Friday afternoons, in preparation for Shabbat, businesses close early, and for the next 25 hours, the place turns into a virtual ghost town. But then Saturday eve, suddenly it comes alive again! I find here a vibrancy of life I haven't experienced elsewhere, even in Canada.

Let me introduce you further to my beloved Jerusalem (ירושלים), that ancient mystical city mentioned nearly 700 times in the Hebrew Bible. My perspective has changed somewhat from the time I first set foot here on a tour in 2007. I originally came with an organization widely respected in the Jewish community. It was a dream to finally travel to Israel, and I was full of wonder as I took in the sights, sounds and scents, as well as tasting and touching the beauty of God's creation. By the end of those couple of weeks, I felt so at home in Jerusalem that I was homesick at the thought of having to leave.

Subsequently, I returned in 2008 and 2010 to volunteer, gaining a deeper sense of identity with this nation as I clad khaki army fatigues as an international civilian volunteer. We assist soldiers with sorting and packing medical and other logistical supplies, as well as helping to clean and refurbish equipment. During time off bases, I explored other regions of the land. Especially rewarding is reading Scripture in the very areas where the events recorded took place. Even amongst the most secular, I find a pervasive awareness of God in the Land of Israel. It is amazing to be here amidst the throngs of pilgrims coming for one of the three annual festivals: Feast of Tabernacles (Sukkot), Passover (Pesach) and Pentecost (Shavuot).

My longest trek across the land was much different from the first. That wide-eyed wonder turned into revisiting the familiar. At first I found this disconcerting and disappointing. But then I relished the idea of living as a local person; after all, that was why I had saved up money to be able to have an extended cross-cultural experience during most of 2013–2014. My employer graciously granted me an unpaid leave to fulfil this dream of a lifetime. I wanted a taste of Israeli life, for a season becoming a part of the history and learning some of the language.

The train that let me off near Ben Yehuda Street took me to the heart of a nation. The ancient Hebrew language was revived, according to the dream of the man after whom this street was named. Adjacent to this street was the ulpan, where I became immersed in the language over the course of a year. Faculty and *talmidim* (students) of this school, along with my comrades with the army, became mishpacha (family) to me.

Section I: First Trip (2007)

Immediately at Home in Jerusalem

Anticipation built over the summer after I signed up for a tour to Israel from September 23 to October 4, 2007. Israel was definitely a top must-see place, and finally I had both the allotted time off and finances to be able to go. The timing seemed right. My fortieth year was coming up, and it was also Jerusalem's fortieth anniversary of being reunited under Jewish sovereignty. I decided to go with a tour group respected by the Jewish community.

The day arrived. We gathered at the airport in Toronto, meeting those with whom we'd be exploring the Land of Israel over the next 12 days. We were Canadians from coast to coast, some veteran visitors and others venturing out for the first time.

I was thrilled to find I had a window seat after all and settled in to enjoy the uplifting journey on the connecting flight from Milan to Tel Aviv. After making my way through the crowded Italian airport, I became acquainted with another newcomer who would become a good friend. Our tour leader and others became concerned when they realized we were not with them while being ushered through an express route. They welcomed us back as lost sheep at the departure point.

Eventually my seatmates and I succumbed to sleep, but I opened my eyes just in time to see the Land of Israel appearing at the Mediterranean coastline. I was so excited I couldn't contain it, and I had to nudge my friends awake to share in this moment. Ten minutes later at 1:50 p.m., our plane touched ground to cheers.

Here I was, about to set foot in the Land of Israel for the first time! Inside the arrivals level was a wall sign welcoming us: "Bruchim Haba'im" ("Blessed [are] the [ones] coming"). My first steps outside would preferably have been onto natural earth, yet despite the asphalt covering, there was something almost mystical about making contact with this ancient turf. I was impressed at walking around this land full of evidence. The Bible came alive and was more real to me as somewhat meaningless place names now became associated with specific scenes.

During the bus ride to Tel Aviv, I absorbed striking scenery such as two-tone green trees with red flower blossoms. On arrival at our hotel, I learned I'd been assigned to share a room with another single gal—the friend I'd met en route. From our eleventh-floor balcony, we had a grand view of the Mediterranean. We eagerly dropped off our luggage. Then under the setting sun, we took a dip in the sea's soothing warm water with curling waves splashing up over us. At last, still wearing the clothes I'd arrived in, I made my first steps barefoot on the created land through the silky sand.

Back at the hotel, I discovered the salt water had removed the orange stain off my linen pant leg from the beverage I'd worn after the airline tray had slipped off its hinges. We got ready for our first supper in Israel—an abundant buffet with amazingly decorative and tasty wide variety. Afterwards, nine of us took an evening stroll along a multicolour lit promenade.

That first morning, I looked out over the balcony with a prayer of thanksgiving for the revealing presence over the land. I had shared news of my arrival with family and received an excited response. My grandmother even sounded choked up with tears of happiness. I was up before the 6:00 a.m. wake-up call and read from the prophet Hosea:

Yet the Israelites will be like the sand on the seashore, which cannot be measured or counted. In the place where it was said to them, "You are not my people," they will be called "children of the living God." (Hosea 1:10 NIV)

Afterward the Israelites will return and seek the LORD their God and David their king. They will come trembling to the LORD and to his blessings in the last days. (Hosea 3:5 NIV)

After breakfast, we were off to ancient Jaffa. We saw an original Tel Aviv settlement after driving past embassies. Our local Israeli guide acknowledged with thanks a Christian Zionist organization that had the only embassy based in Jerusalem. The governments of nations had pulled out and moved to Tel Aviv to satisfy world opinion. (Update May 14, 2018: The relocated United States embassy was opened in Jerusalem.) A couple of Canadian musicians were instrumental in establishing this symbol of international support, which has remained steadfast now for decades, advocating for and providing practical aid to Israelis as well as to Diaspora Jews.

Our first day, our guide informed us of local news. The Israeli army captured some terrorist leaders, averting their plan to blow up a crowded part of Tel Aviv this Yom Kippur. Already we were confronted with the reality of Israeli life.

Going back in biblical time, we passed a modern rendition of Jonah's fish monument in front of a flat-roofed, multilevel building with gold-tinted white stone. Later, we visited The Museum of the Jewish People, which depicted the multiracial Jewish nation through history surviving against hope, symbolized by a light pillar in the midst of a black cage-like structure. There were also models of international synagogues, each unique design influenced by local culture. Here, I discovered the current black clothing worn by the Orthodox community is styled after seventeenth-century Poland.

On the road, we passed by fields of banana plants, olive groves and fig and date trees. I was utterly amazed by the fruitfulness of this terrain, which drinks in so little natural rainwater over the course of a year. I was eyewitness to such miracles of growth.

A featured stop on our tour was a medical facility at Kfar Saba. A doctor gave a presentation, expressing gratitude for help funding their work there. He recounted an experience with a Holocaust survivor, where he determined this patient who had survived such an ordeal should not die for lack of medical attention.

The hospital provided us with disposable green scrubs that we donned to tour their ICU and watch a live operation through a window and monitor. A patient's lungs were being reinflated following a heart procedure. At this centre, as with other Israeli hospitals, once the line is crossed onto the premises, everyone is simply a patient. That includes even a terrorist wounded in the process of harming or killing others. Israel, the Jewish community, places a premium on the value of life.

Along the coastline, our tour group stopped at the old Roman city of Caesarea, from where we caught a stunning view of blue and white waves riding high and sloshing against rocks. Across the way was a chariot track, as well as some stone arch aqueducts and small pools. Nearby, we sat in an amphitheatre that we learned was an ancient venue for sadistic entertainment. Life certainly didn't have the same value here.

Next on our itinerary was our ascent of Mount Carmel. What a panoramic view looking out at Mount Megiddo over into the Jezreel Valley, popularly known as site of Armageddon. Below was the Kishon River, where biblical prophet Elijah ordered slain the false prophets of Baal. Earlier he had issued them a challenge to demonstrate which was, in fact, the true

God (see 1 Kings 18). As we descended Carmel, a man with a guitar led a group singing "Shema Yisrael."

I stepped into a chapel, where a friend passed me a candle. We both lit ours and placed them in front of a stone altar. There, I declared from the words of Elijah the prophet: "The God who answers by fire, He is God." (See 1 Kings 18:24 NASB.) My friend replied, "Amen!"

That evening at our new hotel, I sat in a window ledge gazing out upon the Sea of Galilee (better known to locals as the Kinneret). I saw pointed umbrellas under moonlight in the foreground off the beach. Being the experiential person I am, I just had to go over and take a late-night wade into the water. I felt little fishes tickling my toes and noticed lots of larger fish near deeper shores, jumping about.

From the prophet Obadiah (1:15 NIV) I read, "The day of the LORD is near for all nations. As you have done, it will be done to you; your deeds will return upon your own head." While I was here in the land, scriptures came alive, and the words seemed to carry more weight.

The next day, our tour group took a boat ride on Lake Tiberias. Someone aboard explained that following a typical abrupt storm, with little or no advance warning, waves would continue to roll wildly for awhile afterwards—but here they instantly calmed at Jesus's word! Our next stop was the town of Capernaum, whose name derives from the Hebrew words for *village* (*kfar*) and *comfort* (*nahum*). There, I climbed on the ruins of a synagogue built overtop one that Jesus reportedly taught in, claiming to be the Bread of Life come down from heaven. Near these ancient columns was an old olive press. Our Jewish guide explained that virgin oil is what runs off at first from the stone resting on olives before the press worked them further.

Continuing along the way, our tour entered Tabgha, site of the multiplied loaves and fishes, otherwise known as the feeding of the 5,000. According to our guide, the feeding of the

4,000 took place elsewhere, in pagan territory. With respect to the religious site there, one main memory stands out. Inside was a colourful mosaic of the bread and fish.

As I was gazing about, I wasn't paying so much attention to what was in front of me. Suddenly, I whammed full force into the back of a teammate, who fortunately was sturdy enough to withstand the accidental blow. We both burst out laughing. The caretaking priest approached. "Señoritas," he addressed us. "This is not a place for laughing."

I apologized for the unintentional outburst, explaining what had happened. Yet I had to wonder whether Jesus would have seen the humour in it and been amused along with us.

So much there is to take in from this tiny land. We travelled farther northeast and saw Mount Hermon from a distance. At almost 3,000 metres, it is the largest mountain in Israel, shared by three countries (also Syria and Lebanon). Our guide led us around Banias, the Pan Temple area, which in contrast to the tranquillity of our last place had a somewhat eerie and empty feeling as we looked at pillars and a large cave dedicated to idolatry. Here was the alleged site of virgin sacrifices. What brutality these false gods require! This place came to be known as the Gates of Hell. Relieved to leave this atmosphere, we had a longer trek ahead to an anticipated highlight: from the springs of Banias to the famous River Jordan.

Our Jewish guide accompanied us to the Yardenit site, where many faithful flock to be immersed in the green-hued waters. It was definitely tranquil here at this wide mouth of the river, where a large willow branch hung. For those who wanted, white robes could be rented to ensure modesty and to provide a visual image of holiness and purity. For whatever each person's personal reasons for entering the waters, the joyous look on faces was something to behold. Now, several years later, I associate my initial Jordan River immersion as an early mikvah, wading into a sense of Jewish identity even before I realized where I was heading.

Another natural wonder was found later in a factory, during a tour of the diamond manufacturing process. The on-site guide showed us a video of God's creation met by human interaction with stones. What a tedious process indeed, to come to the spectacular end result of these prized gems! A cowboy friend endearingly once called me an easy keeper, so I was content to simply admire from a distance without any compulsion to buy. That evening I chatted with a travel companion outside on our patio. We both expected more of our trip in terms of experiencing God, until she sensed we were to simply draw near to Him as we enjoy His land.

Next morn around six o'clock, I was the first one of our group to be up and out for a swim in the Galilee. How warm it was even at that hour. This day I admitted to taking God for granted, and I acknowledged the privilege of hearing His voice. How amazing that the holy God of Israel desires to be so close to us! I prayed for a return, with our upcoming Days of Awe, to a desire to listen and obey.

Over in Nazareth, we were taken to an outdoor and indoor replica of what life was like there in a village 2,000 years ago. Our designated staff guide was a personable Arab Christian young man. He pointed out the rocky, dry terrain, full of weeds, lending to the hard work of preparing the undersoil to prevent erosion in vineyards. He illustrated an ancient parable of planting seed in good soil to ensure it takes root (see Matthew 13:1–9, 18–23 NIV). In the near distance, I remember white buildings staggered on the hillsides of the town. Up close I saw olives and pomegranates growing. Staff guides in era costumes wandered about, tending to their re-enacted trades or doing household chores. As I petted some donkeys in their pens, our guide explained these gentle animals were integral in planning road infrastructure because they naturally find the easiest path on slopes, bearing their loads full of goods. What an enjoyable hands-on experience employing all the senses.

As we left, each of us was given a gift of a little clay oil lamp, like what would have been in use back then. The most intriguing part of this excursion for me was our gathering in a replica first-century synagogue, listening to our guide's teaching. He noted that Moses's seat was in the centre. He painted a picture of being part of the crowd back then, imagining the weekly portion read from Isaiah 61, followed by the startling announcement by the appointed reader: "Today this scripture is fulfilled in your hearing." (Refer to Luke 4:16–21 NIV.) How to respond? How could this be? Anointed one?

Our next stop on our journey was Megiddo, crossroads of many wars, ultimately pointing to end times. Time was tight, so one of our tour co-leaders indicated we would not be going atop the hill. I expressed my disappointment but then heard one of my teammates call out from partway up, and I hurried to join two of them for fast photos of ruins and waterworks. Then we quickly rejoined the group in time to board the bus.

Onwards we travelled through what many call the West Bank, our local guide pointing out checkpoints and triple-wired electronic fences. I spotted a mine warning sign. In contrast we also saw flocks of sheep with shepherds on increasingly large hills, on sandy dunes and by caves. We drove by the lush green Jordan Valley on our right.

Eventually, we passed along the Dead Sea with its beautiful blue hue and arrived at our hotel, an oasis in the desert alongside the beach. In the immensely salty water, it is hard to manoeuvre without resurfacing and splashing, trying to avoid eyes and mouth. At our buffet supper, I learned that liver and other organs are kosher if from a categorically clean animal. Nonetheless, I don't do organs, leaving my portion for others to partake! Complimentary sweet red Kiddush wine came in mini bottles, and a waiter kept offering more to our large table of friends.

I awoke by 5:30 a.m. without an alarm, in time to watch the sun rapidly come up. I relaxed in the warmth on our balcony. Then it was off to Masada, up the gondola, and around the ruins of King Herod's former palace afterwards occupied by Zealots. I looked over a water aqueduct and reservoir, observing below the terrain outline of an ancient Roman camp, where Zealots tossed rocks down at this enemy trying to come up and attack. We also spotted the Sodom and Gomorrah salt patch in the distance, and our guide told us Hebron was beyond the hills behind the Roman camps.

Seated atop Masada, our guide read a copy of the ancient rabbi's oration recorded by historian Josephus. Faced with the ultimatum, the rabbi encouraged death—and faced some opposition. Believing one risked no resurrection if one committed suicide, they decided for husbands to kill wives and children, and then lots were drawn for 10 men to kill the rest. That way only the last one remaining fell on his own sword. Somehow this end was more honourable than succumbing to martyrdom at the hands of one's ruthless enemies. How do we know what happened up there so long ago if everyone involved died? Actually, some women and children survived to tell. School groups and training soldiers continue to be told. Even a famed orphans' choir was up there that day to hear what happened on Masada. The motto resounds: "Never again!"

Toward the end of the day, a tour friend and I made a jaunt to a desert crossroads for a photo feigning hitchhiking. There were signs of destinations pointing in various directions. The problem was my friend's foot attire was not the most conducive to hiking, so we hitched a ride partway on a golf cart full of seniors! On the mention of hitchhiking when we returned, our tour leader looked alarmed until we reassured her by the context. Several of us took another dip in the Dead Sea. I ventured far out and ended up with salt in my eyes, trying to swim to shore with eyes closed.

What an amazing land is Israel, with such diverse topography packed into that tiny sliver on an international map! And some would want to take away even that. But at this gathering in the desert, thousands show open support for this nation. Our tour bus made its departure for Ein Gedi. Excitement mounted as other busloads pulled in, and nations of the world were represented there. It was the opening night of the Feast of Tabernacles.

Surrounding the growing crowd were mountain silhouettes with lit-up palm trees, changing with the coloured lights, the full moon over us. Later, live camels came down the aisles with a Joshua character, along with a circling procession of shofar blowers, culminating in a group shout reminiscent of claiming the land. After the music and message, a dramatic performance, we enjoyed a meal in the desert. Then the crowd dispersed, and we made it back to our hotel in time for a late-night last swim in the sea with my assigned roommate. It was so calm and peaceful. We shared of our experiences and our dreams of meeting husbands of God's choosing.

Sukkot celebrations continued at historic Kibbutz Ramat Rachel the next day. We watched a video clip of the 1967 Six-Day War, which translated expressed feelings of Israeli soldiers as they entered Old City Jerusalem and came upon the famous Western Wall. Our bus journeyed farther south of Jerusalem, back into the desert, where we met a Canadian artist who encountered God through learning about the Holocaust. His sculptures depict a series of interactions between concentration camp captives and a figure suffering right along with them. As we returned to our bus, I discovered over a sandy ridge three dromedaries (one-humped camels). Two came closer and drank from water in a tarp their master set out.

Next stop was Qumran, cave sites of the famous Dead Sea Scrolls discovery in 1947. Here once lived the strict Essene community, with their emphasis on purity. To think how God preserved these ancient records of His Word all these centuries, to be discovered "accidentally" by a Bedouin shepherd boy who didn't recognize the true worth of what he found in earthen vessels! This priceless discovery brought us much earlier sources than we had and showed the accuracy of transmission over the ages. When it came to our Creator's revelation, meticulous attention was given to ensure each letter was correctly copied for future generations.

By late afternoon, we were heading through the Judean hills, bound for Jerusalem! I recall my first sighting of a sign as we drew closer. We read Psalms of Ascent as our bus climbed the hill. Various tour members were called upon to read. Excitement mounted until our arrival at Mount Scopus for a panoramic view of the city, with golden dome on Temple Mount. Strange, how the later advent of a mosque came to represent the Jerusalem skyline. Centuries prior stood there the Jewish Temple, the house of prayer for all nations.

Upon my first steps outside the bus, I touched the earth with my fingers. Wow, I was actually here! The holy city of Jerusalem, centre of the world! We took photos with Canadian and Israeli flags. Our hotel had "Jerusalem" inscribed in English and Hebrew, and our guide welcomed us home. By that I sensed meaning more than our temporary abode, but rather a deep spiritual significance. How that unfolded would become more than I imagined at the time.

Inside, I noticed ritual hand-washing stations. Water is poured over each hand as a Hebrew blessing is recited. Also, the elevator automatically stopped each floor for Shabbat and other holy days. This mechanism puzzled me for some time, and I did not understand how merely pushing a button could be construed as work. I later learned it had to do with the belief that by activating electrical or electronic equipment, that was likened to striking a fire, forbidden by Scripture on Shabbat.

We had a vast food selection at the kosher buffet, where I enjoyed Jaffa oranges, pomegranate and persimmon fruit. Olives were a staple of every meal, green and black, the stems still on some. Also, a meal is not a meal without bread.

Shabbat in Jerusalem: September 29. Four of our group took a morning stroll around a Jewish neighbourhood, looking for Ammunition Hill. We passed a grapevine ripe with fruit.

Orthodox Jews were walking as families to synagogue. Eventually we found the 1967 site with help from a local man. We walked through the rocky plain up to a metal fence wrapped in large, very sharp razor wire. Here, our lead friend, ducking amidst boulders, recounted for us some of his experiences volunteering as a civilian with the Israeli army. I wondered how he, as a Gentile Canadian, had this opportunity. That was the first I heard of such an international volunteer organization.

We left for our large group tour to another museum, at which was a model of the Temple. Our guide pointed out various sections from David's and from Solomon's eras, as well as the Valley of Gehenna, a fire site of idolatrous child sacrifice. Mount Moriah was to the north of the Temple. In contrast, when Abraham was ready to offer up his son Isaac as a sacrifice, God intervened to stop him from carrying it through. Abraham's willingness to offer up what was most precious to him was enough; even then, he believed God would have brought his son back to life. (Read Genesis 22:1–14 NASB.)

At the Israel Museum was the Shrine of the Book, with a black wall opposite a white dome, representing the sons of darkness versus the sons of light. The longest scroll of the prophet Isaiah (a facsimile) is in the centre, wrapped around a post. Shortly after discovery, the scrolls were sold by a Bedouin, and the price later increased dramatically as their significance and worth were realized!

En route this museum, first we went up to the Mount of Olives for another panoramic view of the city. One of our guides explained this vantage point looked out to where Jesus wept over the city: "O Jerusalem, Jerusalem..." (See Matthew 23:37 KJV.) From this place, my wish was granted to ride a camel; the gentle animal knelt for me to mount and trotted across the lookout point.

We were dropped off by the Old City afterwards, so our small group went exploring again, entering via Jaffa Gate. First we went through the Christian Quarters, past the Ministry of

Tourism and around into the Armenian Quarters, with carpets hanging on display and a poster referring to the genocide committed by the Turkish Ottoman Empire. From here we continued into the Jewish Quarter, we three women heading to our section of the Western Wall. Upper arms covered out of respect, we waited our turn and then found a spot to face the wall near the right side. After touching the wall with hands and lips, I recalled how thousands have shed tears over centuries here. I watched as others read Scriptures in Hebrew, prayed, and cried, arms stretched out toward the wall. After a few minutes, I stepped back to make room for others, prayed, reflected further from a distance and observed plants growing in tufts through the upper wall, a loudspeaker up in a corner to the left. On exiting the Kotel plaza, I was struck by the words on a posted sign: "The Divine Presence never departs from here."

Next we walked along the Via Dolorosa (way of suffering), an ancient stone path with shops on either side. A sign above one doorway mentioned Simon of Cyrene, a possible Passover pilgrim designated by Roman authorities at the time to carry the execution beam of the one publicly sentenced, Jesus of Nazareth, accused in the governor's writing as claiming to be King of the Jews.

Moving forward a few centuries, in the adjacent area were the Muslim Quarters, a busy marketplace with tiny shops carrying all sorts of goods, such as men's loose-fitting long shirts and trouser sets, women's head scarves, olive wood drums, Turkish figs and open bowls of aromatic spices. Vendors called out in Arabic their offer of fresh-squeezed pomegranate juice; others carried trays of small glasses of tea. On exiting the Old City, we were relieved to have space to move!

Our extracurricular adventure group reconnected with our larger tour group for the evening's opening session at a large convention building. There was a procession of flag-bearing representatives of over 170 nations. The next day, our guide and bus driver took us to Yad Vashem, a Holocaust memorial museum. We passed through the area dedicated to righteous Gentiles, remembering the likes of Corrie ten Boom and Oscar Schindler. We went into a darkened place of remembrance, with names of various concentration camps and locations marked on the ground, as well as a monument with flames protruding. Afterwards we were introduced to the children's memorial, a cave-like entry with sticks of assorted heights on a rock above. These were to represent lives cut short. Our guide noted a single candle refracting light across hundreds of mirrors positioned inside. We walked about in silence, hearing the piped-in announcer of children's names and ages; in another section were young ones' photos on display. Outside we paused at a smokestack monument, adding a remembrance stone.

Unfortunately we had to hurry through the main museum with less than two hours to see what we could, zigzagging from side to side into each subsection with different themes, artefacts and descriptions. In passageways were other displays, such as a cart that carried the dead, rail tracks leading to a dead end and piles of dispossessed books. Some displays that affected me most were piles of shoes under a glass floor, typed lists of names and identification numbers, and archived footage of starved victims being dishonourably buried with bulldozers.

We solemnly returned to the bus and from there rode to Mount Herzl. Noted above the entryway are the words "World Zionist Organization." Buried there are prime ministers such as Golda Meir and multitudes of soldiers, including those unknown by name. Back at the conference centre that evening, I bought a small shofar and signed up for a tour of an army base.

By October, we noticed several small and large sukkah structures erected around Jerusalem, in anticipation of the week of commanded rejoicing. Some were of tent-like material, others of plywood and all had partially open rooftops—to allow for a glimpse of Messiah coming in the clouds, if this be the year of redemption. In the Christian Quarter of the Old City, we paid a visit to the Church of the Holy Sepulchre, revered by many Christians as the site of Jesus's death. I tried to look past the cluttered iconoclastic decor to examine this claim.

Later this day, we were taken by bus to an Israeli army base. We entered the grounds and watched as soldiers were called to form a rectangle (the Hebrew letter *chet*), and we were invited to interact one on one with these young men and women required to serve three years and two years, respectively. One soldier told me he embraced as his motto: "Not by might, nor by power, but by My spirit, saith the LORD of hosts" (from Zechariah 4:6, JPS Tanakh 1917). We learned that these soldiers were all rookies, training for frontline combat. When someone asked about a pouch with a symbol around a soldier's neck, he replied that was how he'd be identified if he died. He pulled out and revealed the silver-coloured numbered tag inside.

While going about, I asked a male and then a female soldier about foreigners volunteering with the Israeli army, and neither had heard about such an opportunity, but they were impressed Canadians would want to help them. Upon overhearing my inquiry, a man with a provincial police cap spoke up and answered my questions. He told me of a third-party organization, outlined how to apply and referred me to the representative in Toronto who was involved in the volunteer selection process. I sensed this opportunity was something for me to pursue, especially after an unexpected exchange on our tour bus. The rider in front of me had not been with us on our walk to Ammunition Hill the other day and had not heard another volunteer telling us about his experiences with the Israeli army. Therefore I was surprised when this fellow turned around in his seat and made what seemed a random remark to me. He said he kept getting a picture of me wearing an IDF uniform, and he felt impressed to tell me that. Before leaving the base, I stopped with our tour leader by a candle and star memorial and listened to a lone soldier share how he and his comrades daily passed by this place. As a lone soldier, he voluntarily came over without his family from his home country, the United States, to enlist in the IDF. Such is the love for this nation.

On our first evening when we checked into our hotel in Jerusalem, I found the concierge staff very helpful with booking a small group tour to Bethlehem. Our tour leader had agreed the four of us could go, provided we were back in time to join the Jerusalem March. That morning our little group met in the lobby for the van to pick us up. Outside the entrance to this ancient town was a tall grey concrete wall with a watchtower and barbed wire. Amidst graffiti promoting Palestinian causes with incitements to violence were references to Yeshua as Messiah being the way, truth and life. A huge banner of Yasser Arafat was prominently draped over the side of a large building.

We travelled along Manger Street, the main street of town, where there were numerous shops. We stopped first at the Shepherds' Field, looking out from atop ruins of a Byzantine (fourth- to sixth-century) monastery. We explored inside the shepherds' caves; next, our guide took us inside the Milk Grotto, reportedly the place where Mary nursed Jesus, and where they hid out from Herod before fleeing to Egypt.

We continued on to the Church of the Nativity, where I recognized the bell tower. My maternal grandmother had shown me a circa 1930s photo from my grandfather, then a British soldier. Up here was the place Grandad was stationed on Christmas Eve, Nana told me. Inside this historic building, we patiently waited in line to descend a few steps into a room, where marked on the floor was a 14-point star of Bethlehem, representing the 14 generations in Messianic lineage. Our guide ensured we took time to browse and buy in one of the many souvenir shops before heading back for the security crossing. Our driver spoke of persecution and martyrdom within his family heritage. Upon leaving Bethlehem, we had impressed on us the sense that the Christmas message was no longer so welcome there.

Picture this: thousands of pilgrims from around the world participate in this civic event, the annual Jerusalem March. Excitement mounts as representatives of the nations head toward Sacher Park. A passerby asks what this is about, and why Jews and Christians would be together. She seems impressed, but not all are reportedly in favour. Suspicion of ulterior motives still lingers. After a long and painful history, over the past decade or so, a trusting friendship is growing between the expressions of faith in the God of Abraham, Isaac and Jacob.

We had more than two hours' wait on the hill in the park, visiting, resting on the grass, taking photos and listening to live music. A sea of green and yellow garbed Brazilians appeared to outnumber the mix of various countries' colours streaming down the grounds. People in tribal dress from as far away as Papua New Guinea had come. A woman from Poland wanted to give me a small flag of her country; that reminds me of the young man in Poland who, later in 2012 (during the 25th March of the Living from Auschwitz-Birkenau), wanted to swap his larger Polish flag for my Canadian one. There was something powerful in the exchange. Our tour leader wore her traditional parade Mountie outfit, a symbol of Canadian authority. A petite, spunky grandmother from our west coast kept in step with the younger crowd. As we left the park distributing small Canadian flags and pins, children came flocking, eager to receive.

Now I'll try to convey to you my impressions en route the march. Young and old, male and female, religious and secular lined the streets and were on balconies and on rooftops. People were smiling and waving, welcoming the nations to Jerusalem. What a sight! My friend broke out in dance with her large Canadian flag, which received cheers from the crowd. I proudly waved my Canadian with Israeli flags together. It was an honour to walk by the platform with the mayor and veterans.

Later, we received a fortieth anniversary of reunited Jerusalem keychain, as well as a signed poster thanking us for being in the march. Near the end of the route, a man in a hockey jersey blew a shofar, along with two male trumpeters. The impact of the experience was beyond words.

On our last day here, our whole group toured further sites in Jerusalem. My roommate and I chatted on our balcony the last evening. She admitted to crying over it soon being time to leave Israel. I wanted to rejoice over the remaining time here and feel sorrow later. That last morn, I read from the prophet Zechariah:

> The LORD says this: "I will return to Zion and dwell in the midst of Jerusalem. Then Jerusalem will be called the City of Truth, and the mountain of the LORD of armies *will be called* the Holy Mountain." (Zechariah 8:3 NASB)

> On that day, when all the nations of the earth are gathered against her, I will make Jerusalem an immovable rock for all the nations. All who try to move it will injure themselves. (Zechariah 12:3 NIV)

> Then shall the LORD go forth, And fight against those nations, As when He fighteth in the day of battle. And His feet shall stand in that day upon the mount of Olives, Which is before Jerusalem on the east, And the mount of Olives shall cleft in the midst thereof toward the east and toward the west, So that there shall be a very great valley; And half of the mountain shall remove toward the north, And half of it toward the south. And ye shall flee to the valley of the mountains; For the valley of the mountains shall

reach unto Azel; Yea, ye shall flee, like as ye fled from before the earthquake in the days of Uzziah king of Judah; And the LORD my God shall come, And all the holy ones with Thee. (Zechariah 14:3–5 JPS)

And it shall come to pass in that day, that there shall not be light, But heavy clouds and thick; And there shall be one day which shall be known as the LORD'S, Not day, and not night; But it shall come to pass, that at evening time there shall be light. And it shall come to pass in that day, That living waters shall go out from Jerusalem: Half of them toward the eastern sea, And half of them toward the western sea; In summer and in winter shall it be. And the LORD shall be King over all the earth; In that day shall the LORD be One, and His name one. (Zechariah 14:6–9 JPS)

And it shall come to pass, that every one that is left of all the nations which came against Jerusalem shall even go up from year to year to worship the King, the LORD of hosts, and to keep the feast of tabernacles. (Zechariah 14:16 KJV)

On our last day of touring Jerusalem, I caught my first glimpse of the Eastern Gate (aka Golden Gate) via the bus window. While peering from the corner at Jericho Road, I was amazed to consider one day Messiah will appear there! The sealed stone entrance will be opened again. Our Jewish guide pointed out the Jewish graveyard along the Mount of Olives, and the Muslim one added outside the Eastern Gate. He related a Muslim belief that they can, by this strategic placement, stop the Jewish Messiah from coming and resurrecting the dead. How remarkable one can believe so far, yet not embrace this Messiah!

We walked around the parameter of the Garden of Gethsemane, marvelling at the ancient olives trees with wide gnarly trunks, branches full of green olives. I imagined Jesus being so stressed over what he anticipated facing that he actually sweated drops of blood. From Kidron Valley to Mount Zion Gate, I rejoiced over being here, looking up at the ancient stone full of pockmarks from ammunition rounds. We visited the traditional Upper Room with ornate architecture, where the famed Last Supper took place and where the apostles experienced the Holy Spirit at Pentecost. We paused at what nearby is regarded as King David's tomb. Close to the high priest Caiaphas's house was a rooster figure, reminiscent of the impulsive disciple Peter's denial of knowing Jesus. Our group entered a pit where Jesus was reportedly lowered through a hole in the ceiling and kept overnight, awaiting trial.

Over in the Old City's Jewish Quarter, our tour leader had taken us into a souvenir shop. At first I was disappointed we were losing sightseeing time, but some pieces of a puzzle came together for me. The shopkeeper spoke of a language barrier that exists between Jews and Christians; sometimes we use the same words or phrases but with different meanings. One illustration especially stands out. He described how approaching Sukkot, one finds Jewish men meticulously shopping for the perfect plants for the lulav ensemble. To an outsider, it can appear legalistic and unnecessary. But when you understand one is searching for the best gift for the Lover of one's soul, that gives the activity new meaning. He explained that for many of us in Israel for the first time, we may feel natural being here. That's because we're in our Father's house! I anticipated feeling a part of my heart being left behind in Jerusalem. Surprised and honoured to be singled out to pray for the Jewish shopkeeper, I uttered a few words I do not recall.

Afterwards, I noticed our host and others in our tour group were visibly touched. Before we headed out, I bought a copy of this author's book, which he signed for me: "Carrie, I like your heart."

Our tour group's last stop was at the Garden Tomb, a picturesque area tucked inside East Jerusalem. The British site guide showed us through this tranquil park, where birds were singing amidst the flowers and trees. We paused at the lookout point over the bus station below, noting a skull formation in the cliff wall ahead. From descriptions in the Bible, many believe this is more likely Golgotha, the site of crucifixion, than the traditional Church of the Holy Sepulchre which is within the ancient city walls. A replica of a round stone was across the path from the tomb opening in the cave wall. A few at a time, we entered in to find slabs of stone to the right. Here is believed to be where Jesus was laid. A sign inside read, "HE IS NOT HERE FOR HE IS RISEN."

As the sun was setting, after a reflective time together, we were about to leave when suddenly we were startled by a loud, explosive blast. I looked at our assistant leader, who also had a look of dread, wondering what may have just happened. Our British guide hurried over to assure us this was simply the signal to end Ramadan, telling Muslims they could eat! Couldn't they settle for a dinner bell?

Sadly, we left on our bus back to our hotel for our last meal together, catching our last views of Jerusalem by diminishing light. Four of us, the Bethlehem crew, later cracked open a bottle of wine to toast, "Lechaim!" meaning "To life!" I blurted out in error, "Heimlich!" eliciting laughter. My roommate and I made it to the lobby by midnight, postcards dropped off at front desk. We boarded our red tour bus for the last time, making my last steps in Jerusalem. The sad reality of leaving had not yet fully affected me emotionally, and we arrived at the airport around one in the morning, bidding farewell and final "Todah rabah" ("Thank you very much") to our driver.

It took most of three hours to get through all levels of security. Some of our team had to rummage through a lot of our luggage to locate a gift of a clay oil lamp given to each of us at Nazareth Village. I held mine up as it was examined by a guard. Someone from our tour group was selected from the line for further questioning. Occasionally I glanced over to see her with a perplexed look, nodding. We went through more X-ray machines, this time with my backpack and a bagful of film. (My 35mm had konked out on the Sea of Galilee, and for the remainder of the trip, I used disposable cameras.) At the boarding area, I lingered to the last, reluctant to leave Israel.

Something that the Christian Zionist organization, who facilitated our tour, strongly emphasized in teaching was that replacement theology had no place in the truth of Scripture. In other words, the Church has *not* replaced Israel!

> This is what the LORD Almighty says: "In those days ten people from all languages and nations will take firm hold of one Jew by the hem of his robe and say, 'Let us go with you, because we have heard that God is with you.'" (Zechariah 8:23 NIV)

See the sure promise of Jeremiah 31:31–36 (JPS):

> Behold, the days come, saith the LORD, that I will make a new covenant with the house of Israel, and with the house of Judah; not according to the covenant that I made with their fathers in the day that I took them by the hand to bring them out of the land of Egypt; forasmuch as they broke My covenant, although I was a lord over them, saith the LORD. But this is the covenant that I will make with the house of Israel after those days, saith the LORD, I will

put My law in their inward parts, and in their heart will I write it; and I will be their God, and they shall be My people; and they shall teach no more every man his neighbour, and every man his brother, saying: "Know the LORD"; for they shall all know Me, from the least of them unto the greatest of them, saith the LORD; for I will forgive their iniquity, and their sin will I remember no more.

Thus saith the LORD, Who giveth the sun for a light by day, And the ordinances of the moon and of the stars for a light by night, Who stirreth up the sea, that the waves thereof roar, The LORD of hosts is His name: If these ordinances depart from before Me, Saith the LORD, Then the seed of Israel also shall cease from being a nation before Me forever.

Section II: Return (2008)

A Deeper Identification

I treated my first time in Israel the previous year as though it may have been my only chance to explore the land, but I was back sooner than expected. I recall the feeling of my first involvement as a civilian volunteer on an army base. We arrived at the designated spot to meet the Israeli coordinator and receive our assignment. Until that day, we did not know where in Israel we would be serving for the next three weeks.

After laying down the law of what was expected of us, we were sent off with soldier accompaniment to each international team's allotted base. Soon after entering the base, we were donning khaki fatigues. I remember emerging from our humble barracks and proudly posing for a photo.

After hours, our leisure time was spent in our sandpit living room, surrounded by a communal laundry line, with aircraft often roaring overhead. One morning I watched an F-15 fighter jet fly over the memorial site of rocks and trees. From this distance, it resembled a housefly. We met our first madrichot (leaders), most of whom are young women lone soldiers who voluntarily came from their home countries to serve in the IDF. They were our main point of contact, providing translation and instruction on daily duties. Israelis are quite multitalented, as one soldier snacked on chocolate while chatting on her mobile phone and playing guitar.

Each morning began with flag raising and a news report. Our little team of comrades soon bonded. One who especially left an impact on me was an encouraging father figure who later went on to his heavenly abode. Another was a young woman who grappled with the history of her home country, Germany; her act of service was her way of showing empathy with the sufferings of the Jewish people.

Outside our weekend army hostel, several of us gathered around a fountain to share evening snacks we had purchased at a nearby grocery store. We toasted a glass of sweet red wine, and in the dark we discovered the bag of cheese twists I thought I had contributed was actually a popular peanut butter flavoured snack. Prepackaged army fare was provided for all three meals, so eating out was a treat. One morning during breakfast, outside our sunny window, I noticed a sprinkling of raindrops—the first time seeing rain here in Israel.

While out exploring more of Tel Aviv, I spotted a magnificent large cloud with sunrays poking through. Along Rothschild Boulevard, I noticed a tree that had hangings that resembled *peyot* (side curls of hair worn by some Orthodox boys and men). On this picturesque street stands a rather bland-looking building of great significance. There at Independence Hall, the nation's first prime minister, David Ben Gurion, announced in 1948 the rebirth of the State of Israel.

My new friend came with me that day in search of the Canadian embassy, where I expected my voter package to have arrived by then. We stopped in a drugstore to ask directions, and I found its store layout and logo familiar. Upon inquiry, a clerk informed us this Israeli chain was founded by a Canadian who had made aliyah (immigration according to the Jewish law of return). For seven years, I had worked for his company, both in Eastern and in Western Canada. On finding the embassy, we had to turn in our mobile phones and take a number tag, even though we were the only customers there! After a substantial wait, I was called into an office only to find out that my voter package was held up in customs. (Some time later, I received a call while atop the Mount of Olives in

Jerusalem advising that if I came to the consulate building early the next morning, I could still vote!)

On arrival, one of the staff remembered me from the previous day and inquired why it was so important for me to vote. I answered that our Canadian prime minister supported Israel, and I wanted to keep him in office. When asked his name, I answered, and the consulate staff in unison began to enthusiastically chant our PM's name. After emerging from casting my vote, he and his colleague cheered me on, waving mini Canadian flags.

The first day back at the base, our clean uniforms were already dirty. One of my tasks was to remove grime and then apply oil to the tracks on tanks. We climbed in and out of tanks, cleaning them, and we also painted parts of military vehicles. My late friend used to muse that he was wearing his "cleanest dirty shirt." That second week, we received our first epaulettes, blue tags affixed to our shoulder straps, which signified that we were international volunteers.

Our final week, they took us to a kibbutz in Rehovat, which now operated as a museum. Prior to the mid-1970s, its function was largely unknown to the public, because it was an underground ammunition factory, accessed through a secret trap door and stairwell beneath the laundry room. Here, a select group of early volunteers stepped forward for an assignment they were about to discover. These pioneers came to call those outside of their circle "giraffes," those above ground on the kibbutz who knew nothing of their daily endeavours. To conceal their untanned flesh, which would make them stand out from others working in the fields, a doctor prescribed them supplements, and each took a turn in the tanning salon!

We walked through the factory, moving from successive work stations, including the cutting of metal and shaping of bullet shells. The final task was entrusted to a woman, with the theory she would not bang down too hard on the loaded bullet cap, causing the whole place to explode! Before the workers could blend back in above, at the end of every work day they carefully helped one another remove any trace of metal from their hair, clothing and boots. To alert to coming British inspectors on the kibbutz, a light signal was installed, and the officers were stalled over complimentary offers of cold beer, prepared ahead in the ice box. What an operation to remain secret all that time, as not everyone back then (or now) see Israelis as having the right to defend themselves!

While on a weekend off, exploring Ashdod, I had stopped into a pharmacy to purchase some peroxide. My Hebrew being very limited at that time, I pointed to the bandage on my shin (from an aforementioned army prank gone awry), and the woman in the white lab coat responded questioningly: "Ee-oh-deen?" And potent iodine that was, much stronger and more effective than I've found since.

In Ashdod was a traffic circle with fake trees and human figures lit up at night. I also found traces of Canadian charity, with a Zionist youth centre dedicated. As the sun was setting, I stood on the shore of the Mediterranean and called a friend, telling her I was looking south in the direction of Gaza.

On various occasions as I looked about Jaffa, Jerusalem and Haifa, I wondered where in these old cities my grandfather once trod during his service with the British military. Between 1936 and 1939 were the Arab revolts. Israel was called Palestine back then under British rule, a misnomer tracing back to Roman times. My nana told me that Grandad did not always go along with British policy of the day. She showed me some of his photos. If only he were still alive so I could compare experiences with him, now that I had completed my term of service as a civilian army volunteer.

At the southern tip of Israel on the shore of the Red Sea lies Eilat, where temperatures can soar above 40 degrees Celsius. Eilat is a popular beach destination amongst tourists and Israelis. Having met and received assurance from an instructor at my travellers' hostel, I decided to try a scuba lesson. However, upon completion of the required Hebrew form—with the help of his boss translating into English—it was determined that due to my having a cat allergy, they would not allow me to scuba dive without a doctor's note. It mattered not my reasoning that cats are not generally found under the ocean, so my breathing would not be affected.

Instead, I took up snorkelling at Coral Beach, where I could rent equipment for a few shekels a day. Only a short distance from shore, just beneath the surface, I could watch stunning colours of fish, some striped yellow and purple. As the name indicates, there are coral reefs underwater which are quite abrasive, as I found when my foot scraped against one. My travellers' shelter was a cozy place, with international guests mingling in the centre common area outdoors, surrounded by the dorm units and indoor kitchen facilities and office. From this point, I ventured out for a day trip across the border.

A note of caution: this method is not recommended for most travellers, especially the younger novice! Before leaving Canada, I had tried booking a spot on a day tour to the traditional Mount Sinai in Egypt. The company told me to call back, because at that time they did not have enough participants to run the tour. So I did again and again, receiving the same answer. Then it was time to fly to Israel. From there I kept in contact with the tour company. Finally, one day they advised they now had enough to run the tour—but no more room for me! I'd explored other options to no avail. So plan B: I'd simply walk across the Israeli-Egyptian border from Eilat.

Before heading out that morn, I did let a couple of fellow travellers from my hostel know where I was going, claiming that they could expect my return by day's end. While going through customs at Taba border crossing, I exchanged just enough shekels for pounds as I thought needed. I'd first checked with an official who seemed to have no vested interest in how much I'd spend. As it turned out, due to a Muslim holiday, buses were not running that day, so my only option was taxi.

After receiving a reasonable estimate, I ventured out to the awaiting row of drivers. One tall man in a long robe looked at me expectantly, tapping a stick across the palm of his hand. His eyes looked crazed. Nope, not going with him. On to the next one. I scanned down the row, sizing up the drivers and searching for one that I discerned would safely transport me to the base of Mount Sinai. There he was. The only problem was we'd upset the taxi pecking order.

Even though I'd discreetly communicated to this driver I wanted to travel with him and not the guy with the stick, as soon as we began walking over to his vehicle, the argument began. The driver advised I wait in his taxi as he appealed to the other drivers to let him pass through. A circle formed, and from inside the vehicle I heard shouting and saw angry motioning. My eye was on my driver. How would he react? Would he pass my test, or would I get out and return to customs? There, bright white uniformed tourist police stood by. They surely would have a vested interest in ensuring this tourist had a good experience and would want to come back or recommend visiting to others. I had already approached one officer to let him know in whose taxi I planned to go, asking him to watch out for trouble. After minutes of yelling and another younger driver attempting to push my driver, passage was cleared, and my driver passed the test. He kept his cool and merely blocked his assailant. Onward to the mount.

At its base lay Saint Catherine's Monastery. Getting there was under a three-hour drive through desert road and around mountainous terrain. On arrival my driver paused, and out his window, he addressed a young Bedouin man. He apparently agreed to be my guide and recommended enlisting his elderly acquaintance, also for a reasonable fee, so I could ride up on camelback. It was explained the camel could only go so far near the top, due to the narrowing path. From there the youth and I would hike to the top and back down. My taxi driver gave me his card; his plan was to rest at his friend's place and then return for me when I was ready to call.

Off we went, robed Bedouin guide leading the way. I was on a grouchy grey camel, and the elderly man wearing a traditional red and white keffiyeh (head scarf) trailed behind. The rope dangled from the animal, who turned his head toward me and seemed to snarl. Normally furry creatures like and trust me. I trusted that this beast was not suicidal, because he had a tendency to frequently veer toward the edge of the unguarded path, which narrowed as we got nearer to the top. The trek was mostly in silence because I did not know Arabic, and my young guide spoke limited English. The camel owner's main audible contribution was the sound of his periodic spitting. He was far enough back that nothing hit me.

The view was spectacular. Increasingly people and animals down below began to shrink to the size of ants. The rock surface in the sun ranged from different shades of reddish brown, with flecks of green where there was some vegetation growing. Eventually the camel could go no farther, and I dismounted, thanked and paid its owner, and proceeded onwards by foot, following the robed fellow.

This was the month of Ramadan, when devoted Muslims fast from sunrise to sundown over a 30-day period. In this blistering heat, the youth did not partake even of water as he faithfully carried out his job as guide. Occasionally I tried to discreetly sip at my water bottle, because my mouth became dry as the air got thinner, and both my guide and I stopped at intervals to catch our breath. Before setting out, a food patron near the base of the mount invited me to order. I politely declined, having observed no running water in any of the sink basins. Was I ever glad I'd filled my water bottle with fresh Israeli water!

Most of my surroundings were natural rock formations, but there was some evidence of human ingenuity. One amusing example was the "emergency station" carved in rock. I saw neither an attendant nor any supplies of basic first aid. There was not even an apparent mode of communication! At another place was an archway, marking an entry to nowhere obvious.

The path continued to narrow until we reached the top. What a sense of awe, reading from the book of Exodus the account of Moses and the community receiving the Torah, the Ten Commandments! I tried to imagine what this was like: the atmosphere of thunder and lightning, the sound of trumpet blasts. What was it like for those first-hand witnesses? For Moses? I had new appreciation for him at his ripe age to be trekking up and down—twice—schlepping stone tablets originally inscribed by the finger of God. These vital instructions were revealed foremost to the growing Israelite nation, but the basics were also meant for all humankind.

Once I was satisfied with a period of reflection atop Mount Sinai, I returned to my patiently waiting guide. It was just us and birds up there. A few small edifices indicated signs of prior human gatherings. The Bedouin and I began our long hike down, making big steps over boulders, a different path than what we took going up with the camel. Saint Catherine's Monastery was visible off in the distance. My guide, seeing I was getting tired, assured me only two more minutes. He mentioned this a few times, so I concluded the Egyptian "two minutes" was in a different time zone! Eventually we both safely reached bottom, and I thanked and paid my guide. Then I contacted my taxi driver, who returned for me as promised. On the drive back, I fought to stay awake and take in the view of dancing shadows as the sun set over the hilly, sandy earth. Back at the border, I thanked and paid my driver, and I was ever so glad to cross over by foot, again on Israeli soil.

North of Eilat in the Negev is Beersheva; there remains Abraham's well. Earlier in Jerusalem, I'd met an *olah chadasha* (new Jewish immigrant) who'd offered to take me around her new hometown. I rode a late-night bus there, which was so crowded we had soldiers reclining on the floor, machine guns pointed in various directions, necessarily strapped onto each uniformed figure. With no time to toss my duffle bag below the bus, it and my backpack sat on and under my legs. Despite the cramped quarters beside a big fellow, I somehow dozed off and awoke in Tel Aviv. That was not my destination. Off I got, and I bought another ticket to backtrack south to Beersheva. By morning I reached this ancient city, and the bus station was also brimming with people. Upon discovering my mobile phone battery had run out, I sought to access a payphone I noticed inside a restaurant, but I was not permitted inside. A young man in a long line noticed me and explained in English that there was a bomb scare in effect. Oh.

After walking to a nearby mall, I managed to connect with my new friend, who showed me around as planned. First I found Abraham's well on my own, but it was closed, so I settled for climbing the fence high enough to take a peek down over the top. Wells had been a real point of contention. A huge, neatly rowed cemetery testified to that. So many young lives lost, valiantly. Many were from Australia or New Zealand, like my guide.

They were part of the famous charge of the Light Horse Brigade, which in 1917 assisted British General Allenby in recapturing wells from the Turks who'd ruled the area for centuries under the Ottoman Empire. Allenby was considered a hero by many, and a monument stands here in his honour. There are remnants of the bygone era: a red and white crescent flag flaps by the old Turkish train station. In recent times, a welcome centre was built for new olim to move into and gradually adjust to living in their new home country. My guide also took me around the city core and the outdoor market, and we enjoyed some fresh-picked carob and melt-in-your-mouth gooey dates from local trees.

Upon returning to Jerusalem, at Kibbutz Ramat Rachel I met up with a Canadian friend I'd made during my first trip to Israel. From this historic place were stationed the early defenders of the reconstituted nation. Inscriptions lined bunkers. On a high ridge overlooking the skyline was a chuppah, the traditional Jewish wedding canopy. There, I dreamed that if I ever had a chance of getting married in Israel, I would like to stand with my groom.

At Ramat Rachel were gathered another kind of defender of this now sixty-year-old nation: prayer warriors from around the world. We were assigned to set times, covering around the clock up in a tower. I was relieved that Canada was part of a 4:00–6:00 p.m. watch. But I soon learned that we too would be roused during the wee hours of the night, awakened by the large contingent of Asian participants who were camped out on mats in the same auditorium. On the mat adjacent mine was a sole representative of a tiny European country called Liechtenstein. During mealtimes and on excursions, I also met a smiling and colourful bunch of Polynesians, and even some Alaskans. What everyone had in common was a desire to see Israel protected and thrive.

One of our excursions headed north, stopping in Nazareth. A large church building was in a prominent place, behind a tall, wide banner announcing Allah as the one before whom to submit. In another spot, we were shown another unusual combination: a tiny synagogue-church, where services reportedly rotated shared space. That night I got little sleep between having to share a room with a sweet elderly woman whose snoring ripped through my eardrums, and moving my mattress out onto the balcony from where the muezzin (Muslim call to prayer from a minaret tower) reverberated throughout the atmosphere before sunrise. I looked forward to moving on from here, and I went to board our bus by the lobby. But the lobby was not there—from the elevator button marked ground floor. By the time a few of us realized the exit was from a higher number level, the bus had left without us! So here we were. Now what? We tried to make the most of it, walking around and conversing in our common language of Français. At least we knew the bus was due to return by day's end.

Farther north awaited a new adventure: travelling to the Lebanese border. The international spiritual defence force gathered to listen to instructions from our local guide. In the event an alert siren sounded—warning of an incoming Katyusha rocket—we were to rapidly run to safety. That day seemed quiet and peaceful. Rich green trees lined the border. Through the fence I could touch the foliage of another country. Some participants brought with them colourful banners—not exactly a form of camouflage! The silhouette of one man standing at attention on a rock resembled to me an Israeli soldier. We came. We prayed. We left without incident.

Like the wells of Beersheva earlier, the Temple Mount in Jerusalem later became another place of contention between Muslims and Jews. I wanted to see it for myself but was advised I must go up there with a licensed guide. One found me at Jaffa Gate. We negotiated a fee, and he told me where to meet. After waiting in line, security asked in an anxious tone where my guide was. I assured them he would be on the other side, and he was. There was an expansive open area surrounded by gates, each with an Arabic name.

The guide took me around the perimeter of the mosque with the shiny golden dome, telling me of various Islamic exploits. For faithful followers, nearby were pre-prayer washing stations, where hands and feet and certain orifices were purified. I recall no mention of the actual existence of two successive temples, which predated the site of this blue-tiled, rounded edifice constructed in the seventh century. I tried to imagine the former days. The Temple Institute in Jerusalem contains reconstructed implements like those used in priestly service in bygone days, in anticipation of the future "house of prayer for all nations" (see Isaiah 56:7 NIV).

Departing from Jaffa Gate entrance into the Old City, free walking tours were offered on a regular basis. Our guides took us through the main arteries as well as down winding side streets and onto roof tops. They gave us a wide sampling through the ages of the major cultures living there: Jewish, Muslim, Christian and Armenian. After our excursion, four of us—another Canadian gal, an American (with whom I've remained friends), and a tall guy from Switzerland—decided to go eat shawarma. They took up the invitation to join me afterwards atop the rampart walls, offering a spectacular view over Jerusalem. We were eye level to luscious date palm clusters. We females were thankful for our tall male acquaintance, who protectively came between us and some Arab youth who at first welcomed us (apparently mockingly, as they followed up with expletives) and then tried trailing us on the walls. We continued our way around and then returned to ground level without incident. From there we bid our Swiss friend adieu, and we entered the obscure opening to Zedekiah's caves, believed to be the site of the temple quarry. Artificial lighting gave the shallow cavern an orange glow, with shadows of other human figures dancing about.

Farther south in the desert, I ventured along the Ein Gedi nature path, coming across a beautiful icy mint-blue waterfall. Nearby were rows of caves, amongst which young David hid from King Saul, who was obsessed with taking his young rival's life. Nevertheless, as Scriptures tell us, David was eventually anointed as Israel's new king, and he first reigned in the ancient city of Hebron.

A new Australian friend agreed to accompany me there to explore the old quarter. We took public transit and had to go through the Bethlehem checkpoint. I assumed my travel companion would always keep her passport on her person as I did in a foreign country, so I was taken by surprise to discover she'd left all her identification back at her guest house! Now what was I to do? To travel alone would not be wise. There would not likely be another chance before flying back to Canada, so I appealed to the military personnel. They permitted us to enter on the condition the Australian remained by my side and exited the checkpoint along with me and my Canadian passport.

Upon arriving in Hebron, a young man was very eager to show us around, despite our repeatedly declining his offer. He politely insisted on tagging along, and he did guide us to the oldest part of town. When my friend needed public facilities, he brought us to a school director, who let us use her *sherutim*, an enamel basin sunken into the ground. Afterwards, the director introduced us to her hundred-year-old mother, who sat on the floor of their abode, baking flat bread on an electric appliance. They invited us to join them for fresh bread and tea. We accepted their hospitality with thanks.

Much of old town Hebron was like a ghost town; not many tourists came here. When at one point there was a pedestrian traffic jam, with heavily garbed soldiers on standby, I asked our young guide what was going on. He explained the soldiers were ensuring safe passage of the Jews. My photographer's eye caught the image of a short, stocky soldier with the most serious look on his face beneath the helmet. Seeking the permission of the taller, older-looking soldier, I used my limited Hebrew to ask, "Beseder (okay) photo?"

He replied with a curt "Lo," so I didn't argue. But then he continued in fluent English. "Your lens cap is on." Oh! Didn't I feel sheepish, yet I was glad his "lo" was not absolute. Once I removed the cap, it was okay to snap, so I did. It remains one of my favourite photos, capturing a serious reality of Israeli life amongst those who call themselves Palestinians.

Another day, with a group of tour participants, we visited the ancient tabernacle site at Shiloh. We heard a former mayor's personal encounter with terror, his close brush with death. He led us on a pilgrimage to the rock formation, which formed the base where the Israelite place of worship was erected. Not far from here, we stopped and heard from a radio broadcaster why a certain hilltop was being repopulated. Bethel was where Jacob had his dream of angels ascending and descending from heaven. In Hebrew, the new name he gave this city means "house of God." The covenant promise was reiterated here to Abraham's grandson, extending north, south, east and west. From a water tower lookout point, we could view a rock monument depicting which geographical places extended in each direction.

Near the end of this trip to Israel, when I'd all but given up on including a tour of the Golan Heights, I received a call back from the tour company that it was going after all. I headed out on a day trip with our hippy guide. Our little group in the van was shown an architectural sampling of the vital importance of a cornerstone, strategically holding together a large stone archway. If that capstone were removed ... you get the picture. Our hippy guide took us up on a military viewpoint, showing us the bunkers, remnants of a former war brought on by Syria. Just before time to leave, I quickly asked the guide to take a picture of me. Not until we had boarded our tour van did I look at the results of his shot. I'd unknowingly stood in the foreground of a painted silhouette, causing it to appear I had a rifle aimed at the side of my head! Up on this vantage point was also a sign pointing in various directions, including the way to Iraq, from whence Abraham came.

My second trip to Israel would have been incomplete if I'd not taken the opportunity to visit the oldest city in the world, Jericho. A Canadian friend and I were invited to travel along with a group familiar with the turf. There, while refreshing our feet in Elisha's stream, we met one courageous woman and listened to her heart for the people of this place. Her vision to counter hatred demonstrated love for Israel and the nations surrounding.

The finale, our last eve in Jerusalem, was with Israeli guests, including those who had recently immigrated. The event organizers put on a quality performance of song and dance at the large conference centre. Dignitaries, including the mayor, welcomed us to this great city.

Section III: Whetting My Appetite (2010)

First 24 Hours in Jerusalem

The time arrived for my departure to Israel for the longest duration yet: the spring of 2010. My late friend, a Holocaust survivor, and our mutual younger friend accompanied me to the airport by bus. One of my best friends and her parents met us there, and we shared laughs together until it was time for me to go through security. With this airline, I was questioned both at check-in and again in the boarding area. They even swabbed the sole of my boots!

This trip had been several months in the making, from obtaining a leave of absence from work to taking care of all the little details of preparing to go. I believe this will be a time of exponential spiritual growth, a time for enlarging vision, finding further direction.

On arrival at Tel Aviv's international airport, I discovered my backpack had been rummaged through, and a missing item turned up on the conveyor belt. No matter, though. I was here, my third return to the land.

Greetings from Jerusalem, this city where God placed His name!

While gazing over a lookout point, I learned there was a site called Hill of Evil Counsel. That was where the United Nations building stood.

A Canadian friend had planned to take me to Sderot (near Gaza), introducing me to a media spokesperson there, but I learned the other night that plans were postponed. That was okay; I was sensing that God wanted me to begin this trip by really pressing into Him, being willing to keep laying down my own agenda. I looked out over the skyline of Jerusalem, asking Him to show me what He wanted me to see and hear what He wanted me to hear.

In the land, I live such a sense of adventure, exploring and observing as a freelancer, as a Canadian accessing areas denied to Israeli Jews. Note the big red signs, for instance, and imagine if you were told, as a citizen of your country, that certain patches of ground were off limits to you simply because of who you are! Scripture became more vivid to me while I sat in Shechem and read the passage referenced there, Genesis 12:1–6 (NIV), the promise of blessing to those who bless Israel. Sadly, from posters plastered about, many of the current inhabitants of this ancient city revere heroes who curse and fight against God's people.

Similarly in Bethlehem, Yasser Arafat's image is prominently displayed. This late leader was a far cry from the ancient leader David, who from wells here received water brought to him by his mighty men at the risk of their own lives (see 2 Samuel 23:15–16 NIV). In humble gratitude, David poured it out as an offering before the Lord.

Transition from Israeli Army Life

Tonight I'm writing to you from Jerusalem, from an organization which counters hate propaganda. Two days ago, I completed my first three weeks serving on army bases. I feel right at home here in the land. It's also been a place of testing, of learning to identify at a deeper level with some of the pain experienced here.

Along with fellow Canadians, volunteers from the United States, France, Germany and Switzerland were assigned to a base assembling medical supplies. (The team to Haiti was sent from this base. During the Holocaust, Haiti took in Jewish refugees.) Each morning we joined in formation with the soldiers for flag raising. Before each weekend off base, everyone scurried to prepare for inspections. We were urged to keep drinking water because temperatures ranged in the mid-thirties Celsius, and we younger ones were doing a lot of heavy lifting (several pallets of cases of IV solution).

Let me introduce you to some of our team: F of Montreal and P of New York, who asked and were deeply moved over why non-Jews would help Israel; B of Berlin, who like Abraham is a friend of God; G and R of Cleveland, who after courageously battling cancer came to serve; P, a retired Texan cop moved to tears over learning from Jewish friends; M, of Western Canada, a retired math teacher and a natural comedian; and G, of Western Europe, a member of our warehouse dream team. Our madrichot were top notch.

Outside work hours, our madrichot arranged for special activities to teach us more about history and culture pertaining to Israeli life and the army. Speakers included a general and an officer expressing appreciation for our coming to help and inspire them. An author in her eighties shared of her early days in the defence of the nation. I recall her story of being told to meet a man holding a newspaper while she carried some cargo under her top! She was there, surviving the siege in Jerusalem, initially unaware that from Tel Aviv it was declared the rebirth of the State of Israel in 1948. One evening outside the barracks, our madrichot joined with us in a song and dance circle, including, by request, the Canadian and Israeli national anthems!

That last evening together, with my spunky, grandmotherly comrade from Queens, we put on a couple of skit performances for our soldiers. I wrote and directed a spoof of an old sitcom, casting characters who learned to adapt on an army base rather than being shipwrecked on a desert island. The idea was spawned after I observed at flag raising a fellow volunteer who, in his wide-brim hat, resembled the star character.

My comrade wrote and directed her comical skit on a revised history of Israeli wars won, featuring characters such as Moshe Dayan wearing an eye patch. She reached back in time to include David versus Goliath, the giant struck dead via a slingshot. What differed in these accounts were the crucial role of our army volunteers and their innovative use of base medical supplies to save the day!

Our last day, the commander and deputy commanders, both examples of strong and gentle authority, decorated us with medical brigade epaulettes. Each of us also received dog tags (army ID necklaces) with our names in Hebrew. God has given me such a strong sense of identification with His chosen people.

Outside my army adventures, on weekends off, I visited some places I hadn't been during my last time in Israel. Accompanied by a seasoned army volunteer, we arrived in Sderot less than three hours after a Kassam rocket hit the area; I learned this news en route. We had a meeting with a journalist there, and I saw the unedited footage of the damage. Thankfully everyone got out of the building in time. Those rockets are very heavy; I held one. We also talked with a mother and daughter who experienced a rocket hitting near their home. They pointed to a wall full of shrapnel marks and related that a boy sought refuge there, and no marks were left on him! At least four Kassam rockets have hit the area this month, one killing a Thai worker. One also struck Ashkelon 11 days after I was there. Hamas (the Islamic ruling party in Gaza, whose name in Hebrew means violence) has reportedly called off their ceasefire.

Hamas also recently incited some Muslims in Jerusalem to riot, declaring a "day of rage," following dedication of a restored ancient synagogue in the Old City's Jewish Quarter. Police and military presence were increased as rocks and floor tiles were tossed from the Temple Mount. A field trip with our soldiers was cancelled as a security precaution. We went to the Western Wall the following week once peace was restored.

Last weekend, I visited Petah Tikva (the fifth largest city in

Israel), Bet Shemesh (literally, "house of sun"), Kiryat Ye'arim (where the Ark of the Covenant temporarily rested), Abu Ghosh (an Arab town which has been supportive toward Israel) and Efrat (where I was invited for Shabbat at the home of a prominent rabbi's widow; she is a Canadian who made aliyah).

Then this weekend, I took a train to the ancient port city of Acco; when darkness fell, I tried "blending in" with a crowd of Muslim girls to make safe passage out the gate toward the bus station. I stayed overnight in nearby Haifa, at one of several soldiers' hostels around the country. Yesterday morning, in pouring rain, I continued on to the old mystical city of Safed, browsing through the artist colony and around Orthodox synagogues, then stopping at a popular cheese shop. There, I met a server whose name means "life."

The last bus back to Jerusalem before Shabbat took a meandering scenic route. On arrival at the volunteer house, I received a warm welcome from director and team. After goodbye hugs with my previous team and invitations to visit them back home, I'm adjusting to my new neighbourhood. Last night I was invited for a Shabbat supper at a rabbi's home, where several tables were crammed into their living and dining area, lined with buckled bookshelves. A warm welcome was extended to all, including a man whose faculties were in need of restoration. It was such a beautiful picture of joyful singing amidst chaos, with a wide spectrum of practising Jews and Christians sitting together and partaking of spiritual and physical food. They served the largest loaves of challah I've ever seen! One Jewish woman related she sensed the presence of Ruach Hakadosh (Holy Spirit).

The rabbi's teachings, alternately in Hebrew and English, offered hope for freedom from our personal Mitzrayim (Egypt). He used an analogy of matzah (unleavened bread) to demonstrate humility, and challenged us to seize opportunities to do mitzvah (obedience to what God commands) while urging us to procrastinate when tempted to sin. He explained the reason why in Scripture the sin and donation offerings were presented together: that way, no one could tell who was presenting what. In Jewish values, to embarrass another is likened to murder. God made provision to protect our dignity.

After a needed ten-hour sleep, this morning I awoke to my new alarm clock, the next-door rooster! I enjoyed a quiet time up on the roof, and then I went out to orient myself to the neighbourhood, which bustled with business activity on Shabbat. From French and Hebrew, now I heard the sound of Arabic. Through one of the gates of the Old City, in the Muslim Quarter, a small boy tried blocking my path with his tiny bike. When I went to walk around it, he slugged me. I sternly told him no hitting, and then I smiled and wished him salem (peace). How sad that young children are indoctrinated toward hatred. Before heading back to this volunteer house and joining the director for supper, I walked along a path through a Muslim cemetery, up to the Eastern Gate overlooking Gethsemane. There, I stood between a place of pain and a place of joy.

> For thus hath the LORD spoken unto me, Like as the lion and the young lion roaring on his prey, when a multitude of shepherds is called forth against him, he will not be afraid of their voice, nor abase himself for the noise of them: so shall the LORD of hosts come down to fight for mount Zion, and for the hill thereof. As birds flying, so will the LORD of hosts defend Jerusalem; defending also he will deliver it; and passing over he will preserve it. (Isaiah 31:4–5 KJV)

> Drop down, ye heavens, from above, and let the skies pour down righteousness: let the earth open, and let them bring forth salvation, and let righteousness spring up together; I the LORD have created it. (Isaiah 45:8 KJV)

Building Oil Reserves

Before I head to my next army base tomorrow, I wanted to try to summarize the past couple of weeks volunteering with an organization dedicated to combating hatred. More is caught than taught! I arrived expecting full days starting with prayer, seeking God for the day's agenda, then serving where assigned. Instead, it seemed the message was more like "Do nothing!"

Actually, the main service was to worship, and to build oil reserves like the five wise virgins in a parable. As the atmosphere is changed, doors open. For example, our director has received considerable favour: access into Gaza. I was hoping to go in but found out the army generally approves only longer-term staff. The director models for us a posture of ready obedience—no turning back. Together as a team, we're learning to dedicate ourselves, calling forth God's purposes. On a more personal level, the Lord's been answering my prayer to be undone in His presence, but not how I thought. He's ploughing up ground. I've asked for fresh circumcision of heart. Passover Monday, I gladly received freedom, followed by an abundant amount of oil literally being poured on my head!

Over in East Jerusalem yesterday, the director appointed two of us to paint some of a building interior in preparation for filming international teachings. She hung out with us, and we enjoyed lots of laughs. Afterwards, she invited us to join her in Shabbat supper. This building is where we spend each morning, dwelling in God's presence, sharing insight and song, chewing on His word, partaking of matzah and grape juice and experiencing unity and a contagious enthusiasm for the things of God. In the midst, we have periodic walk-ins off the street because the doors are always open (literally) to the community. We also have international visitors join us, such as the five Inuit women from Greenland. Our team consists of our leader, with her transparent passion for God and love for people, and a handful of energetic younger and older adults from the United

States, Singapore, Australia and Canada. (Presently I'm the only Canadian represented.) We also have a local Israeli young man and an older Arab citizen to round out our diverse team.

Except for the local members of the team, the rest of us live in community at the volunteer house in Jerusalem, about a fifteen-minute walk to the Old City. Our rooftop (my favourite spot) looks out over the Temple Mount and the Mount of Olives, for the perfect view awaiting Moshiach! Frequent background sounds are the minaret, often followed by the rooster day and night. We share meals together, some prepared for sitting around the table and some for standing around the kitchen chatting.

Strong roots are in Jericho. As our leader remarked, what happens there in the eastern gateway impacts the land; what happens in Jerusalem impacts the world. Last week we prepared fortified rice packages which, with local leaders, were distributed in what some term refugee camps. These places are breeding grounds for hatred. One of their leaders came forward and made public his decision to no longer be a part of this way of living.

Thanks to everyone who continues to pray for the people in Israel—all the children of Abraham. And thank you to those who remembered me as well. I landed on my feet after a fall in Jericho, where a wall partition gave way, and I went sailing backwards from the porch of an ancient house! The local people nearby screamed and looked over the edge, amazed that I was not harmed! Thank God for all His mercies.

> At that time they will call Jerusalem "The Throne of the LORD," and all the nations will be gathered to it, to Jerusalem, for the name of the LORD; nor will they walk anymore after the stubbornness of their evil heart. (Jeremiah 3:17 NASB)

Passover Passion

What is it like to celebrate Passover in Jerusalem? Not what I expected. Interwoven in all the peace and joy I experience being here is also a deepening identification in our Saviour's pain. He was misunderstood, falsely accused, hated and rejected. He is grieved over our sin yet longs for restoration of relationship.

You know when your innermost being rises up and prays things that you know your natural self won't like? Have you ever asked God not to listen to your preferences but to do whatever it takes to make you more reflective of His nature? As with others in Bible times, sometimes He even uses what our enemy meant for evil.

Recently I visited a congregation and was impacted by the message conveying acceptance, forgiveness and grace. We were challenged to not go against God's means of atonement. God's own arm brought salvation unto Himself (cf. Isaiah 59:16; Isaiah 63:5 JPS). When we try to depend on our own understanding and our own efforts rather than letting His Spirit flow through us, we hinder the process of being restored more into His image. A first-century Jewish leader, Shimon, once had the yetzer hara (evil inclination which was influencing his words at that moment) reprimanded by his chief rabbi. Later, this rabbi responded to those who hurt him: "Father, forgive them, for they do not know what they are doing" (see Matthew 16:23 NASB; Luke 23:34 NIV).

Just before the eve of Passover, I was at an outdoor Torah study in Jericho with some from our volunteer team and some local people. Then a sheep showed up with her lamb! As I petted that little creature, I considered how hard it must have been to sacrifice after being in one's home fourteen days. There, I had some matzah and grape juice, tearfully thankful for this little sign.

Some of us from the volunteer house joined in a Seder meal hosted atop the Mount of Olives. The head of the home spoke of one Passover lamb per household, expressing belief that salvation unfolds family by family. As the hostess shared from her poetry, there was that theme again: she affirmed the deeper the pain, the deeper the joy. I accepted her invitation to stay after supper for the all-night vigil in their home. The group declared over Israel—Jew and Arab—"Behold the Lamb!"

At sunrise, before rejoining the volunteer team, I walked down the mount and entered the olive grove. When I asked God what He wanted to convey to me, I sensed the question: "How much do you want to be like Me?" What came to mind was a marred, disfigured man. Again, my *nefesh* (soul) wanted to revolt, and after noticing lilies growing by the trees, I began to sing a chorus seeking less of me and more of God.

The following day, we were back in Jericho, watching a guest drama group portraying Messiah extending compassion to his enemies. Some local Muslim children laughed at the scenes of Roman flogging and crucifixion.

A couple of days later, during some free time, I walked through the Old City walls, exiting by the ancient Jewish graveyard. I discovered a path past Absalom's pillar and stopped to take a photo of some caves. When I asked a woman beside me if she knew their significance, her answer turned into a long walk and talk along the Kidron Valley. It turned out she was a Jew from the same area in London from where my mother's mother originated. She talked of how Yeshua met the requirements of being our acceptable sacrifice. Afterwards I went to pray at the remaining wall from around the ancient temple.

While living here in the community, I am encouraged by example to reflect on how beautiful our King is. Our leader demonstrates that we are to serve first the Lord, and secondarily labour for others. By God's enablement, I'm learning to let love prevail and stay in a humble position, so His life can move more readily through me.

But if serving the LORD seems undesirable to you, then choose for yourselves this day whom you will serve, whether the gods your ancestors served beyond the Euphrates, or the gods of the Amorites, in whose land you are living. But as for me and my household, we will serve the LORD. (Joshua 24:15 NIV)

Yom Hazikaron and Yom Ha'atzmaut

Last evening began a very sad day for Israelis, Memorial Day, and this evening we transition into a very happy one, Independence Day. Soldiers transported us off base for these days, having us join them this morning in a grieving ceremony for their fallen. I was moved upon noticing a mother weeping over her son's grave. An empty helmet hung nearby. Wreaths were laid, and rifle salutes fired. Last night an American Jewish volunteer and I covered a twenty-minute watch of a twelve-hour candlelight vigil on our base. Many continued to pray for the release of kidnapped soldier Gilad Shalit. (Update: Gilad was released on October 18, 2011; he had been captured by Hamas on June 25, 2006.)

This third time volunteering on Israeli army bases, I'm in a more remote region, on a more rustic base. Besides one fellow Canadian, volunteers are from the United States, Australia, New Zealand and Sweden. I had to taper my uniform pants two sizes in using a borrowed diaper pin! When I turned on one tap, the one at the adjacent sink turned on simultaneously. One lesson was drilled into us: Drink, drink, drink (*mayim*, that is). You can become dehydrated quickly. One of our main assignments was to prepare kit bags for soldiers, ready to pick up and go upon notice of war.

Last week we participated in a base-wide drill, donning helmets and bulletproof vests and waiting inside until the siren ceased. When one of our volunteers didn't show up for an evening activity, one of our soldiers went in search of him with an armed paramedic. He was lost and found all right. We were warned not to wander far from our quarters, especially at night, to prevent risk of being shot at if someone inadvertently startled a guard. (They would warn us first, in Hebrew and Arabic, to stop.) I also learned there are vipers and scorpions around the base. Comforting feeling, eh? But really, I'm at peace being here.

On my first weekend off, I visited a goat dairy farm on a moshav (community co-op). It's run by a Jewish family by the same original surname as my maternal grandmother. Our family immigration pattern does not seem to indicate we are related, but there is a possibility I have some Jewish roots. I sampled their delicious cheese and was invited to select eggs from the chicken coop for my breakfast, as well as pick loquats and lemons from the trees.

The next day, I took a bus to Tiberias and stayed at a designated soldier house. From there I hiked into the next town, where I linked up to a part of the Israel National Trail. After finding the painted marker stones, I made my way past big green hills, stopping at a spring; continuing past an olive grove, past a wheat field and through a patch of banana plants; and arriving at the following town. There, I discovered a Canadian flag and met a soldier who had recently finished his term of service, having been in Operation Cast Lead in Gaza. Afterwards, I conversed in French with some tourists from France and Canada who just got off a bus. They introduced me to their Israeli guide, who expressed deep appreciation that I came to serve his country. Next, I went for a swim in the Kinneret. As the sun was going down, I headed back out to the highway and caught a bus to Tiberias, exploring a bit more before returning to my quarters. I had to be up early to head back to the meeting place, from where our soldiers were picking us up to go back to the base.

In a short while, Independence Day celebrations will begin, so I'm heading over to our army hostel and taking a dip in the nearby Mediterranean. Then we'll be joining a gathering at Rabin Square. The celebrations continue tomorrow in Jerusalem on Ben Yehuda Street. There's nothing like being here in Israel.

Honorary Member of the Tribe

My first connection with Israel was through a tour. There, a fellow Canadian told me he had been a civilian volunteer on Israeli army bases. The following year, I arrived on my first base, donning the uniform and living in barracks. Now I've served a total of ten weeks on four bases, each time with superb soldier guides for our international teams. A participant from Switzerland observed, "The volunteers during my service came from nine different nations: French, Swiss, Finnish, Dutch, German, Hungarian, South African, Ukrainian, Russian, Canadian and a big number of the United States. Jews and Christians, all united!"

Real comradeship developed through both laughter and tears. When news came that soldiers from our base were injured, there was a shared grief that it happened to our own. Sunday to Thursday, we provided practical assistance: cleaning, oiling and painting equipment; sorting and packing soldier kit bags, protective kits and medical supplies; and even refurbishing donated tools. As one commander put it, we were helping them reorganize after the last war and get ready for the next one, whenever that may be. But as much as our labour was appreciated, a commander remarked, it was our presence that greatly encouraged them, knowing there are people around the world who stand with Israel.

Complementing the assignments were evening activities where we learned more about the history of the defence force and our civilian volunteer program. We had a taste of Hebrew language and culture. Our guides even took us on educational outings, such as to Palmach Museum or Independence Hall in Tel Aviv. We ate as the soldiers ate, including lots of boiled eggs and bread with cheese spread or hummus, and we drank as the soldiers drank—lots of water! My communications were a mixture of broken Hebrew, French and English.

Given that some of the bases are more rustic than others, what draws people of various ages and backgrounds to come alongside and support Israel this way? We've had mother and son, father and daughter and brothers come together. Those experiencing the program for the first time meet veterans who have returned numerous times. An older volunteer from the United States humbly remarked, "We gave so little in comparison with how much we received from the IDF." For me personally, it's the people who make the experience what it is—a chance to identify in a unique way with what the people of this land face. A family from New Zealand stated, "As non-Jewish Israel supporters we were delighted that the IDF volunteer program gave us the opportunity to come and serve in a practical way. Thanks for making it possible to see your land and meet your people over a longer period than a tourist tour would have allowed."

One of the strongest points of identification came when a Jewish brother and I had the honour of taking a turn with the soldiers guarding the vigil candle the eve of Yom Hazikaron. This American acknowledged the reality of army conditions yet referred to his volunteer experience as "the time of your life!" Recognizing my strong sense of identification with the Jewish nation, I was blessed when one of my barrack mates told me she considered me an honorary member of the tribe.

From Dan to Daphna

I'm back in Tel Aviv-Yafo for tonight, where our team of volunteers was dropped off from the base. My comrades and I are staying at the army hostel, and then I'm heading to Jerusalem early tomorrow. I've signed on for another week at another base in the south, starting Sunday. Then I'm back with media production while the organization director is away in India.

Last time I wrote, I was about to celebrate Independence Day at Rabin Square in Tel Aviv. It was an evening of inflated hammers, spray foam, flashing light trinkets, song and dance and fireworks. One of my Canadian friends invited me to a barbecue at her yishuv near Jerusalem. That was quite the feast after army food!

After a shorter work week, I took a bus farther north to Kiryat Shmona, staying at another soldier facility. My roommate had an M-16 in our room, which she kept by her person at all times. From there I hiked to Dan through a kibbutz, explored the nature reserve, and then resumed part of the Israel National Trail from Dan to Daphna.

At this point, I exited onto a highway where I could catch the last bus to Haifa before Shabbat. On arrival at the soldiers' hostel, I was welcomed as the only civilian volunteer into the dining room to enjoy a Shabbat meal with the soldiers. The next day, I hiked partway up Mount Carmel and then rode up the rest of the way. While en route down, I stopped at a lookout point and danced before the Lord. I thought of Elijah recognizing God's still, small voice.

My last days at the northern base entailed loading heavy kit bags onto a truck, painting an army insignia onto a warehouse wall (using cigarette butts for the finer artwork!), weed whacking dry brush (to prevent fires) and then cleaning freshly oiled equipment. Some of us gave blood donations in a mobile medical truck. Others of us received the chance to raise the national flag. Everyone participated in lively discussions and also went on an outing with armed guards. We presented our madrichot with tokens of our appreciation. Today, it was sad to say goodbye to everyone after three weeks of bonding. We shared tears together with the soldiers while watching a movie inspiring random acts of kindness.

This month I've been going through the book of Jeremiah.

The Hebrew name *Dan* comes from the root to judge. In the midst of judgment over sin, God's heart is still reaching out to His people with hope for cleansing, healing and restoration.

A soldier smiled, encouraged when I shared with her from Psalm 17: "Keep me as the apple of the eye; Hide me in the shadow of Your wings" (verse 8 NASB).

Death of Vision … Into Wilderness

From the crossroads of Jerusalem, disappointment strikes. Where is God's perfect will in the midst?

Back in Jaffa at the army hostel, welcome camaraderie awaited me. A fellow volunteer invited me out and began asking me spiritual questions. Later that weekend, I took a long, contemplative swim in the Mediterranean. On our last evening together, a few international volunteers from our base went out for shakshuka, a spiced tomato and egg dish served in a frying pan.

This week I head to my fourth base, this time in the desert. By now the Tsahal (צבא ההגנה לישראל) fatigues are feeling like my normal attire. I'm familiar with all the beret colours and their division names. I know how to stand at attention and at ease. With this last group, I'm the sole Canadian. Our assignment is to help refurbish donated tools and vehicle parts from North America.

One of my favourite characters was a grandfatherly gentleman who came with his brother, a professed atheist rabbi. He told me he found me very interesting and personable, and he seriously encouraged me to write a book. Another volunteer I met is an author, broadcaster and photographer. She recommended a few tips to me. I need a more creative outlet than I have in my life right now.

During an evening stroll on the grounds, I was stopped by military police—and then commended for helping their country through civilian volunteer service! The organization's founder addressed our group, and the commander of the base expressed his gratitude. Our madricha was so thankful for the card I made (in which everyone wrote her a message) that she burst into tears.

My last weekend in the desert, I did some more exploring. I took in a spectacular view of Mitzpe Ramon Crater, and in Sde Boker I visited the desert home and grave of the first prime minister, David Ben Gurion. Farther south in Eilat, I crossed the border into Jordan for a prearranged tour of Petra. It was booked through a major hotel lobby, so I trusted all the details were arranged. That morning as I waited for my shuttle, a man in an unmarked white van slowed and offered me a ride. I declined. Then when he called my name, I realized this was it! In small, hand-painted lettering along the bumper was the name of the "official" tour company.

An Australian family was next on his route. Upon departing the regional airport, we were informed another man in a car awaited us on the other side of the border. Onwards we went for our two-hour ride to the ancient Nabatean site, en route passing by Bedouin tents, shepherds and sheep, goats, donkeys and camels and barren desert mountains, with occasional spurts of greenery, notably, acacia trees.

After arriving at Petra, we met our guide and began a long, humid hike amidst pinkish red rock formations. They were both stunning and disturbing, with much evidence of widespread idolatry. The key viewpoint is the treasury building, carved into a huge rock. It's estimated over 30,000 people once lived in this city, including some Christians, around the fourth century. A familiar sound was the clip-clopping of horse chariots. Over 80 percent of Petra is believed to be yet underground.

On the way back to the Israeli border, our driver was speeding, taking curves dangerously fast, and following too close. Then we passed the scene of a horrendous accident, where ambulances were just arriving at the scene. After that, our driver showed more respect for the road. For many reasons, I was glad to be back on Israel's side!

After a needed rest at a guesthouse in Eilat, I joined in a Shabbat service. In the afternoon, I walked a small portion of the end of the Israel National Trail, after last month hiking a portion of the beginning in Dan. This wilderness experience was mostly uphill over dirt mountains, around some rock ledges and to a high point, where I rested in a cleft of the rock. Once back to the start, I waded in the Red Sea, asking God to make a way where there seems to be no way.

I got up early the next morning and caught a bus to Jerusalem via the Dead Sea. There, I stopped for a relaxing float. We passed a huge mound of salt. After arriving in Zion, I spotted the Temple Mount at a distance. Before returning to our volunteer house, I explored some more of the Jewish Quarter of the Old City, including the famous Hurva synagogue rededicated this year, having been destroyed twice in its history. Some outside the community nervously regarded this restoration as a sign of the Third Temple's imminent rebuilding. My last stop was the Kotel, the Western Wall. What direction do I go from here?

> Where there is no vision, the people perish.
> (Proverbs 29:18a KJV)

Criss-Crossing Worlds

Welcome to this place of criss-crossing worlds. Almost daily since returning to Jerusalem from civilian army service, I walk between Muslim and Jewish neighbourhoods, taking in the sights and sounds of two very different cultures. One major street runs between the contrast. In the volunteer house, I share space in the "Bedouin room," formerly the filming studio, the walls covered in egg cartons and hanging fabrics. I prefer to sleep on the porch or rooftop, where I can awake to sun rather than pitch darkness. One night I even camped out at the Kotel instead of walking all the way back through another neighbourhood at that hour.

When I'm not involved in a painting project, helping with chores, or hosting a group of students at the volunteer house, I like to be out in the community. A shopkeeper regularly greets us with "Welcome" in an Arabic accent. A younger man one day initiated a discussion of spiritual questions with me inside the Old City market. His animosity toward the Jewish people was evident. I said my piece and excused myself, expressing confidence in our one true God.

Our earlier army field trip to the prayer wall was cancelled for security reasons. Instead, recently I was able to join a group of Canadians touring inside the Temple Mount tunnels, making our way through narrow passages and huge wet stones and standing close to where was the Holy of Holies. Elsewhere, I also caught glimpses of treasures all prepared and ready for the rebuilding of the Third Temple: the golden menorah, showbread table, oil jugs and measures, laver, priestly garments and even musical instruments.

Jerusalem Day was on May 12 this year. A new friend and I celebrated over at the Kotel, where a saxophone played the late Naomi Shemer's classic song "Jerusalem of Gold." The area was well secured with regular and military police, border guards and Golani and Givati units of the IDF. They were outfitted with riot gear, but thankfully peace prevailed. En route to trendy Ben Yehuda Street, people poured down other streets in song and dance with Israeli flags. I stopped in one shop whose owner sought to honour Hashem (God's holy name) by selling modest apparel. We had a very encouraging discussion. The night ended after I inserted a prayer note into a crevice of rock in the Kotel, thereby releasing an area of pain to the Lord. I noticed a shift soon after that.

Another day, I looked around the archaeological gardens where a pile of huge stones remain, traditionally believed to have been toppled by the Romans during the destruction of the Temple in AD 70. Nearby was flute and drum music, with a boy uplifted and covered by a banner, being rejoiced over by the mobile crowd. This was his bar mitzvah. After joining the throng, I climbed steps to gain a panoramic view of the city from the Mount of Olives to the City of David. In the background emanated Muslim prayers from the Temple Mount above me. Inside a nearby museum was a realistic animation depicting a man going to Jerusalem in temple times. Coming from afar, he exchanges his money, buys a goat, enters a purification mikvah, and then ascends steps to the Temple to present his sacrifice through the priest.

One other day off, I ventured up to the ancient city of Shechem, participating in the cultural custom of waiting around until enough people came to fill a *sherut* quota. That's a shared taxi van, quite reasonably priced, but you have to be patient—it's not on a tight time schedule for departure! I eventually arrived in Shechem via Jericho and was surprised to find also a modern city with lots of tall buildings lining the ancient mountains of Gerizim and Ebal, where the blessings for obedience, and cursings for disobedience, were announced (Deuteronomy 27–28). While I was reading these Scriptures, a young man approached, offering to show me around the old part of the city. I did not divulge any of my personal details, yet he informed me that he used to be involved in a movement for which he had been jailed by Israelis. He claimed he simply wrote emails. I advised that in future, he use his leadership for the good of others, following another type of role model. Then we parted ways because the sherut to Ramallah was about to depart, and I aimed to be back in Jerusalem before dark.

A less controversial place to go was Elah Valley, where David slew Goliath. I walked along the dried-up brook, facing the mount where the Philistines gathered, with the mount where the Israelites gathered on the opposite side. I symbolically threw a rock. My Jewish taxi guide read the Hebrew Scriptures to me, engraved on a nearby monument. I thanked him for arranging this special tour, and told him I love Israel and Israel's God. Back in Bet Shemesh, I caught a bus back to Jerusalem, reading the Psalms of Ascent en route.

This week I participated in some prayer gatherings in preparation for the third great pilgrimage festival here in Jerusalem: Shavuot. Hebrew for "Weeks," it is the culmination of counting off forty-nine days from Passover. This occasion recalls the giving of the Torah on Mount Sinai. It also corresponds to Pentecost. One leader spoke of us needing fresh oil and fire. He pointed out sometimes the Lord needs to make us lie down, like sheep in green pastures. There was a strong presence in that meeting as we sang about God being a consuming fire.

Our director and team just returned from India, sharing of their experiences seeing funeral processions along the river. There, the departed were sent adrift. In the face of such a display of death, our team honoured life.

Last night I visited in hospital the widow of a prominent rabbi. She remarked that one of the greatest modern miracles is seeing Christians who bless the Jewish people. She told me she believes we are now living in the Messianic era and that we are very close to seeing him reign from this city of Jerusalem. Then before I left, she gave me a knowing smile, remarking that some believe Moshiach is already here.

Wow, what times we're in. And what a place to be in, here in Jerusalem! My heart is so tied to this place and its people. Less than two weeks remain until I'm due to fly back to Canada. I need the Lord to show me the next steps to take.

Extended Furnace Time

Shalom from this city of the great King! I'm still here, until the end of this month. In May the thought of leaving Jerusalem was hard to bear, so I asked God to give me favour with my employer. For now I sense to linger in Jerusalem.

In preparation for Shavuot, starting the evening of May 18 and into May 19, I joined with some others in prayer, even praying one of those "dangerous" prayers for God to do in me whatever He needed to do. We looked out over the city from a high balcony. One woman had a picture of the Lion of Judah wildly dancing. That night I stopped at the Western Wall, and a mighty wind blew there!

On Shavuot, traditionally the story of Ruth and Naomi is recounted. White clothing is worn, and white foods are eaten. Some of us wore floral headdresses at a country-wide congregational event held at an area moshav. Afterwards, I visited with a Canadian friend who made aliyah, now living in Israel. From her place, we headed into Jerusalem, up the Mount of Olives, and joined with others in a prayer tent before sundown. I continued over to the Western Wall, where multitudes of God's chosen were singing and dancing. Upon exiting the tunnel by security, I let my grandmother and mother hear via mobile phone the harmonious voices of young Orthodox men. My family felt like they were right there with me.

The next day, over lettuce sandwiches (leaves with hummus) back at volunteer headquarters, our director discussed how Israel is hidden amongst the nations. She extended to me an open invitation to come back, even if her organization turns out to be for me a launching pad for something else in future. In Hebron the following day, the team went to the tombs of Abraham, Isaac and Jacob. Then we dunked in Abraham's Spring, receiving blessings.

On Shabbat eve, I encountered at the Kotel a group of female soldiers, officers in training, dancing in a circle at sundown. After chatting with some of them, I headed over to a rabbi's place for Shabbat supper. He and his family open their home each week to those in the area without family. While en route, I met a young man who shared his life views with me. Over at the rabbi's house was an atmosphere of mutual honour. As we thankfully ate the various courses served, he taught on the value of encouragement: lifting people up to a better place than they were before.

En route a trip into Bethlehem, from a distance I had a glimpse of Herodium, the famous king's hilltop fortress. After the taxi driver pointed out to me the water cisterns associated with another famous king, David, I walked about the city centre. A journalist acquaintance of a friend had asked if I could find for him a certain map. On it, Israel is wrongly renamed Palestine, and some of her cities are given Arabic names instead. But as I asked around in some shops, there was denial such a map existed; a reliable source tells me otherwise. Before exiting the security checkpoint, I met two young boys who were selling flutes.

At one of the daily prayer times back at the volunteer organization in Jerusalem, the director urged those present to step forward and symbolically shake off old garments that hamper walking in a new way. She noted a key to being productive is sharing. She pictured us jumping into the water and obstacles clearing. As leader, she cancelled any curses against me, symbolically removed the weapons from my back, pronounced healing over wounds, and spoke versus the lie, affirming I do hear God's voice. In response, I raised my shield of faith and chose to let the Father's love pour in where there's been blockage to receiving.

During my remaining time in Jerusalem, I ventured over to the City of David, just outside the Old City, and descended with flashlight into the ancient Gihon Spring, also known as King Hezekiah's Tunnel. It can take an hour or so to wade through ankle- to thigh-deep waterways, manoeuvring narrow winding cave passages. Near the end, by the Pool of Siloam, is an inscription from the era. From out of this place in a former Jebusite city, David and his army acquired the new capital of Israel.

At the time I didn't know it, but while I was deep underground, an alert siren sounded across the city. I discovered this news while meeting with a respected journalist to hear more about how he got into his field. His organization is one of the most loyal defenders of the State of Israel and its people, aiming to counter false information propagated by many media outlets. While in his office, he showed me a photo release received via a major press outlet. It pictured a man's head and shoulders; the rest of the attacker's body was not visible. Here was a picture of the type of forces Israeli people are up against. It's a battle between those who worship death and those who value life.

Annually for decades, Canada has participated in a walk in unity with Israel. This year I joined my fellow Canadians long distance by mobile phone as I walked with them in Israel. First I proudly watched the live webcast from an internet shop near New Gate in the Old City. There, my nation welcomed the prime minister of Israel and his wife to Toronto. In the crowds was featured a young Canadian who was currently serving in the IDF; during a training exercise, he and the PM had met. As an expression of appreciation for his coming to serve of his own accord, the prime minister arranged for him to take a short leave, and he flew him over to see his family in Canada. After the opening speech and ceremonies, the crowds embarked on the walk. It was an especially meaningful occasion for my friends in Toronto, who passed the phone around, having through me a connection with Jerusalem.

Next day after this uplifting event, news was released that put a damper on the atmosphere. I heard first via a fellow volunteer that there had been an incident on a flotilla at the western shore. Some claimed it was merely a peaceful boat carrying humanitarian aid to the impoverished people of Gaza. But other reports indicated violence ensued toward Israeli commandos, who boarded when those navigating refused to halt for inspections. How would other sovereign nations respond under such security circumstances?

Around Damascus Gate were signs of solidarity with the

so-called Palestinian cause. Shopkeepers had closed their doors. That evening I accompanied a couple of international volunteers into Jericho for a discussion they were leading. The lesson was letting the local people know God had in store blessings for them too, if only they would trust God and not take matters into their own hands. The participants raised their voices, beginning to incite hatred toward their Jewish cousins. The discussion leader tried to curb the heated arguments, to no avail. Then I asked to say something through the interpreter. I admitted to the small group gathered that I felt hurt and angered by what they said, noting almost daily I cross paths with people of both cultures. Maybe it's because I was a new face that they stopped their shouting and listened. Honestly, I don't remember all what came out of my mouth that day, but hopefully it had some positive impact. One young man came outside as we were leaving and quietly admitted that he had a friend who is Jewish.

Some while later, I watched from the Knesset visitors' gallery as the prime minister of Israel entered, and other members of the political scene reviewed the elements that came to be known as the flotilla incident. I wished in retrospect that I had been in Canada amongst those who welcomed him for his historic visit to my country.

We live in refining times. Originally referring to Assyria, I believe the following could apply to other declared enemies of Israel:

> "Their stronghold will fall because of terror; at the sight of the battle standard their commanders will panic," declares the LORD, whose fire is in Zion, whose furnace is in Jerusalem. (Isaiah 31:9 NIV)

From Israel's Capital to Canada's Capital

The world is watching Canada's example. Last weekend from Ottawa, a First Nation leader stated that forgiveness is spiritual; it cannot be legislated. It was a kairos moment as thousands of First Peoples of our land extended forgiveness toward our prime minister, who took responsibility on behalf of past governments' abuses through the residential school system.

Seven years ago, I met for the first time my Métis sister. She and our dad were reunited after 40 years! Personally, I have a strong sense of identification with the First Peoples of Canada, as well as the Chosen People of Israel. Therefore my heart was torn when I sensed I was to stay longer in Jerusalem rather than fly back in time for this historic moment. My new Canadian friend was convinced there was a purpose in us praying from here in the land. I know there's no distance in the Spirit. Just before the gathering began, I connected by mobile phone with a friend present there, exchanging blessing between Israel and Canada.

After an Algonquin leader welcomed the participants to the land, we turned our attention to God, acknowledging, "As far as the east is from the west, So far has He removed our transgressions from us" (Psalm 103:12 NASB). He paid the cost. A later song declared that another day is dawning, speaking of freedom to be who each of us is. Various warrior dances ensued. A featured speaker was one who loyally ploughed the ground during his long years of service in government. His father taught him not to be afraid of any man. A leader, representing the church in Canada, led out in an apology while kneeling at the feet of some First Peoples. An aboriginal woman responded, expressing sorrow for those who did not live to see this day and seeking God to do through us what we cannot do for ourselves. Forgiveness depends on supernatural grace. A female leader, descendant of immigrants, presented a painting portraying the church's posture now is one of serving the First Peoples of Canada.

While witnessing from Jerusalem this historic moment, I was powerfully impacted when one man sang out about an angel lifting his right hand toward heaven, declaring there be no longer delay (from Revelation 10:5–6 NASB). We were asked to imagine God's kingdom coming forth. Inuit and Métis representatives released forgiveness for how the church's message was distorted, while noting from Psalm 130,

> If you, LORD, kept a record of sins, Lord, who could stand? But with you there is forgiveness, so that we can, with reverence, serve you. (verses 3–4 NIV)

Something that particularly impressed me with our prime minister's apology was that it was very specific in outlining injustices done. Likewise, the First Nations chief, leading out in reading the Charter of Forgiveness, was careful to acknowledge each aspect of the apology. One of my friends of the Cree Nation was amongst the twenty-four elders and twelve witnesses who signed the three copies of the charter.

Excitedly I watched the procession of First Peoples, and I rejoiced as a children's choir sang the national anthem in the Cree language. Our PM recognized the obligation to walk out necessary changes to reflect repentance. A cabinet minister demonstrated this new era of mutual respect and honour as he sat while taken through a "capture dance" ceremony along with a First Nations chief. A special commission would be meeting the following week. Another musician impacted me personally as she honestly sang out various wrongs committed against her people, graciously followed by the words "but I forgive you." We can be transparent about how others' actions caused us harm; that does not detract from forgiveness but rather strengthens it.

Observing from Israel, I was thrilled to see flags of the twelve tribes of this land. The words "Come on home, Canada" resonated in my spirit as healing anointing was released across my nation. As Canadians in Jerusalem, we declared over our nation together with those in Ottawa, "Chai," the Hebrew word for *life*. My Cree friend displayed a red shawl with a white maple leaf, rippling streams flowing from its four corners.

Many danced for restoration of fatherhood, and much honouring took place: First Peoples toward a national leader who is a descendant of Ishmael, and between the French and First Peoples. One aboriginal dancer challenged us with the question, "What are you going to do with your freedom?" He noted that governments come and go, and the church will fail us; therefore our security needs to be in God. A female First Nations leader spoke out against an anti-Semitic spirit. My Canadian friend and I rejoiced to see the Star of David on a flag and hear it acknowledged that Messiah is to reign from Jerusalem!

Our live webcast connection went down at a point of blessing Israel, and eventually it resumed at a new point of blessing God's chosen. I'm blessed to have my feet planted here, but still I yearned to join my fellow Canadians in the grand finale of the gathering. A Mauri warrior dancer moved about, scooping up maple leaves strewn on the floor; he was joined by other First Peoples (on drums) and French (on violin). It was a unified celebration of what the Lord did in our midst. The First Nations chief reiterated, "Mr. Prime Minister, we forgive you," and declared all praise and glory to God.

O Jerusalem, Jerusalem ... Oh Canada!

Shalom from this ancient city. Daily I battle to push aside every hindrance to knowing God more. Fear of intimacy keeps trying to intrude. From a Jewish widow, I learned that it's considered a mitzvah to eat the fruit of the land. From that I thought, *How much more to enjoy the fruit of relationship with the One who gave us life!*

Earlier this month, I really wrestled over when to fly back to Canada. I desired to be there in person for that nationwide gathering in our capital, Ottawa. Yet I also sensed a need to lay down that desire, to choose the "better thing." My jealous Bridegroom wants exclusive time alone with me, like an extended honeymoon. That's so hard for me to grasp! A leader assured me in my struggle that I'm on track, indicating I was being storm tossed by the wind of God's Spirit. She pictured the Lord turning our faces, locking onto His gaze. On a day I was sweaty and spotted with paint, some volunteers came around me and spoke encouraging words of God's heart toward me. They rejoiced when I arrived at the decision to stay on in Jerusalem into June.

I returned to one of my favourite places and ascended the Mount of Olives, where I prayed that the Spirit of God would overshadow every part of this city. I blew a shofar facing toward Zion Gate. Later that day, I sat in the public gallery of the Knesset, watching the minister of defence and the prime minister, praying God's will prevail in regards to the no-confidence motion a coalition was bringing forth. Present was an Arab MK (Member of Knesset) who claimed she had been on the flotilla, and the media was zeroing in on her. Beside me, a local woman translated a summary of what was happening. She expressed appreciation for Canada's support of Israel. She related her frustration with media so often casting her country in a negative light. I encouraged her, noting a growing sense I have to become involved in influencing media for righteousness. Outside afterwards, I learned from a staff member that the vote did not succeed.

The atmosphere is really intense here: in the natural, so in the spiritual. Another volunteer and I participated in an anti-terror course at a shooting range outside Jerusalem. Our instructor, an official with the Israeli army, prepared us in drills before entrusting us in turn with three types of weapons. We had to be able to instantly respond to commands, such as when to run and when to halt. We had to demonstrate an ability to balance and not lose our footing, especially while carting a gun! Step by step, the lesson unfolded. Eventually each of us, under close supervision, fired toward the plain paper target with a hand pistol, an automatic rifle and then with a special forces firearm. A protective barricade was behind, ensuring the safety of all. A real soldier, he said, must always be on the alert.

Recently by Damascus Gate, I came across a gathering of Muslim men chanting and bowing on the street corner. I learned from the border guards that access to the Temple Mount was restricted that day. Another day I met a Muslim shopkeeper in the Old City who showed me photos from the 1880s to 1967: Damascus and Jaffa Gates, and the Western Wall. He remarked that very soon things would change. There's a strong sense that Messiah is imminent.

At volunteer headquarters, a friend of the director gave a message about Messiah's longing over Jerusalem, desiring to gather the people as chicks. She related a childhood story of a farmer who discovered in the aftermath of a fire his charred hen. But from under her ran out live chicks! The safest place is under God's wings. "He will cover thee with His pinions, And under His wings shalt thou take refuge; His truth is a shield and a buckler" (Psalm 91:4 JPS). How do you stand firm in these last days? Know how to feed yourself, encourage yourself, depend on God as your Source and endure hardship as a good soldier.

Returning with My Bridegroom

Sadly, today is my last day in Jerusalem. My extension here has been a honeymoon period. I'm returning to Canada with a ring written in Hebrew: *Ani l'dodi v'dodi li*—"I am my beloved's, and my beloved is mine," from Song of Songs 6:3 (KJV). Recently

I discovered a very sweet-smelling, tiny white flower called Jasmine. We carry our Saviour's fragrance wherever we go.

Again I've hiked up the Mount of Olives to pray. Today I beat a native drum for emphasis as I walked around the panoramic view of the city, declaring that Hashem will be King over the whole earth; He is one and His name one (see Zechariah 14:9 JPS). I went away on a short retreat. A friend gave me a book, which has taught me in regards to pain and love, and conquering fear.

In Jericho we had taken cable cars up the Mount of Temptation. As our time in the land was winding down, our volunteer director had consented to my accompanying a younger gal in staying over in Jericho. Each of us had further personal retreat time with God, based at the organization's historic old building. On nearby grounds, I took a dip in Elisha's Spring. Late that night, a man showed up outside carrying a long-bladed knife; it turned out he was the gardener checking up on the property! For breakfast we volunteers enjoyed sweet, crisp grapes straight off the vine. Then a local staff ensured we made it back safely to Jerusalem.

Over in the Jewish sector of Jerusalem, I've made new friends. A rabbi and his family are an exemplary light to the nations, continuing to open their home every Shabbat to whoever comes. This week he spoke on looking for opportunities to show chesed (kindness). One older man I met there kept popping up around the city; initially he didn't remember my name, so the first time he called out to me, "Hey, Canada!" I responded appreciatively to my new name, glad to represent our nation.

This morning I awoke on the roof, watched the sunrise, and pondered Moshiach while glancing over at the Mount of Olives. Later I stood atop the mount, imagining it splitting in two at God's presence (see Zechariah 14:3–4 NIV). After my prayer watch, I prepared to pack and then took a last stroll through the Old City, along Jaffa Road. I am now in the Jewish

Quarter, about to make one last stop at the Kotel before the sherut picks me up for the airport. My Bridegroom's coming with me back to Canada!

After the long flight, friends met me on arrival, going out to eat at a restaurant in the heart of Toronto's Jewish community. Although it's a blessing to see family and friends again, I so miss being in Israel, especially Jerusalem. It was home to me. Just yesterday, my tanned sandaled feet walked its ancient streets …

Sukkot on Media Team

My desire to serve in media in the Land of Israel came true in the autumn of 2010, when I was selected to participate in Sukkot celebrations. Our enthusiastic and friendly team was headed by a kind and knowledgeable director. One assignment was sending a pair of us out to distribute invitations to Israeli guest night, a grand performance of song and dance where the nations honour those in the land—including the mayor of Jerusalem. On our rounds of the neighbourhood, we were invited into the sukkah of an army officer and his family.

Our cohesive team worked between the headquarters office and a makeshift press room over in the convention building by Jerusalem Central Bus Station. We also took turns tending the magazine and radio station display table in the conference centre. Outside organization headquarters, we hosted refreshments for guests in a large sukkah. From the balcony, the son of a former prime minister spoke to the crowds outside, as did the chief rabbi of a nearby city. I was in my element, taking photographs with my first manual focus digital camera.

After hours, we volunteers liked to relax at the outdoor cafe of a gas station near our hostel. We sampled a beverage which tasted of black licorice, and another contained chunks of aloe. We shared a lot of laughs together.

One day each of us was assigned to a special project: mini

tour coverage. I was sent to accompany the busload to Bethel and to Shiloah. Bethel was the ancient site of where Jacob had the vision of the ladder, with angels of God ascending and descending (see Genesis 28:10–17 NASB). There, our guide, the announcer of a popular radio station, posed a question. Consider why our opponents deem as illegal settlements what is built in this place of our ancient heritage. A lookout point sign lists the various regions (north, south, east, west) allotted to Abraham, Isaac and Jacob and their descendants by promise of God. From there we continued on to Shiloah, where the portable tabernacle rested many years. As pilgrims we descended along the path to stand amongst the stones outlining its foundation.

The grand finale of the Feast of Tabernacles, after the tours and guest speakers, was the massive gathering at Ein Gedi. As the sun was setting, colourful lights reflected off the surrounding palm trees. An outdoor meal was served, and then the nations joined in more song and dance, exalting the God of Israel.

This two-week venture passed quickly, and I was back at the airport. Now there were even more questions. Security wanted to inspect my camera equipment and laptop, even requesting that I log on. When they spotted a document referencing the prime minister, they pointed and instructed me to open that! Here was the PM speech he extended in welcome to the nations who came to visit Israel during Sukkot. Our media director had handed me the official disc from the PMO for me to transcribe the video. I did so very carefully, word by word.

Section IV: A Taste of Israeli Life (2013–2014)

Army Mishpacha

In December 2012, I was preparing to leave, at last to embark on my dream of a lifetime: to get a taste of living in Israel for a year. For more than two years, I'd been setting aside funds. My employer approved an unpaid leave so I could gain such cross-cultural experience and expand my media communications skills. For me, it was like a virtual aliyah. I gave away most of my belongings, put away a few keepsakes in storage and brought the remaining items with me. In January it was time to say goodbye to family and friends, assuring I would be in touch by phone or email. Then the day came: January 27. I took off from the ground in Canada and by the next day had arrived back in Eretz Yisrael.

We were sitting outside in the hot sun, large boxes spread over the asphalt, sorting various medical supplies into like piles. As we worked, my New York comrades and I talked and laughed. Ka-*tome*: those syringes in the orange pile. Ya-*roke*: those in the green pile. Thus we practised our colours. "Stop it!" That's what the transliteration of the Hebrew print was on one of the items: an anti-diarrheal medicine. The athletes' foot antifungal cream displayed the same word—pronounced "pee-tree-*yote*"—as a topping many of us enjoy on pizza!

Each morn we assembled for flag raising on our base. Because it was my third time assigned here, it felt like home. One thing unusual this time was waking to find large rain puddles outside our barracks, so much so that we stepped out our door onto a wooden pallet. I pretended it to be a raft and used dustpans as paddles for a fun photo op. My veteran barracks mate returned to this base decades after serving during the 1956 Sinai Campaign; then she was a real soldier, but now she is a volunteer. Israel has deeply meaningful street signs, like those after names of prophets, or one in Tel Aviv which declares, "Am Yisrael Chai" ("People of Israel live")!

Our soldier guides, the madrichot, have such sweet personalities. There's a real connection between the local and international volunteers. A group of immigrant Russian ladies regularly came to assemble first aid kits. One day our warehouse manager surprised everyone at break time by bringing out tasty treats and letting a Canadian volunteer entertain in his clown outfit! You should have seen these ladies' faces light up in smiles over his antics. It was inspiring to see the devotion of veteran North American volunteers, who offer months of each year to serve on this base. One older man remarked to me that I was more Jewish than some Jews, encouraged by my example and eagerness to learn.

My favourite field trips with the army were at two interactive military museums: the Palmach (depicting characters from the early days of defence), and the IDF one by the old rail station in Jaffa (displaying changes in equipment and vehicles over the decades). Back on grounds Sunday, I took what turned out to be my last evening walk around the base.

Now, here I sit at Zurich airport in Switzerland, a place I didn't expect to be, writing a different ending to my army experience in Israel than I anticipated. Early hours Monday in the barracks, I was awakened by my mobile phone. A nurse from Mount Sinai Hospital notified me that my father had died. For the remainder of that night, I stood outside by the eucalyptus trees calling family members until daylight broke, and I heard a rooster crowing in the distance.

After flag raising that morning, I announced to my volunteer comrades the news about my father. They surrounded me with tears and embraces and were truly mishpacha (family) to me. Our madrichot alerted the necessary authorities that I would need accompaniment off our medical base before week's end. Both the Israeli and Canadian offices extended their condolences. Our work station supervisor, the base's second in command, and the commander conveyed the most genuine looks of compassion as they clasped my hands. Soldiers and volunteers offered whatever they could do to assist as I prepared to book a flight back to Canada.

My last evening on the base, I was called forward in a meeting and presented with an honorary beret; attached was a special insignia pin which belonged to my madricha. She knew what it was to lose someone close to her, and she wanted me to have it. I deeply thanked her and told her I would wear it at my dad's memorial. It was at this base where I walked about one evening with my mobile phone, passing nearby my other madricha and announcing to her that I was talking with my dad from Canada. She called out to him that he has a lovely daughter, and he matter-of-factly replied he knew that!

It was still February 10 (Toronto Canada time) that my dad, at age seventy-seven, went home with his Saviour, in whom he'd come to place his trust five years ago. My last visit with him was on the occasion of his baptism, December 30. My last photos of Dad show the joy in his blue eyes. His last words to me by phone in Israel were, "I love you very much. God bless."

From the Tel Aviv airport, I looked at photos of my dad for the first time since his homecoming. My younger sister and I were named as decision makers to carry out his written wishes. We planned his memorial over the phone. One of my best friends picked me up from Toronto airport, hosted me, and took me to meet my sister and brother. My younger siblings and I headed up north to meet our older sister. I dreaded entering Dad's apartment with him no longer there. Northern Ontario is where our dad was born and raised, and where he returned ten years ago after a forty-year reunion with his firstborn daughter.

I remained there most of the time until my flight was due to return to Israel February 28.

A friend offered to take me to plant a tree in my father's memory. That is another fitting tribute, because my last contact with Dad was in Israel, and my favourite childhood memories with him were associated with the outdoors. We spent weeks as a family camping across Canada and the United States during the years Dad was a teacher. Dad would not want us to dwell on his death but to celebrate the life the good Lord gave him. My connecting flight to Canada was just announced, and passengers are lining up to board, so I will continue writing up in the clouds …

Outside air temperature up here is now negative 60 degrees Celsius; it was 17 degrees when I left Tel Aviv. During my second Shabbat off the base, I was walking barefoot along the Mediterranean beaches. I had a chance to try out a surfboard, but I was more successful balancing it on my head carrying it to the shore than I was keeping my feet planted on it in the water! In addition to my base comrades, I made several other friends from other bases at the weekend army hostel. One was a Catholic woman from Japan who came to help the Israeli army in gratitude for how this country helped hers during the tsunami. Another was an Orthodox Jewish woman from Quebec, as well as a Baptist Christian man from France. I remember them for their kind prayers.

Earlier in the weekend, I hung out with these friends in Jaffa, exploring the IDF museum and walking through the Carmel market, which was rich with produce and unique handiwork of local artists. One booth had clay sculpture caricatures of various medical personnel and patients. Old City Jaffa retains traces of British and former Turkish influence. It's from where Jonah ran from God, and Peter stayed there with Simon the Tanner. The previous weekend, I walked about the ancient port as the sun set on Shabbat.

Back at our army hostel, we partook of Kiddush (blessing

over a cup of grape juice), followed by bread dipped in salt, before the Shabbat meal led by soldiers. My Japanese friend and I were invited to join other volunteers and soldiers for evening prayers at synagogue. We didn't have skirts with us, so we had to improvise using army blankets. Initially we thought the service was inside our hostel building, guarded by armed soldiers, accessible only to soldiers and volunteers. But then we found ourselves walking outside in public in our new fashion! There can be amusing moments when finding your way around a new culture and language.

Ending our weekend at the army hostel, my money belt fell on the shower floor, and I hurriedly had to blow-dry the contents before everything stuck together—including my passport! We were to be at the designated meeting spot soon to meet the soldiers taking us back to the base. Suddenly I saw my new Canadian 20-dollar bill shrivel up amongst the similarly green 20-shekel notes which remained intact! A kind couple offered to trade me their paper bill and take my melted money back to a Canadian bank. These international volunteers have big hearts.

If only the world could also see what beautiful people the Israelis are, so full of life in the midst of threats of death. While having to face my own father's death, I was surrounded by so much support there in the land. If such tight bonds could be developed between comrades serving together this short time, how much more for those soldiers who fight in defence of their country's freedom.

I still have over 1,600 kilometres to fly before landing in Canada. Through my father, I am at least a fourth-generation Canadian. It has been an honour to represent our country serving Israel. Now it's time to honour our father by carrying out his last wishes. Each of us children, grandchildren and great-grandchildren will join with his siblings and their children, along with Dad's friends, and do as the Israelis do: faced with death, remember life!

The evening before his memorial back in Canada, I was surprised by the treasures Dad left behind in his apartment: albums of our photos, a carefully organized binder of our letters, postcards, and birthday and Father's Day cards we children had sent him over the years. These preserved mementos, along with the beautiful log cabin quilt Dad made me in 1994, remain symbols of just how much he valued us.

A couple of weeks later, still in mourning, I had a sense of return home as I was greeted at the Tel Aviv airport by a Canadian comrade in uniform. As we drove toward Jerusalem, we passed by almond trees in blossom.

Later on while touching the ancient Jacob's well in Shechem, I was refreshed by cool water I drew up in the pail. Again in Jerusalem, while meeting in the central area, I was welcomed back by an orphan's embrace and squeal of delight. Another meaningful moment was planting a tree on Father's Day in a forest between Jerusalem and Tel Aviv. One day on our medical base, a young soldier girl had belted out in an angelic voice a hope for miracles in connection with believing.

Dad's Memorial

Since my in-flight update, I now sit at a comforting inn with my dad's memorial card on the bed beside me. It's been an exhausting and tense four days, especially yesterday. Today was my dad's memorial.

A flight attendant was touched when I shared with her what I wrote about my father's death. I appreciated the listening ear of this kind Jewish woman. My friend and her mother were waiting for my arrival at Toronto airport, and they brought me to our hometown, where I grabbed a handful of fluffy snow on exiting her vehicle. The day prior, I was gazing across rich green grass within view of Gaza. Her parents treated us to dinner. Her dog was a comfort to me as she was last year when I lost my nana. Much of that evening was taken up in phone calls with each of my siblings.

The next day, while my friend was at work, I tried to track down as many numbers as I could to invite Dad's family and friends to his memorial service. I was so blessed to have this haven to do what I needed to do to prepare. The only thing missing was internet, so I trudged in the blustery weather over to a popular Canadian coffee shop chain to send out my father's online obituary.

I arrived up north, and there were numerous appointments for my younger sister and me to attend as co-executors of our father's will. The first stop was to pick up our dad's remains from the cremation centre. It didn't seem right for me to be carrying my father this way out to the vehicle. He was a whole person. (We had to carry out his wishes.) Here's where the reality of his death hit me. Next we had to meet with his lawyer, to understand what our role was now. The best appointment that day was designing and printing his beautiful memorial card. We met our older sister back at the inn, where we spent the evening together.

Each sibling took a part in making the day come together. Our brother insisted on paying for our motel room, and he treated us to pizza and drinks. Our older sister, besides tending to Dad's apartment and cat, took care of refreshments for Dad's guests the next day. Our younger sister was the initial contact with the hospital and cremation centre until I arrived in the country.

That evening my younger sister and I entered Dad's apartment. We went to look for any photos or memorabilia to display at his memorial. I glanced around his apartment, at his cap and shoes by the door, at the cast iron frying pan setting on the stove (where we'd made eggs together many times), at his table and chairs (where we sat and talked). His cat was now skittish, looking lost without her master.

We had limited time to set up everything before other family began to arrive from out of town, but even my young nephews pitched in to make it all happen. A few volunteers assisted us.

Our dad's firstborn carried in his remains and set the wooden box up front. Nearby that same spot, Dad had chosen to be baptized just six weeks ago.

Dad's two sisters arrived from the Toronto area. I tried to track down his brother's whereabouts with the assistance of the provincial police. We ended up receiving a message from him just as we were leaving the parking lot. My uncle bawled when he learned of his brother's death. Dad's first wife's sister also came, as well as friends and congregation members. I introduced several who were meeting for the first time.

The service began with a dear man singing a cappella "Amazing Grace." My sister shared a poem, and I read a message I'd asked God to give to my dad. We also played an audio recording of Dad reading a passage from Luke 2:1–14 concerning good news announced in Bethlehem. "Glory to God in the highest, and on earth peace, good will toward men" (verse 14 KJV). A member of the congregation conveyed some kind words about our dad "just scraping" into Heaven in his last years. Next, the message noted how we all have rough edges, but one day we'll all be perfected as we come face-to-face with the Saviour.

Downstairs we gathered to meet one another and exchange further memories of my father. We set out his framed pictures and photo albums, just as he had arranged them. I played my photo slideshow to country music and then read out my list of key memories spanning my lifetime with Dad. His older sister gladly received Dad's reading lamp, under which she now lovingly knits. We'd set on the table a jar found in his apartment on which he'd handwritten, "Laughter is the best medicine." His younger sister cherished this memento of him.

After Dad's memorial, some of the family gathered at one of Dad's favourite local restaurants for Chinese food. My brother and sister then left for home, taking Dad's cat with them. The motel offered me a complimentary second bereavement night, for which I'm very grateful to have a place to rest and reflect before sorting Dad's apartment. The staff have provided exceptional service and shown tremendous compassion. Earlier, the sun was shining through the forest outside my window, snowmobiles whizzing by as I looked through Dad's photo albums. The sun's now setting, and this evening I'll be heading to Dad's empty apartment alone. Tomorrow I'll be visiting our family graves.

My Father's Chair

Shalom from Jerusalem this last day of February. Thank you to everyone who expressed compassion over the loss of my dad this month. It still doesn't seem real that he's gone. Knowing he is in God's hands makes all the difference.

A friend picked me up from the airport this afternoon, took me out to eat and drove me to my new stone home here atop a hill not far from the Old City. First I stopped in at the volunteer centre for a time of prayer with some of the team I'll be with the rest of this year. There was a sweet sense of God's presence with us as we shared Scripture together. I read from my dad's Bible.

Yesterday in Canada, I made my way by bus from one aunt to another just as a big snowstorm was brewing. Nonetheless, my flight was only briefly delayed, long enough to de-ice the wings. I flew via Vienna. It was good to spend part of the past three days with Dad's living relatives, including his brother we hadn't seen in over 20 years! He's now reconnected with his sisters.

Up north, I'd gone to my great grandparents' grave; in Toronto, I went to my father's mother's grave. Those of us still alive carry in us something of those who've gone before us into eternity. The small town where my father was born and raised, and where he returned the last ten years of his life, has left an impact on me. Those who knew my dad, including staff at the local shops, remarked how they'd miss him. It was a difficult yet honouring task of sorting through my father's belongings that week, setting aside keepsakes for different family members and donating most of the rest to charity. When I locked up the apartment for the last time, I recalled an old song while glancing at my father's empty chair.

Back in 2003, I found my older sister (firstborn of our father and her late mother; I am firstborn of my mother). She and Dad were reunited and had the past ten years together. Last Father's Day, we presented him with a beautiful wooden plaque, to which we now added an engraved marker in his memory.

Now I'm back in Israel, the land where I received word of my father's homecoming. Early tomorrow morning, I plan to go pray at the Western Wall. Shabbat begins tomorrow eve, and I'll be ready for a rest.

You Never Know

Back in the spring of 2010, I heard a song about having to say goodbye to closest family and friends, following the path God leads in my life. Again that song echoed through the sanctuary in the background from the media room where I now serve. This week as I commemorated the first month anniversary of my father's death, the words have new meaning. Now I know Dad is fully healed, safe in the Lord's care.

Here in Jerusalem, I have been partaking of daily bread, fresh from the local bakery. It is often sold with za'atar, a savoury green powdery substance made from a mixture of spices. We live in a kosher dairy volunteer house, along with a family from the former Soviet Union. The hilltop stone house looks a bit like an archaeological artefact. Our side entry is lined with olive, lemon and loquat trees. This week the internet was down for awhile, and then the electricity cut out. We made do with candles in the meantime. Finally, this week I've begun nesting, cleaning and further unpacking in our new home.

In this part of Jerusalem near the Old City is the Arab market, where cars are parked in every inconceivable way, boxes of produce are strewn all over the boulevard, and merchants loudly beckon, competing for customers. Also a short walk from here off main Jaffa Road is the shuk, a much larger market complex. Come buy chalav and *d'vash* (milk and honey), almonds (still in the green bud), figs and pomegranates.

Last week I finished my media basic training in video editing software. This week I've been digitizing archived footage. Our producer, with twenty years' experience filming and editing, asked me to write up a blurb about partnering with an Israeli hospital. When our director returns from the United States, I look forward to going out on the field and shooting some fresh footage to edit, whether in Jericho, Hebron, or here in Jerusalem.

Staff are expected to participate in a vegetarian form of fasting. All staff are also part of regular prayer times. One day as I emerged from the adjacent media room, I was informed I was playing guitar that evening, and later I was called up front to the microphone to lead singing. Talk about being stretched! That night was a memorable joyful noise, as others beat drums and piped in with other languages.

This past Friday, my roommate and I joined one of the teams from Jericho on a trip to the Jordan River crossing, which was recently opened to the public. Soldiers stood watch as we entered the waters where an ancient prophet named Yochanan urged repentance, and where the Nazarene he called "the Lamb of God" was immersed. There crossed the prophets Elijah and Elisha (see John 1:35–36 NASB; 2 Kings 2:1–15 NIV). As we were leaving, I spotted three white doves on a rooftop.

The next day, I went up on the ramparts surrounding old Jerusalem for a bird's-eye view of the city. My teammates later learned why they were prompted to pray for my protection. While caught up taking photos from one of the higher ledges, I temporarily forgot the level I was on had no guardrail, turning around and noticing just before I would have taken one big step down!

For my first Shabbat after my return back from Canada, I was invited to a friend's place just outside Jerusalem. I met this rabbi's widow through another Canadian volunteer who helps on army bases. This widow made aliyah from Montreal and now resides by where the prophet Amos once lived, Tekoa, in the Judean Hills. We rested and feasted, walked and talked. She eagerly awaits Moshiach. After sundown Saturday, we visited some of her neighbours in nearby Efrat (where King David grew up). The room was filled with immigrant American Jews enjoying a lively music jam session.

The following Shabbat, I reconnected with other friends from 2010 at a rabbi's place nearby in Jerusalem. Each week this family hosts yeshiva students and international travellers for an extraordinary meal and time of teaching and singing alternately in Hebrew and in English. Together sit Jews of many stripes: Orthodox, Conservative, Reform and Messianic. Last Friday our table was comprised mostly of Gentile believers, a group from the Netherlands. The next day, after some of us visited one of our local team in hospital, we encountered a group of young Jews on a heritage trip, linking arms, singing and dancing by Ben Yehuda Street. Then I turned, and beside me was a Canadian musician. I learned that this fiddler actually lives on a roof! After she returned home, someone called my name. It was the group of 10 from the Netherlands again. They invited me over for a late-night gathering around their table. Oh, the other night after leaving the rabbi's, one of my friends invited a few of us over to the home of a millionaire. You never know where you end up in Jerusalem!

Through Fresh Eyes

Monday evening as the sun went down, it marked the end of the week-long Feast of Pesach, the first of three main annual festivals when pilgrims from around the world come up to

Jerusalem. For the first time, as a spiritual exercise, I tried cleaning up what traces of chametz we had around our home. The Lord had already been showing me leaven that He wanted removed from me, especially pride behind fear of man! I agreed with God and asked Him to burn up any fear (*yirah*) in me that was not the good kind of reverential fear of Him. This Passover was for me a time of deliverance from my personal Mitzrayim.

Multitudes of God's chosen, more than I'd ever seen there before, gathered at the Kotel one day. Kohanim (priests) had come to this remaining Western Wall which had surrounded the Temple. That Thursday I went up on the Temple Mount, where the famous Jerusalem landmark stands: the Golden Dome. Long before any mosques were built here stood the Holy of Holies, the innermost place of God's temple. I went up there in remembrance of the veil which ripped open upon the sacrificial death of the Passover Lamb.

Earlier that morning, I went to the empty Garden Tomb, first stopping to look out at the skull-like image on the side of the rocky hill, known as Golgotha. According to the Jewish calendar, Passover begins on the fourteenth of Nisan; that's when the lamb was slain after four days' inspection. According to some calculations, the one many call Jesus rode on a donkey into Jerusalem on the tenth of Nisan. Further, that would place resurrection day this year on Thursday morn, the sixteenth of Nisan. Celebratory worship music flooded the nearby streets of East Jerusalem on traditional Sunday morning, where the minaret reverbs five times daily. Many believers gathered in the garden to share a time of communion.

We had a new arrival at our house, a volunteer from France with whom I can parler Français in the midst of all the American accents. It had been my desire to see this city via fresh eyes. On her first day, I had the chance to show her around Jerusalem through the Old City gates to Gethsemane, hiking up the steep Mount of Olives. As she snapped pictures left and right, I tried to capture her expressions of wonder at the places she saw. I lost track of how many times she said, "I'm so happy to be here!"

Next Friday I went to meet one of my Canadian friends who had made aliyah; she was delayed arriving at her kehillah due to a roadblock caused by the American president's visit. While waiting, I overheard two guys seated near me mention Canada, so I went over and met these Cree brothers who had come to Israel to pray spiritual protection over the land. As we chatted, they received a text that the person they were expecting had just arrived; she turned out to be my friend! Our mutual friend invited us all over for Passover Seder near Bet Shemesh; it was the first such experience for our brothers on their first visit to the land.

Before Passover Shabbat began, I happened upon a blood donation vehicle sponsored by Canadians. The medic who received my gift had been a sniper in the IDF, so his aim was exceptional! Later, I met up with one of my Israeli friends from 2010, and he ended up inviting a whole international contingent of guests to a local supper. We enjoyed our cultural exchange with visitors from England, Austria, Germany, Poland, the United States and Japan. The Buddhist girl had her first taste of a traditional Shabbat meal, which I explained to her. Several of us hung out afterwards with a Bedouin host, introduced to us by my Jewish friend.

The day before, I had a very surprising encounter returning from the Temple Mount. I was delayed getting back to volunteer, trying to get my Bible back, which had been confiscated from inside my purse at the security gate upon orders from Muslim authorities. (I was not aware that in this democratic Jewish state, I could not take my holy book up there to do personal reading.) After walking about the mount, I was directed to exit through a different gate, and by the time I reached the original gate through the crowds, it was locked. After a long wait, my Bible was released. As I hurried through the Old City market and back to our volunteer house, a Muslim man suddenly called out to me to pray for him. That got my attention. I stopped and asked if he meant now, and for what. He stretched out his arm and invited me to pray in the name of Mohamed or any prophets. So that he was free to choose, I advised I would pray only in One Name. Still he insisted I pray for him, so I did. It will be interesting to see what happens from here.

Then another strange thing happened over the weekend. Two of my Orthodox Jewish friends asked me to come with them to a meal hosted by a church. I questioned them on that. We ended up going together, welcomed by Filipinos, and discovered they had a guest speaker from Toronto Canada presenting a message on the Passover Lamb. The last evening of Pesach, I joined one of my other Jewish friends for another supper. A Brazilian girl there invited us afterwards to her apartment inside the Old City. We learned she had previously studied witchcraft and was now grappling with what she believed. The atmosphere in this eclectic city is something else. We faced down intimidation from Arab boys pointing a toy gun at us as we stopped to look out at a sight, and mockery from Arab girls waving a cell phone in my face as I walked by dressed up like most Jews are for Passover.

Now, you may be wondering what I'm actually here for between all these adventures. Yes, I do put in a week of full-time service with the media department of an international organization. In fact, I completed my first video using the new editing software I have been learning. It's comprised of my own still shots, mixed with archived footage I digitized from tapes. Our producer said we can use it for an online promo. Now we're getting ready for a new series of televised online shows. Two others have joined our volunteer staff house, from Ukraine and Taiwan. I remain the only Canadian, but I'm not alone. Recently someone I know from my army connections happened by the area and handed me a loonie (one-dollar coin) to remember my home nation.

You've heard the saying "the cooing of doves is heard

in our land" (Song of Songs 2:12b NIV)? Well, I hear it quite frequently. Two mornings in a row, a dove was perched on my window. Amidst the climate here, there is peace and joy. This week I enjoyed picking olives from our tree. It was during Passover 2008 that my grandmother decided to apply the Blood of Yeshua to the doorposts of her heart. I miss not being able to call my dad or my nana from Jerusalem. My mourning is gradually turning to joy, longing to be closer to God than ever before, yielding afresh as a living sacrifice to Him.

Three Yoms

Israel sure knows how to commemorate and celebrate. Since Passover, we've had three more holidays, two sad and one happy: Yom Hashoah (remembering the Holocaust), Yom Hazikaron (honouring fallen soldiers and terror victims) and Yom Ha'atzmaut (rejoicing over Independence Day). I've been following along with the Jewish community's weekly Torah and Haftorah readings during these days leading up to Shavuot.

The previous Shabbat outside the rabbi's house, one of my new friends and I met a young Arab man who shared his story of how he turned from Islam and embraced Yasū' (يسوع); his life is now at risk from his family. He loves his Jewish brothers whom he was formerly taught to hate, and he was accepted to eat with the rabbi's family and guests. You remember that other Muslim man who asked me to pray for him? Well, I crossed paths with him again, and he responded, "Hamdulillah" ("Praise be to God"), because his arm is better!

Our rabbi reminded everyone that God is not looking for rote prayers coming to Him with a negative self-view. Rather, he encouraged us that our prayers do make a difference. This rabbi also urged us from 2 Kings 7 (verse 9) to spread good news, noting it's a sin to hold back. During another study, he rendered that the woman prophesied in Isaiah 7 (verse 14) was not necessarily a virgin, as the same Hebrew word *almah* indicates a young maiden. But would God have given a sign that was merely a pregnant young woman? How unusual would that be? So when I listen to anyone's teaching, I measure to see what lines up with the overall context, the truth of God's word and character. With the much more intense spiritual climate here, I'm determined to keep pressing into God as never before. As Abraham decided when faced with the enemy (Genesis 14:23 NIV), he would accept "not even a thread or the strap of a sandal."

We are to encourage one another, especially in these times. Another of my Jewish friends showed me a book that depicts scientific wonders that reflect Scripture. There was described an experiment I had heard and taught about. Dr. Masaru Emoto, a Japanese scientist, put ordinary water in Petri dishes separated into two rooms: one full of curses, the other full of blessings. After a period of time, the microorganisms responded accordingly: the ones exposed to curses turned out grotesque formations, the ones surrounded by blessings became beautiful designs. Hmm ... what are the implications for our human bodies, which are comprised largely of water?

One day as I sat in our yard and worshipped while playing guitar, I rat ran by my feet. My shalom remained undisturbed. I've been taking a stance against a spirit of fear. Reminiscent of a song I heard long ago, I hail Moshiach as king. Another favourite is from the Hebrew name for God Almighty; the lyrics paint a picture of God's heart for Jew and Arab here in the land.

It's not easy to love an enemy who seems to hate you just for who you are, or whom you represent. One evening some boys on the adjacent property threw a brick-sized rock at one of our young Jewish orphan girls. Another time at midday, I went to exit our gate, and some Arab youth barged their way in. One of our male staff directed them back out. While in Jericho, another of our male staff contracted a painful illness; thankfully following persistent prayer, he was completely restored. Strangely, one day I woke up with a numb arm, which lasted the day but gratefully was back to normal by next day. Recently someone came against me with Satan's native language of accusation, but a witness came to my defence; the one who accused later repented. The key is to not get rattled by enemy attacks. According to Revelation 12:10–11 (KJV), we overcome the accuser "by the blood of the Lamb" and by what we testify.

Our team continues to expand, with four others from the United States. We had to shuffle rooms. Now we have ten in the house, and just one sherutim. We're grateful to have even a little lukewarm water in which to wash. Our Russian housemate can regularly be found in her favourite spot by the hotplate, making homemade soup or borsch. My Canadian specialty is fluffy stovetop popcorn made with olive oil.

Camera, lights, action! Sound check? Our media producer and I ran our first live test stream using the improvised computer video system in lieu of a switcher. Although there are some learning advantages to a small team here in the land of my calling, still I miss the camaraderie of our larger camera crew back home. On April 12, I received an encouraging call from someone who has a significant background in media: a high-ranking government official from my home province. Yes, really! Someone from my dad's hometown knew his honour from years back and contacted him to share words of wisdom with me over here in Jerusalem. He advised I seize the current opportunity and run with it. Until another door opens, I should stay where I am.

In addition to this favour shown to me, this week I also had the chance to take our equipment and film three key figures in Israel: the president, the prime minister and the IDF chief of staff! First I had our HDV camera on a monopod at the Western Wall for the evening remembrance ceremony. The next day, I took the train up to Mount Herzl, where I underwent almost an hour-long security check. Minus the monopod, I entered the grounds and was instructed to go to the media platform, where major news outlets were situated. I followed orders, but then someone else in security redirected me elsewhere upon finding I didn't hold a government press pass. It was just as well, because I didn't have a clear view from there. I followed behind a big commander, who cleared a path through the crowds right up to the gate. From there I found a nice place to perch by a tree, the prime minister only a few feet away, speaking at the podium. It was good to be amongst soldiers again too.

By nightfall, out on the main street of Jerusalem, the atmosphere had changed from sombre to festive. A friend joined me, and we roamed amidst the multitudes, they wielding spray cream and inflatable hammers and I wielding the video camera. Picture this: light rail transit continued to run down the unguarded core as pedestrians packed the street dancing and waving blue and white flags. I dodged about capturing B-roll holiday footage, keeping watch for oncoming trains. Being a videographer requires not only an eye for the moment and composition, knowing the technical aspects of the equipment, but also quick reflexes while sometimes precariously balancing oneself in tight spots. The next day for the national holiday, I enjoyed a barbecue reunion with a couple of army buddies at our Canadian friend's place. She told me her apartment is my home away from home. She took me to a special event where the organizer approached me and was interested in using some of my footage in a documentary. More favour, and open doors?

Besides this widow friend, God has demonstrated His love through a little Jewish orphan girl. She comes running up to me with a big smile and hug, sometimes taking my hand and talking away to me in Russian. You don't always have to understand the language to communicate. This Shabbat morn, I climbed atop the Mount of Olives and found myself amongst a group from India. I sat with them as they cried out to God. The day before, I stood beside a young woman weeping aloud at the Wailing Wall. And the day before that, I entered the Kotel tunnels and was amongst Orthodox Jewish women there in that tiny, cave-like shul believed to be close to where the Holy of Holies stood above. Believing our Great High Priest already made access through the veil, there was such a strong sense of the presence of God in that place. As the other women quietly prayed through their siddurim, I found a book of Tehillim (Psalms) in dual Hebrew and English.

Countdown to Shavuot

From the second day of Passover, the Omer countdown of 49 days began, in anticipation of the giving of Torah on Shavuot. In temple times, it referred to the interim between barley and wheat harvest offerings. This year I celebrated the day atop Mount Zion, amongst a diverse Jewish community, some of whom looked straight out of the 1960s with their colourful garb. Picture this: myriads of tents set up on a dried grassy plain; campfires burning perpetually; young and old, Orthodox and not, discussing matters pertaining to the Bible, joyfully praying, singing and frequently feasting. We entered the grounds by King David's tomb, finding people crashed out in various places, because not everyone managed to stay up all night and day for Torah teaching. In a makeshift shack kitchen adjacent the tarp overhangs, willing volunteers prepared the next meal. My friends and I sat down on mats in the company of the crowd and joined in group conversations. A sweet young gal taught me Hebrew blessings over each category of food which God provided. No one lacked, and one handsome man smiled and replied when I thanked him at day's end, "When you come to the King, you have everything—all the house."

Leading up to the fiftieth day—Pentecost—in another part of the Old City, pilgrims from around the world waited in hopes of being included in the limited number of people allowed into the Church of the Holy Sepulchre that day for the annual Holy Fire phenomena. An American diplomat explained to me the belief that the patriarch goes into the area designated as Jesus's tomb and receives fire from heaven. He then emerges into the expectant crowds and passes along the flame, which quickly multiplies throughout the building then into the ancient streets. I happened upon these hungry souls who held out candles and prayed they would receive true revelation from above. Three sweet Russian babushkas (Lida, Lida and Luda) invited me to sit on the grass with them. We communicated despite not understanding much of each other's language.

On a more personal note, I commemorated another significant date: May 11. That marked the one-year anniversary of my nana's homecoming to Heaven, and also 15 years since Grandad went there before her. Last year I had two evergreen trees planted in their memory atop Mount Carmel near Haifa, where Elijah challenged the prophets of Baal. My grandmother's family name is rooted in Elijah's name, so I thought it fitting to spend that weekend up there where the trees were planted. A local family hosted me; on Shabbat morn was held a musical rendition of the book of Ruth, a traditional reading for Shavuot. En route hiking up the mount, I encountered Druze hospitality and enjoyed a couple of tasty meals, one made over a roadside woodstove by a widow and her son. After a time of reflection by the Carmelite monastery, one of the staff welcomed me to place a small wooden memorial of my grandparents in the garden. Before Shabbat ended, I headed down to Carmel beach to a spot known as Camel. There I enjoyed the relaxing atmosphere and went through my family photo album, watching the white waves roll in under the moonlight. Nana loved being on a beach. I decided to stay there until sunrise, before taking the bus back to Jerusalem.

Before the middle of this month, I joined a trusted new friend in a tearful last Shabbat together at the rabbi's place. Another guest, not knowing my friend soon had to return to her country, raised an innocent question: Why would anyone want to leave Jerusalem? May the door open for her to return in God's perfect timing. Before her flight, I wore some clothing she gave me, and we walked around our beloved Jewish community.

The director of where I volunteer returned from her speaking engagements overseas about a month ago, and she often reminds us of atoning sacrifice: the blood is enough. During team prayer watches, we are challenged to declare God's promises. One day, she unexpectedly announced in front of everyone that God has a husband hand-picked for me. It's hard to be single, especially after a couple of other volunteers recently married each other here. The team keeps changing, with short-term ones coming in and going back. Our small long-term core is stretched at times; two of us cover media, with the occasional assistance from a former soldier. Another long-term couple joined us as maintenance crew, as well as a talented young American musician. The newest addition to our house is a Sephardic gal. Our Jewish orphan neighbours recently obtained their citizenship, and they continue to be a real blessing in our midst. As one of the leadership encouraged me, maybe one of the purposes I was redirected to serve here is to represent Jewish interests in media.

One of my favourite projects was to make a short video for our director to present to some high-ranking army representatives during one of her strategic meetings with them. I had the privilege of attending one of these meetings on a base, and I heard the soldier welcome more volunteers to influence the region, because the results of the educational programs are beneficial to Israel: less violence to deal with in those areas. Earlier, our team put together a rushed clip comprised of messages urging righteous choices within the nation of Malaysia. It ended up circulating around their national media. It was a lesson to us of how far God's anointing can take something simple we do.

During the Pentecost tour which soon followed, one of our Malaysian guests showed me her passport. I was shocked to read that it was valid for all countries—except Israel. Still,

Israel welcomed these tourists, providing a visitor visa on a small slip of paper. Foreign passports are not stamped, and therefore they wouldn't have trouble going back to Malaysia. Our media team took to the road, filming at some of the key places on the tour: Elisha's Spring in Jericho, Tomb of the Patriarchs in Hebron and Jacob's Well in Nablus. There in ancient Shechem we drank from that well; we also declared blessings from Mount Gerizim.

There was some mix-up with transportation, so five of our staff ended up hitchhiking back into Jerusalem before the eve of Shavuot. We were blessed by an Armenian Belgian tour group to find room on their bus; their leader was a Canadian priest with whom I communicated in French. Locally in Jerusalem, our media team accompanied the group of predominantly Asian tourists to the outer wall of the Old City, where they danced as a wall of fire with their colourful flags. The tour also took us to the Knesset (federal government building) and to Yad Vashem (Holocaust museum). I collected on video several of the participants' impressions afterwards.

Most of my time is spent in Jerusalem, where I live—as long as the Lord wants me here. I have taken a couple of other small treks outside the city on days off, like the day I went to Ramallah to take personal photos of what I observed. (As a Canadian citizen, I can enter places that Israelis cannot.) The late Yasser Arafat was revered there, commemorated in public photos such as at the entry of a so-called refugee camp, inside which was parked a Jaguar. I was amazed at the amount of wealth in the city: gold jewellery stores galore, frequented by shoppers, and lots of new building construction underway. The governing body received a mass of funding through overseas taxpayers' dollars, particularly from the United States. One boy expressed resentment that Canada was not so eager to fund their cause. A street near an administrative building was named after the Islamic word for holy war. As I walked through a ritzy neighbourhood, a couple of boys approached me presenting initially as friendly, but I was on guard. Sure enough, one suddenly jammed his hand into my front pocket, and I just as quickly grabbed it and yanked it out, loudly calling for police. At that, they ran. They didn't even manage to steal the piece of scrunched-up peanut bag I had in that pocket. Before I caught a bus back to Jerusalem, I did encounter a couple of gentlemen, youth who let me speak blessings over them to become true leaders in the right way.

I've seen Gaza only at a distance, while volunteering with the army, and once accompanying our director and two other staff to a border crossing. They were going in to bring back a medical patient whom a Jewish hospital agreed to treat. Hopefully more and more will be brought to repentance through the kindness shown by their Jewish cousins. Recently I took our youngest staff on a trip to Bethany, that village where Jesus visited friends Martha and Mary and their brother Lazarus. Their house no longer stands in the spot people remember, but Lazarus's tomb remains, watched over for centuries by generations of a family member we met. He pointed out the original opening, as well as the inner window through which Jesus would have peered down at his friend for whom he wept. From there he was called forth, apparently to find his way out of the cave, still wrapped in grave cloths, where his loved ones waited for instructions to unwrap him. There inscribed in the tomb we read, "He is the Resurrection and the Life." Across the path, I showed our young volunteer just how small mustard seeds (of faith) really are. I broke open a tree pod, and out spilled what looked like tiny grains of sand. Earlier she joined me in entering a mosque, sitting on the floor with the women, heads and arms covered, silently praying for true, heavenly visitations.

Now back to Zion. Early on May 8, I joined with soldiers at Ammunition Hill and then walked up Mount Scopus and over through Lion's Gate into the Old City, where there was rejoicing with flags at the Kotel. It was Jerusalem Day, commemorating when, in 1967, Israel won against all odds against her enemies who initiated war against her. The city and the ancient temple area were finally back in Jewish hands after almost 1,900 years. Last weekend, I returned to Mount Zion, the grassy plain where I celebrated Shavuot on May 15. This time only a few Jewish souls strolled by, and I found a quiet spot of much-needed rest. I sat on an overhanging bough and read the Torah and Haftorah portions for the week. I had stopped by the Upper Room, where a special Pentecost was once experienced. At the place where I usually eat on Shabbat, the rabbi's wife recently expressed her belief that we're in the "final moments" before Moshiach appears.

Yes, these are exciting times, and I'm in an exciting place. Still, things have come my way to discourage me. But this afternoon I was encouraged as I entered my Canadian friend's shul and experienced the soothing presence of Ruach Hakodesh. Joy re-emerged as this friend invited me to join with the circle of dancers to the Hebrew Scripture in song, accompanied by anointed violin. The message was just what I needed to hear: we are mighty men and women in Moshiach's army. It's in the Jewish community that I most feel at home, loved and accepted. There's a sense of honour there for God and people. I was also blessed by a visit with another Canadian who has a big heart for Israel; it was with her that I first explored this land. God has been showing me His kindness, even through strangers, and providing for me food and clothing. He's even lavished me with gifts expressing His value of me. That gives me confidence I don't need to depend on my own resources to carry me through as long as He has me here in His land.

Fatherly Protection

June 16 was Father's Day in Canada, my first one without Dad here. That weekend I went to Tel Aviv–Yafo. I hiked the long trek along the beach to where the sea meets the Yarkon

River. I stood in the Mediterranean and let the large waves crash over me. When I stopped by the army hostel where I had stayed, a Canadian Israeli soldier was guarding the door. After I explained to her the purpose of my visit, she let me in to pause at the spot of my last phone call with my dad, and she extended to me a genuine hug of condolence. As Shabbat came to a close, while seated outside at ancient Jaffa Port, I looked through photos and remembered many good times with Dad.

On Sunday, a way was made for me to join a group of American Jews going to Nachshon Forest, about halfway between Tel Aviv and Jerusalem. There, a forest ranger handed me an evergreen sapling, a sweet elderly rabbi spoke blessing over it, and I planted it with my own hands in memory of my father.

The month of June has been for me one of special recognition of my heavenly Father's protection and provision as well. I just completed a type of faith fast without others knowing at the time what I was doing. I set out to not buy myself any food for 30 days, but to trust God to provide. And that He did. Here are a few examples. A friend left me her canned tuna before she returned to her home country. A member of our prayer watches bicycled in with a bag of bread and offered me some. The tree in our yard yielded sweet juicy yellow loquats. Former tenants left behind a can of tomato paste as well as onions and garlic, with which I made a tasty soup.

Three times in one day, I learned that an area which I'd passed through later had something happen there. A riot had occurred at Zion Square, some Arabs threw rocks at police at Damascus Gate and a Druze security guard tragically shot to death a Jewish man across from the Western Wall. That guard was being investigated for murder, having fired at least 10 rounds into an unarmed man. That man was known in the community as one who served at a local soup kitchen, where some friends and I visited during Passover week. Now his 16-year-old daughter is without her father.

One Shabbat as I was reading my Bible at the Kotel, I noticed a little bird feasting on a crumb of bread. Then another small bird came along and helped itself to part of that crumb. I watched as the original bird did not try to fight or resist this intrusion on its meal. It contentedly continued to eat what was left of the crumb, while the second bird peaceably ate its portion in close proximity. How much we can learn from God's feathery creatures.

I so enjoy connecting with the Jewish community that gathers at a local rabbi's house each Shabbat. I have made several friends from there of various backgrounds. Recently I was blessed by a conversation with the rebbetzin, and I thanked her for the way she reflected an aspect of Hashem's character to me. *Hashem* is a reverential term referring to God's name, believed too holy to pronounce. I experienced our God as El Shaddai through her compassionate example.

Two weeks ago, I entered yet another area of identification with my people here. I began Ulpan Alef. Translation: it is one of four formalized levels of learning Hebrew by immersion. Our *morah* (female teacher) is superb and makes our twice weekly three-hour classes a lot of fun. In fact, tonight we learned how to say, "Have fun"; it's "Oseh chaim". Literally, it means to "make/do life". Every bit of instruction from the moment it started has been in Ivrit—all speaking, reading and writing (without vowel markings)! I hope to be able to complete next the Bet level here in the land.

Last week we shot and edited a couple of debut talk shows for a possible new series, featuring our media soldier. It was his idea to field questions, as a Jewish man, to our director, a Christian. I really enjoyed putting together the multi-camera video. My main task is to continue to produce promo ads for the upcoming new TV season. These ads give people a taste of Israel and what volunteers are doing in this land. I am getting some new B-roll footage (in HD), as well as digitizing and seeing what old SD footage we can use to illustrate our director's messages. Over the next few months, I hope to be able to glean from additional learning opportunities, some of which our director will try to set up. There is a sense of anticipation of things expanding, and our director prayed I'd have supernatural downloads of creativity and understanding how to do media.

Our household recently added people from England, South Africa and Norway. We also have an adorable American family headed by an emergency room nurse, who's been helping to coordinate contacts and patient visits between Israeli hospitals and outlying areas. Her children have been a real blessing here, and they'll especially be missed as they return home this week. Our staff house presently holds eleven of us—with only one sherutim, and one fridge!

The Norwegian volunteer invited me to join her on a weekend off to go to Eilat. En route through the Negev, we saw sheep and goats wandering on a barren plain, and later we saw lush palms along the Red Sea. We camped out in a travellers' hostel, Bedouin style. Bamboo siding was covered in hanging rugs, with matting on the ground for bedding. Soaking up over 40-degree sun on the beach, we looked across to Jordan's mountain range. We snorkelled over underwater caverns and around sharp coloured coral, marvelling at the tropical fish. Next eve, we joined in singing at another multicultural shelter. These are amongst my memories of the southernmost tip of Israel.

Another leader from Canada was in town to do some teaching and afterwards had some time off to do some touring. I showed her around for a day and was blessed by our time together. She wanted to pray in a shul inside the Kotel tunnels closest to the Holy of Holies. We also went to the renovated Temple Institute, where is prepared most of the articles for the third temple. Mystery still surrounds the location of the Ark of the Covenant, but some believe from a late archaeologist's work that the excavation where it resides is located only a short distance from the Garden Tomb.

When people ask me how long I'm here, my standard answer now is, "As long as God has me here." My visa is soon up for renewal. I sense there's a much larger purpose in why I'm here for a longer time; I have yet to discover exactly what that is. I'm learning so much from the Jewish community, and this is my home for now. Still, Canada will always remain my home country. I'm honoured to be the sole Canadian representative in most of my circles. Happy Canada Day tomorrow to all my family and friends there, as well as those who've made aliyah here.

About the People

On July 1, Canada Day, I went to the City of David to film some of our staff fourteen metres below ground. We waded through natural cold spring water ranging from ankle deep to above the knees, starting at Gihon Spring (where David and his mighty men established the former Jebusite city as the capital: Jerusalem) and ending at the Pool of Siloam. The 533-metre-long tunnel, during the reign of King Hezekiah, diverted the water supply in preparation for Assyrian attack. Chisel marks and an inscription remain. It was pitch-dark down there, so the only way I could get clear footage was to hold a high-powered flashlight right next to the video lens, my other hand steadying the camera on a monopod, while keeping my footing on the wet rocks!

Our director was impressed with the results and is taking my video clip on the road during her speaking tour across the United States. An Orthodox Jewish group behind us overheard a young boy testify of how God healed his eyes so he didn't need glasses; their leader approached to confirm this was a real, modern-day miracle. Later on July 1, my international housemates requested I sing our national anthem as they enjoyed some cake with me. Afterwards, I went for supper with a rebbetzin, who had made aliyah from Canada; I looked more Israeli, and she looked more Canadian in her red and white attire.

In contrast to Canada's celebrations, here I joined with my people in the day of national mourning known as Tisha B'Av. It refers to the ninth day of the month of Av in the Hebrew calendar, a repeatedly tragic day throughout history. Both temples were destroyed around that day. The eve before July 16, I sat with a group on the floor of a yeshiva (rabbinical seminary) as someone sang the book of Lamentations in Hebrew. We joined in the other sorrowful yet beautiful songs, including the final one crying out for Moshiach and redemption. A rabbi originally from Canada shared how this day was not so much about mourning the loss of buildings as it was about not letting the light of God shine through us to the nations.

Late that night, the leader took us around rooftops in the Old City. I lingered at the Kotel before finding floor space to nap alongside Orthodox women inside a wall tunnel synagogue. Next day along the way home, I joined some yeshiva students as they stopped to exuberantly worship the Lord at different access points to the Temple Mount, which they are not permitted to enter. I took in a film at a local learning centre sponsored by Canadians. They offer a number of free classes on the essentials of Judaism, so I've been discovering further what various rabbis believe. An Orthodox woman in one class invited me over for Shabbat supper, and I joined the table of eight from Toronto and New York. God has given me such favour and acceptance in the Jewish community as I explore my roots.

My favourite place of learning has been the rabbi's place where I often go for Shabbat meals. This July they received the biggest crowd ever. That day especially exemplified the language of love, of unity, of honour. The rabbi defined a wise person as someone willing to learn from anyone, and he gave each of us opportunity to teach. One recognized the responsibility to be a positive Jewish example to the Muslim community. Another spoke of a Hebrew word for vision. Everyone celebrated with a group of new olim who moved here from different parts of the world. A table of female Torah students cheered me on as I spoke, and I identified with their story of one deeply impacted by such generous kindness in the Jewish community.

Media communications? Yes, of course. That's why I'm here: to expand my skills. And that I've been doing, becoming more technically proficient and creative at using the video editing software. Our director gave me positive feedback on the introductory clips I've produced so far, and it's been a team effort with our producer to prepare prospective TV shows for broadcast across the Middle East. Although it's not the full-fledged media training I thought I was coming to learn, this door has several advantages, key ones being less cost (just rent and groceries) and more flexible time to participate in other aspects of life in this city. A leader from another organization recently invited me to pitch ideas for freelance magazine articles. I spent part of a day cycling around the oldest city in the world, Jericho, gathering material for a story he wants covered.

Apart from my 30-plus hours per week in the media department, not counting any freelance opportunities, I continue to really enjoy my Hebrew course two evenings a week. On top of that, I have homework almost daily. The class has deeply bonded, and some of us hang out after hours. Through a classmate, I discovered a local hostel that also hosts Shabbat meals for international travellers. Everyone pitches in on the preparations under supervision of a comical chef. I ended up joining a table of fellow army volunteers. A different Shabbat I was invited to a friend's new apartment; in preparation we shopped together at the shuk, reviewing Hebrew words, and enjoyed Filipino cooking. An Israeli she knew invited us to the Dead Sea, so off we headed to float in the salty water under moonlight.

Another Israeli, who knew little English, took me to the library regularly to encourage my Hebrew vocabulary. Last time, we stopped at an outdoor table on main Jaffa Road, and next thing we knew, our table grew, joined by others who recognized us from the rabbi's house. I managed to keep up a conversation with a young man in his twenties, and afterwards he wanted to ask me out! Actually, I've discovered that studying Ivrit out in public places attracts attractive guys who want to invite me out to converse. Maybe I'll meet my husband this way? I have a long way to go before being fluent in the language, but God willing, I'll be here long enough to make real headway.

Outside my Jewish circles is the immediate world around where I live: East Jerusalem. The Muslims continue to carry out their Ramadan thirty-day fast, which began the evening of July 8 and ends the evening of August 7. Here's how it goes: about 4:00 a.m., a loud canon blast awakens us from a deep sleep to alert their fellow Muslims they may have their last meal before sunrise. Throughout the day, it's business as usual, except in some respects where it resembles Christmas. Festive lights and lanterns are strung up, and gift ideas are more plentiful.

Despite their fast, merchants still openly display even sweet delicacies for sale. Additional crowds here on a pilgrimage press through the narrow streets of the Old City. Young boys join older men in exercising their lungs, vying for customers. The prayer call five times a day over the minaret loudspeakers can be heard even at the Western Wall. Then by sunset another canon blast reverberates through our neighbourhood. It's quite a thing to see the crowds rushing toward the food vendors. For a short while there's virtual quiet as hungry Muslims gobble down meals. Even shopkeepers briefly lose interest in sales as they huddle over makeshift tables to fill their bellies.

But the quiet soon erupts into boisterous behaviour around Damascus Gate. Boys race donkeys to and fro outside the walls. Late into every night, we hear shouting and horns tooting. Taxpayers foot the bill for increased police surveillance along strategic points. Border guards stand by with horses and trucks, their extra protective gear, clubs and guns ready if needed. Several times Jewish friends and I have been rerouted the long way around, because certain gate entries and parts of roads in the Old City are restricted to Muslims only. The reason: to protect us from potential violence. Meanwhile, Muslims can freely enter the Kotel area and Jewish Quarter so long as they pass through security.

It is sad for the necessity, but it is reassuring to see soldiers roaming about this country. Last week I had a special invitation to gather in a large conference centre in Jerusalem. There, the Israeli army honoured volunteers, those in actual national service with the army, and us international civilians. Imagine a packed hall, joyful music streaming from soldiers singing and dancing for us on stage, much like in old wartime big band era. The president, through video, thanked us for serving his country. The commander addressed the crowd of volunteers, sincerely grateful for our efforts to serve alongside them on bases.

Earlier this year, this same man shook my hand and expressed deep condolence to me over the death of my father. A young female soldier rushed up to hug me; she was the one in charge of my group when I received this grievous news. I had brought along the beret she gave me to honour my father, the one with the special pin. She was blessed to know I cherished her gift and wore it to Dad's memorial. Our Israeli coordinator, an energetic woman who welcomed me back to serve this fall, reinforces the sense of family that the army has been to me. After the army volunteer reunion was over, I approached a couple of commanders to thank them for doing all this for us. One of them responded in a gentle but authoritative voice, emphasizing more so thanks to us! What humility. What honour. That's the Israel I know.

Late night July 31, I perched outside our garden door, connecting by live video between Jerusalem and Edmonton. There, at 2:00 p.m. in Canada, was our friend's memorial. She was part of my original circle of friends when I moved west. We were part of the same congregation and volunteered at the same organization. We enjoyed sharing meals with friends in common and going hiking in the vast river valley. Just before I moved back east, she received shocking news that she'd been diagnosed with cancer. Instead of giving up, she chose abundant life, and she invested all she had to make the most of whatever time God gave her.

Our friend outlived the prediction of doctors, taking into account their wisdom, adding natural treatments and undergirding it all was faith in our Saviour. You know, I don't recall her ever complaining or showing resentment. She demonstrated gratefulness and continued to serve others. And God brought along others in her neighbourhood to serve her in her time of need. She went home with her Lord on July 9. Her memorial was a beautiful time of remembrance, and I am very thankful for the sweet couple of friends who enabled me to be a part, carrying around their laptop so I could interact with others of our circle of friends. Now we look forward to the day when we are all reunited in the world to come. In the meantime, following Laurie's example, we choose to live life here to the fullest.

On the topic of gratitude, I want to thank each and every one of you who takes the time to read my writings, to come alongside me on the journey through this holy land. This is a land of pomegranates and grapes, freshly picked from our yard. Fig and cactus fruit are plentiful in the outdoor markets. Presently I'm sipping *sahlab* (a creamy warm Arabic drink with nuts and fruit) as I sit writing to you in a sidewalk cafe. People mill about outside, every evening celebrating life here. This time, being here is really about the people.

Genizah

Do you want to be fit for the New Year? Then walk through the streets of Jerusalem. A fellow volunteer remarked, "It's always uphill around here!" It can seem that way, but my muscles are accustomed to the steep inclines and the many stony stairs.

Have you heard of a genizah? There is one in or near many synagogues around the world. It refers to an archives box in which tattered holy books or any letters containing God's name or word are stored in preparation for reverential burial. We learned this in Hebrew class around the six-month mark of my father's death. During break time, a classmate shared something about one of her relatives, which God utilized to bring freedom to me. I was still haunted by memories of how I wished things could have been different, carrying around guilt that I wasn't there in my dad's last hours of life. This ulpan friend invited me out after class, listened and cried with me in identification. I've since been able to move forward, cherishing the good times with my dad, and I even had a couple of dreams about him. As learning Hebrew becomes more challenging, I persevere, recalling my dad's words to me: there's no such thing as *can't*!

My Hebrew ulpan course is wrapping up. We have our farewell meal together this Sunday, and our big exam is September 11. I plan to continue on to the next level. Being with the media production centre provides me with the flexibility to pursue such additional learning opportunities. Some volunteers have returned from Australia and the United States and will be serving primarily in Jericho. Out of our Jerusalem studio, we just submitted our first set of shows for broadcast, and I continue to work on promotional videos and learn more audio editing tools and other special effects. Recently I inquired at a local media school about part-time course options; our producer welcomes this pursuit. One of their staff (during his student days) produced an award-winning film, which we viewed in Hebrew class. This is a season of being immersed in Jewish learning.

Last month a friend invited me to The Great Synagogue in Jerusalem, where Rebbetzin Esther Jungreis from New York was speaking. I've since been reading her book: *The Committed Marriage.* The organization she founded in the United States has a Jerusalem branch. I'm invited to check out their Torah studies and relational matchmaking classes. This rabbi's widow considers it one of the greatest mitzvot to be an instrument of introducing people to the marriage partner of God's choosing.

As much as I love Canada, I really like living in Israel. For the last Shabbat of the year 5773, I headed north by bus and then hitched and hiked the rest of the way into Kibbutz Harduf, located between Haifa and the Galil regions. My objective: to be immersed in *teva* (nature), *sheket* (quiet) and Ivrit (Hebrew). I heard of this communal society from my ulpan. It was founded on anthroposophy, a philosophy of Rudolf Steiner, providing those with special needs a sense of integrated community involvement. Resident artwork is proudly displayed. The grounds include renowned programs for the disabled, staffed by volunteers from around the world.

Originally, no machinery was used in organic agricultural production. Today, however, the cows are milked mechanically. It was still a treat to try fresh, warm milk. The kibbutz has full amenities on site, including quaint shops selling local crafts, and I enjoyed conversing with the local residents. They invited me to join them for a special Shabbat ceremony, where a young girl, hands shaking, was assisted by staff to light the candles. We all sat in a circle, singing and sharing. What a beautiful and unique experience this day of rest. This kibbutz even had a huge community pool, where I joined others finding refreshment from the heat. For *motzei* Shabbat, I had received an invitation to a forest play featuring Jewish and Arab actors in an adaptation of a musical about ethnic rivalry.

Over the weekend, I walked about the land, stopping to see the cows and horses, sheep and goats, roosters and donkeys. I chose to sleep outdoors my second night, and unexpected mosquitoes (scarce in Jerusalem) readily found me there. In addition to sampling the sweetest, juiciest pomegranate straight off a tree, I brought back a bagful to share with my teacher and classmates. With gratitude I remember the welcome atmosphere of Kibbutz Harduf in the north.

Although many places around Jerusalem are so familiar to me, it's the people who make the difference. One day I was reflecting at the Kotel about how usurping powers try to take over what God has given to His people. Consider the Temple Mount and the Mount of Olives. Compare the beauty now as a foretaste and imagine this place as the kingdom of God during Moshiach's reign!

With the Word of God written on our hearts, He wants us to be guided by His eye, not having to be controlled as a horse or mule by bit and bridle (see Psalm 32:8–9 NIV). This past week, I experienced the consequences of going against my own better judgment, bypassing that brief sense I had not to proceed with downloading a media player onto my laptop. But I was trying to improve my Hebrew by watching a recommended film. Instead, I experienced a hard object lesson. Moments after completing the free download, a suspicious icon appeared, so I quickly uninstalled it. A couple of days later, after doing some banking, I realized my browser had been hijacked by spyware, a form which others found particularly difficult to remove. I had to contact my bank in Canada to temporarily freeze my account and change my passwords. That momentary decision cost me hours of research by trial and error to finally remove all traces from the registry of my computer. Thankfully, this was not a life-or-death situation. Next time it's far better to recognize and instantly heed promptings of the Holy Spirit.

Today until nightfall was day two of Rosh Hashanah, head of the New Year 5774 in Jerusalem. We celebrated the beginning of creation of humankind. Throughout yesterday and today, the blowing of the shofar (ram's horn) was frequently heard. Ten days later is Yom Kippur, the Day of Atonement. The first eve of Rosh Hashanah, some of my housemates and I had a special supper at the rabbi's place. Next morn I prayed at the Kotel, where people danced about in white garb. Noon meal with some new friends was hosted by Chabad (a Hasidic Orthodox outreach, based on a Hebrew acronym for wisdom, understanding and knowledge). Then last eve and this morn, I participated in a special New Year's service, which emphasized intimate relationship with our God the King. This afternoon I'm about to head to another gathering at a friend's kehillah, and I've invited some visiting Canadian friends to join me at the rabbi's for a first Shabbat meal. God has given me so many connections here with the Jewish community and other believers.

What's in a Lulav?

A week ago, the last and greatest day of the fall feasts came to an end. It was the culmination of seven days of commanded joy. (cf. John 7:37–38 NIV). Back in temple times, water was taken from the main source in Jerusalem, the Gihon Spring, which feeds into the Pool of Siloam, and was poured out on the mount. Also on this day, Hoshana Rabbah, worshippers plead with God to save them. Afterwards, five fresh willow branches are taken and beaten on the ground, an enactment of judgment complete. On Rosh Hashanah, the hope of the Jewish community is to have one's name written in the Book of Life. On Yom Kippur, it's to have one's name then sealed in the Book of Life.

In the days leading up to Sukkot, the Feast of Tabernacles, the faithful are out searching for the perfect gift for the Lover of their souls. Each etrog is carefully inspected to ensure there are no black specks and that its *pitom* and stem are intact. This bumpy yellow citrus fruit has both fragrant scent and taste. Next are two willow branches, which have neither scent nor taste. Then there are three myrtle branches, having scent but no taste. And finally there are date palm leaves, which have no scent but do have taste. The latter three species are bundled and held in one hand, and the etrog is held in the other; together they are waved (three times in each direction) before the God of Israel each day, except Shabbat. One rabbi explained the species represent the community; each one plays a crucial part, with the strengths of some rubbing off on the weaknesses of others, so they must function together.

But what's really in a lulav? To someone on the outside, it could seem a strange custom carrying one around in public. Well, this Sukkot I recognized what power there was in this tool of worship. Disappointed I hadn't found one sooner, I felt great joy in discovering I could still obtain one in the Orthodox neighbourhood of Mea Shearim. As I was nearing home with it to drop off a bagful of groceries before Shabbat, suddenly a big Muslim woman rushed up to me in a rage, seething with hatred. She was shouting and waving her arms, pointing toward the lulav and demanding I get off of what she regarded as Arab land. I tried to use my crisis intervention skills to calm her, because I had to deal with many irrational clientele in my workplace back in Canada, but there was no reasoning with this woman. I proceeded home to leave my groceries, and two friends accompanied me back out of that area of East Jerusalem. Walking down stairs was a bit challenging with the lulav concealed in my outer pant leg, protruding from ankle to above my shoulder, the hunch hidden under a jacket and scarf! As we neared Kotel security, I informed a couple of soldiers of my encounter with that Muslim woman and the reason why I was now withdrawing my lulav from under my clothing.

A couple of days later, one of my housemates informed me she was approached by an Arab man on the street demanding to know who in our house wore a Star of David. I don't want to yield any ground spiritually, but I decided I want to live freely, not having to hide my lulav behind a sukkah (festive shelter) across the street. Therefore I took a friend up on her earlier offer to move in with her in her new apartment in Jerusalem's central core. I moved in the bulk of my heavier belongings before Shabbat, and last night I moved in with my remaining items. Now I'm out of earshot of the muezzin's prayer call. No one urinates outside our front entrance. And I won't be able to hear gunshots and see rubber grenades explode as border guards twice last week had to pursue troublemakers by Damascus Gate.

Nonetheless, I will miss many things about that old stone house I shared with up to a dozen others. First, I'll miss the camaraderie there, but we are keeping in touch. Our new apartment has no yard with fruit trees, although the marketplace has many quaint places to sit and relax, often with street musicians playing enjoyable tunes. We don't yet have internet access, a washer, or beds for the other room. Last night I slept on a wooden pallet with padding. We do, however, have a built-in fitness program: there are ninety-five stairs to ascend into our place!

Baruch Hashem, I scored 85 percent on the Alef final exam. Now I go on to the next ulpan level: Alef Plus. Another training opportunity arose with a local film school. A team of educators from there will be participating in training and producing short documentaries with the Jerusalem facility starting this January. I'm trusting for much favour to continue volunteering and learning from God and people in this beautiful land.

Trust is truly a gift to be honoured. I have received much of it in the Jewish community. One evening I went to a Torah study in someone's home; there, someone from a different organization recognized me and invited me to the home of another rabbi whose classes I attended. In the sukkah, I was warmly welcomed by a group of Orthodox women. It was a very enjoyable evening where blessings were exchanged. One woman asked me to hold her baby, and her other children were eager to help me learn and correctly pronounce new words (such as butterfly: *parpar*). At the home of the rabbi where I regularly go for Shabbat, his wife is now letting me help to set up and clean up (aware I'm not yet familiar with all the kosher rules), and even to watch their youngest child while they briefly slipped out of the house for a walk together. They also encourage me to share inspirational teachings with other guests at the community meals. One morning in the Kotel sukkah, a couple of brothers ensured I had grape juice to join in the Kaddush, and they offered to walk me through the special holiday Hebrew blessing over it.

Throughout this month, I've had the most visits with fellow Canadians I've had since my arrival in the land. Two of them were friends I made from my first plane ride to Israel. One couple is mutual friends with one of them. Several others travelled with the other friend, and we connected up at their temporary apartment here. They visited where I volunteer, enjoyed meeting my rabbi's family, went up on the Temple Mount, and watched the annual Sukkot Jerusalem March as I filmed the participants and crowds welcoming the nations. Our producer has been providing some very encouraging coaching tips in field videography. Besides Canadians, running into others I know here is a regular occurrence.

Have I mentioned before how much I love this place? Where else in the world do you find such wide-scale passion to pursue God? By the Kotel yeshiva students formed a circle, duos laying hands of blessing upon each other's heads during the finale of Sukkot: Simchat Torah. Hands reached out to touch the Torah scrolls, reminiscent of that grand day when the Creator of the universe personally delivered His life-changing message to His people at Sinai. I was invited to follow the procession through a human tunnel of upraised hands, up into the Jewish Quarter of the Old City. Later that eve, a sweet young man recognized me and called out with a smile to wish me well, addressing me as friend. I stopped into the famous Hurva synagogue and watched an elderly man rejoicing, holding up the crowns that cover the scrolls. The first night of Sukkot, I slept inside the Kotel sukkah, remembering that time in the wilderness when God's people lived in booths, looking at the stars and awaiting Moshiach.

So many fond memories I have of sitting sukkah with my rabbi's family, watching them honour one another, arm in arm, rejoicing exuberantly in dance. Some of us were blessed to join them in a special commemorative meal on the occasion of their newest grandson's brit milah. He was born the first day of Sukkot and circumcised on the eighth day of assembly (Shemini Atzeret). As the guest rabbi, a mentor of our rabbi, taught through the story of the etrog tree, one person can make a big difference! Hashem in and with us, the nations joining with Israel; the rebbetzin acknowledged His presence in our midst as we danced in a circle to the Lover of our souls.

> May the Merciful One send us his faultless Messiah, in the merit of those related by circumcision, to bring good tidings and comfort to the unique people, scattered and dispersed among the nations.

> May the Merciful One send us the righteous priest who remains unseen until his shining and sparkling throne is ready; he who enveloped himself in his mantle; he who has God's covenant of life and peace. (*The NCSY Bencher: A Book of Prayer and Song*, 90)

Amazing, eh?

Hiking Herman

Presently I write to you in uniform from outside my barracks at an undisclosed location in Israel. My fellow volunteers have gone to bed early, and soldiers roam to and from the sherutim (bathrooms) in their pyjamas, toting M-16s for which each is personally responsible at all times. For some of the girls, the guns are almost half their size! Earlier this evening, I was invited by some young female soldiers to join them in a training run around the base. I kept up with a group of 18- to 20-year-olds! Our volunteer team is comprised of people from the United States, Italy, Spain, Holland, Germany, Finland, Sweden, South Africa and Argentina. One of our madrichot is a lone soldier from Canada.

In case you're wondering, I am still training and volunteering in media communications with the same organization. It's just that I've been granted time off to serve again on army bases as I have several times now since 2008. By October 17, I will have completed 16 weeks altogether on five bases. Although there is often a mix of soldiers from different units, mostly I've been with artillery and tanks, medical, logistics and home front command. The latter specializes in preparing the citizens for emergency response, such as distributing gas masks and rapidly securing safe shelter. We are given various tasks to do that free up the soldiers to do that which only they can do. Today we were relocated to a different base. This one's much more lively, with more soldiers here in training.

After supper, a group of gals gathered around me, sharing in some laughter and asking questions in English, French and Hebrew. I'm still surrounded by too many English speakers, but I'm getting to practise some more speaking and reading in Hebrew. The day I finish this round with the army, I start my next level of ulpan back in Jerusalem. Days afterwards, I have an interview with a program director from New York about the possibility of taking part in a documentary filmmaking component at a Jerusalem film school.

My first weekend off base, I travelled north toward the Lebanese border and stayed in facilities built for IDF soldiers with no family in the area. I arrived at Mount Hermon, the tallest mountain in Israel, its famed dew mentioned in the unity Psalm 133 (verses 1–3 NIV). For most of the upward journey, I was the only hiker, passed by a team of cyclists ascending the paved road travelled mostly by military and United Nations vehicles. The cyclists and I exchanged en route friendly greetings and words of mutual encouragement in Hebrew. Then a couple of young guys joined me about halfway up; they were reservists in civilian clothing.

Before starting out at the military checkpoint at the bottom, I confirmed with one of the guarding soldiers that it was okay for me to hike up. He indicated I was free to do so, providing I stayed on the road and ended at the next checkpoint, which was close to the top. From the strategic Golan Heights I was able to take a ski lift farther up and look over into the neighbouring mountains of Syria, covered by looming black clouds. I uttered a silent prayer for God's will to be done, hoping that true peace would be ushered in. From near the base of the mountain, I caught one of the last buses before Shabbat and headed to Tiberias.

On Saturday, I went for a swim in the Kinneret, a lake in Galil region. Tiberias was like a virtual ghost town during Shabbat. Many old houses were long abandoned and in shambles, remnants of a pioneering era. Then there's what remains of the ancient black stone wall from the time Tiberias was a fully fortified holy city. Two very famous rabbis once lived there, and their tombs are frequented by those who hope to yet gain some inspiration from them: Maimonides (aka Rambam) and Akiva.

This Sunday morning, day two at this new base, we awoke while still dark to the sound of a drill sergeant beginning training with her troops. We spent most of the day outdoors toning up our arm muscles, hauling out of storage various types of equipment for inspection, inventory and reorganization. It's fairly quiet here right now, just before suppertime; I hear birds singing and leaves rustling in the light breeze. I think of those who ask me, "Aren't you afraid to be in Israel?" I wish they could experience the peace I have being here. Even if in the future dangers unfold, I am ready to remain as long as God has me. Canada is my home, yet Israel is my nation too.

The end of week two, our madrichot took us to a military museum, displaying how uniforms, vehicles, weapons and other equipment have changed over the decades. It featured profiles of key figures in Israeli government. In one building, a loudspeaker proclaimed the results of the 1947 United Nations vote; our guide smiled as I resounded a "Yes" when Canada was announced as accepting the Jewish State. That weekend I stayed at the main volunteer hostel in Jaffa, taking daily plunges in the nearby sea.

Friday morn, I went to the Canadian embassy in Tel Aviv to pick up some papers. Most Israelis are so kind and patient, willing to assist when asked directions. Still, it's best to have the confirmation of two or three witnesses so you don't end up on a wild goose chase against the clock. Finally I found it, with minutes to spare before it closed. En route I came across a memorial display marking the anniversary date of Prime Minister Yitzhak Rabin's assassination in 1995. Before it closed early for Shabbat, I also revisited Independence Hall, the humble-looking historic building where David Ben Gurion, as head of the Jewish Agency in 1948, proclaimed the rebirth of the State of Israel.

During Shabbat, I conversed over simple army meals mostly in Tsarfatit, as many veteran volunteers come from France. In my earlier days of learning Hebrew, French would readily come to mind to fill in the gaps. But lately, Hebrew has been overtaking my French. I guess that's a good sign I'm making progress. However, humorous mistakes can happen, like when I remarked at meal time that the men are very spicy! The words for *men* and *carrots* are similar: *gevarim* and *gezarim.* We have an Italian member of our team who knows virtually no English, but he understands some French, so I've acted as his interpreter at times. This man reminds me a lot of my grandad, especially when he treats us to live music at the jobsite: Italian opera a cappella. He's also very talented in imitating various birds. We have flocks of parrots flying over our base quite often.

On the weekend, my Italian friend joined me on a free walking tour of 4,000-year-old Jaffa. There, Eichmann was imprisoned, the Egyptians conquered, Napoleon ruled and the British took over from the Ottoman Empire. Jewish presence increased during the late 1800s, when many made aliyah. Jaffa is also famous for its small green oranges, which were out of stock when I went to get some refreshing juice from a local stand. While walking along the seashore, a very elderly man in a dapper coral shirt got out of a scooter and suddenly broke into a hip-swivelling and arm-raising dance! My Italian friend coined a cute quote: "Thank you very gratia."

Again Sunday morn, all of our team met our Israeli coordinator at the designated spot, where we go back with the soldiers to our respective bases around the country. For a few minutes, she appointed me to assist her in a task, which I felt showed her level of trust in me. Back at our base for our third week, I joined our barracks' soldiers for pre-breakfast prayers at the little *beit knesset* (synagogue). Guns were laid down, siddurim (prayer books) taken up. Then before supper, shooting practice could be heard in the near distance. Around our work stations, we observed rescue drills, the soldiers wearing hazmat suits. We were warned of the possibility of encountering snakes or scorpions lurking in containers in the warehouses we sorted. Only one volunteer found the latter. The soldiers here were so good to us, even bringing cold water to us to ensure no one became dehydrated in this October mid-30s Celsius heat.

An officer came and sat with a couple of us over lunch; then today one of the trainers also ate with us. They explained to us many interesting things, answering whatever questions they could divulge. We've been receiving feedback: they feel we're a part of them and would like if we could stay on. The other day while awaiting further instruction, I picked up a bolt nut lying on the ground, placed it on my right elbow and then caught it with my right hand. The soldiers present were amazed at this childhood talent I learned from a popular American TV character, and several of them began trying it as well. Perhaps it'll be a new skill of the soldiers of this base long after I leave.

Tonight's my last night on the base. Earlier, there was a party atmosphere outside our barracks with the soldiers in basic training. We heard lively music and laughter. A girl in pyjamas, rifle slung over her shoulder, came to our door and offered us volunteers plates of cookies. The previous week, we'd shared our cookies with them. What a sweet exchange. Some of them wanted me to eat my last supper at their table. Later, we hung out at the *shekem* (canteen shop) with our madrichot. Through the week, we received gifts from our work station supervisors: unit hats and posters. Our group signed cards and photos in appreciation for our leaders here. In the morning, we have a farewell meeting with the commander, where we will be presented with certificates. Then we sadly part ways: some go back to their home countries; others continue to volunteer in the land in various capacities. Most plan to return and serve again.

It's quiet now. The crickets softly chirp as I peck out the last words of this update. It's such a beautiful night that I almost don't want to go to sleep. But I will climb into my top bunk, to ensure I'm alert to make the most of tomorrow.

Move to Merkaz

Since moving to the *merkaz* (centre), we've had men climbing up our walls! Now, hold on, no need to be concerned. Let me explain.

Before leaving for another period of army volunteer service in October, I had moved out of the old stone house near the Old City into an apartment by Zion Square. The next morning, I left for my army base. It wasn't until I returned three weeks later that I unpacked and settled in. While away, we had more used furniture donated to our cause, so now we're equipped with all we need—with real beds! A third roommate, a young Filipino widow of a Jewish man, will be joining us in November. I did a pre-Shabbat cleaning and freely displayed my Jewish and even army decor. That Friday morn, my housemate and I discovered water coming down outside our window that wasn't *geshem* (rain). We contacted our new landlord and found the boiler had burst. You see, in Israel boilers are installed on rooftops to allow solar heating. Most businesses close early Fridays to give people time to prepare for Shabbat, so our landlord found some Arab workmen.

Now picture this. They arrived and were about to cart the boiler up several flights of stairs because this building has no elevator. The access point to the roof is through our ceiling. They brought no ladder, so the workmen stacked our four kitchen chairs atop our table, reached up to grip something in the ceiling opening and then pulled themselves up by literally walking up our wall! They left footprints as evidence. The new boiler was too wide to fit through the ceiling hole, so they ended up hoisting it up outside the building with a rope. While removing the old boiler, it swung such that rusty water splattered through our kitchen window, so we had some additional cleanup before Shabbat. Other than that, the installation was eventually successful, with no one harmed in the process.

The weekend after volunteering with the army, I headed down to Beersheva and searched out the seven wells marked on the map. Back in Abraham's and Isaac's days, herdsmen quarrelled over access to these life springs. Then fast-forward to 1917 when the Australian Light Horse Brigade, assisted by New Zealand, England and Wales, made their famous cavalry charge to win back these wells from the Turks. A large graveyard is dedicated to the memory of these national heroes, yet sadly, today these wells for which many laid down their lives are again stopped up as they were in times of the patriarchs. There in the Negev is where Israel's first prime minister, the visionary David Ben Gurion, made himself at home on a kibbutz. He and his wife, Paula, are buried nearby in a national park overlooking a spectacular view.

In the historic building in Tel Aviv where Ben Gurion announced the rebirth of this nation, a guide recounted a humorous anecdote to our army volunteers. In reference to the United Nations Partition Plan, which the majority of Arab nations rejected, preferring rather to push the Jews into the sea, our guide noted, "Jews don't swim." He went on to cite proof. Moses entered the Nile in a basket. Later, he and the Israelites crossed the Red Sea on dry ground. Joshua led the troops across the Jordan, which also parted for them. Even Jesus, who was Jewish, walked on the water! The guide said, "So you see, Jews don't swim!"

But Israelis certainly can communicate passionately in Ivrit. Now at the Alef Plus level, I'm understanding our new teacher's more rapid and soft-spoken speech. It took some adjusting, as we miss our original teacher's humour and theatrical style. Last class, our text topic was weddings, and I discovered I may have been giving off the wrong message all this time. In a Jewish wedding, the ring is placed on the bride's right hand. I rapidly wrestled my ring off my right hand and placed it on my left, to advertise to prospective suitors I am available.

I hope to remain in this land for another several months. My interview with the New York director went well. He's accepted me to join his master's students for a five-month film production program starting in January, held at a top-notch Jewish film school in Jerusalem. And he's letting me participate for a fraction of the cost of what another place would have charged! In the meantime, I continue to learn from online tutorials and my more experienced video producer with whom I volunteer full-time. We're about to start editing the next season of online shows.

Besides expanding media communication skills and progressing in Hebrew, there's more to be discovered in my spiritual journey. What would it look like to worship God without the extraneous man-made religious confines? In essence, what do the Scriptures actually say? Which traditions are a meaningful component, and which are an unnecessary hindrance? I appreciate that leadership within the volunteer media organization give me the freedom to explore my probable Jewish roots. While I was away with the army, I heard that friends were asking after me, missing me at the rabbi's house. I really have a sense of belonging in this community. Recently I checked out a synagogue near my new neighbourhood, comprised largely of Canadians and Americans over here. The service liturgy and Scripture readings are in Hebrew, and the message is in English.

Remember that the one whom many call Jesus was Jewish. He taught in synagogues. When asked by some religious people of the time what was the greatest commandment, the response was prefaced by reciting the Shema. "The most important one," answered Jesus, "is this: 'Hear, O Israel: The Lord our God, the Lord is one. Love the Lord your God with all your heart and with all your soul and with all your mind and with all your strength.' The second is this: 'Love your neighbor as yourself.' There is no commandment greater than these" (Mark 12:29–31 NIV).

Some Gentile believers are so ready to judge some Jews as not having a relationship with God. Yet I've met many who reflect more Christlike qualities than some Gentiles who judge them, and they seem to have a closer walk with God. Sometimes the tiniest of mitzvot can have the biggest impact on a person. Elohim is ultimately the judge of our fruitfulness, and often He uses us unawares. That way we cannot become proud over what a great deed we think we've done. A leader recently noted that often Hashem chooses those whom others may deem least likely to succeed. That was the most encouraging point I recall from his message. In the midst of this journey, my Saviour's been assuring me of His love as the Good Shepherd. He is the one to guide me, to guide us, into all truth.

Shalom Yerushalayim

Hayom (today), sadly I say shalom to this great city of Jerusalem. We've been snowed in since Thursday, December 12, and the inhabitants who rarely see snow here are just starting to move and open roads and services again. In a short while, I'm about to head to the airport for a flight out to the United Kingdom to spend some time with family.

And now I sit in an airport in London to give you an update since my *yom huledet* (birthday). I arrived here on a low-budget flight, sleeping from take-off to landing, staying awake long enough to see the night lights of both cities. I was surrounded by Orthodox families, a group praying aloud at the airport before departure. One train stop from here is a major Jewish community. Perhaps after going to the embassy in the morning, I'll stop by Golders Green so I won't feel so far away from Israel.

Later on, I'll be visiting with a cousin in a northern England village; she has neither phone nor internet. But I got a local SIM card, so I'm not totally disconnected from the rest of the world! Earlier I had to relay a message of my coming via a local shopkeeper. My cousin's gift—fitting in view of the recent storm—is a snow globe set upon an Old City Jerusalem model!

While away renewing my passport and visa, I plan to keep up on my Hebrew text and assignments, which my teacher has agreed to email me. I am awaiting results of my midterm exam;

I hope to be back well before my final exam, January 23. She and the ulpan director are very supportive of my return, as are the overseers of the film program, which begins January 19. I also very much want to be there for our Canadian prime minister's first visit to the land around mid-January.

This week has showed me who my true friends are. Amongst them are the rabbi's family where I spend many a Shabbat. He has offered to write me a character reference. An American friend living in Jerusalem is taking care of my post box there. A local Orthodox friend, who earlier turned to me when she had something to confide, checked in with me and cheered me up. A friend from Canada who made aliyah listened and prayed for me. A Russian couple provided me a peaceful place to stay last Shabbat when there was no transport available to get to another Canadian friend's place. Their family even helped carry my luggage several blocks through the snowstorm, when not even a taxi was available! My Canadian Israeli friend will pick up my additional luggage after the snow clears and keep it at her place outside Jerusalem. Another Canadian who volunteers with the army said to let him know if I need any help financially. Such friends have shown me welcome and acceptance, encouragement and blessing, wisdom and humour.

At the end of November, a tour group came through from Canada. They invited me to join them on Friday as they went about the Old City, including the Mount of Olives and the Kotel. They treated me to a tasty shawarma and blessed me with birthday hugs and prayers. Saturday eve after being on the phone with Canadian family and friends, I met back with some new friends from the tour, who celebrated the last hour of my birthday with me on Ben Yehuda Street. A Canadian musician later shared with the tour group similar experiences to mine. She too noted an often arrogance amongst those who call themselves Christians, and she expressed genuine appreciation for the light to the nations that her Israeli friends have been to her.

One of the tour group personally delivered to me from another Canadian friend a gift microphone for my DSLR camera, for which I am much appreciative. Also in preparation for my filmmaking courses, still another friend brought back for me from Canada a new laptop on sale. It has the specifications necessary to operate the video editing software provided by the Jerusalem training school.

Experiencing my birthday in Israel for the first time was very unique. My mother, siblings and other family and friends sent me birthday wishes. In lieu of cake, I had a Chanukah doughnut (powdered with filling). Children from my friend's kehillah sang "Yom Yom Huledet" to me. One of my Canadian Israeli friends came over with garden flowers and candles for the *hanukkiah* my aunt had given me; we shared some challah and wine for Shabbat eve. For Shabbat lunch, I joined friends at the rabbi's, where the rebbetzin embraced me with a motherly blessing on this day of giving to others, and a kohen kept pouring out exuberant blessings over each area of my life. Rain came down as we were outside lighting Chanukah candles at the close of Shabbat. Sunday I had another birthday lunch (and doughnut) with a local friend. My favourite birthday doughnut was the toasty, hot, oozing jam-filled one which I wore during break in my Hebrew class!

One of the key Torah teachings that stuck with me was of Joseph re-embracing his brothers who did him grievous wrong years before. The rabbi emphasized the Hebrew word beckoning them to come closer, and he noted the danger of viewing others only from a distance. On another occasion, this rabbi demonstrated respect toward a misunderstood German guest, whom another guest wrongly accused of being a Nazi. It was an unusual, awkward scene, one in which I had opportunity to be peacemaker. When afterwards I challenged the attacker outside, an Orthodox young man gave his nodding "nachon" to what I said. Hashem wants us to rise above the level of those we perceive to be our enemies, and not succumb to hatred. I publicly thanked the rabbi's family for being a light to the community and for reflecting God's heart toward me.

At Rosh Chodesh (the start of the Hebrew month), I was invited by the rabbi of a Conservative beit knesset I've been attending to make an aliyah. What an honour—my first time in Israel to come up front and read a Hebrew blessing over the Torah reading! Previously, only once in Canada was I asked to read a transliteration of such a blessing in my late friend's shul; that was during the holiday of Simchat Torah in 2011. A new friend from the local synagogue here welcomed me to come along and shoot photos with her on the last night of Chanukah lights in a historic neighbourhood.

As I mentioned, Jerusalem experienced a historic snowfall this past week. Just before the end of November, I was still wearing sandals. Last Wednesday we had a large downpour with high winds and hail. Abandoned, mangled umbrellas lay strewn on the streets. I walked into a travel agency soaking wet to inquire about economical flights to London, and a compassionate staff member offered me a warm meal! The next day, I awoke to fluffy snow falling outside our window. Being a first for me in Jerusalem, I had to get out for the photo op!

I walked along Hillel Street, and green branches were bowed under the weight of wet snow. Ben Yehuda Street was covered by fallen branches. One bough came crashing down a couple of seconds after I'd walked under it! Thursday eve, which was usually bustling with weekend celebrants, saw few shops open. Jaffa Road train tracks were covered in snow, and from that day until Sunday in the city, bicycles, motorbikes and cars were left where they stuck. Pedestrians donned grocery bags over their boots and hats. A huge tree by Jaffa Gate was completely uprooted and lay across the wide walkway. My last visit to the Kotel saw a woman davening with a snow-covered umbrella sheltering her against the wall.

While I was en route to the airport, on the outskirts of Jerusalem, snow banks lined the streets. On arrival in Tel Aviv, there was no trace of snow. Yesterday morning in Jerusalem, a Givati soldier and an army volunteer sitting outside a snowy cafe heartily welcomed me to come back soon. That is my hope and desire, God willing.

Kindness of Strangers

Wherever you are, whatever you are doing, may you enter this new year wonderfully refreshed in surprising ways. May you find a true connection with the God who created us all.

December 15 I was heading off to the United Kingdom for some holiday time with family. First I renewed my passport at the Canadian embassy, receiving the fancy new one in record time. Then I revisited a few tourist places around London before taking a train northeast, to the area where my grandfather was born and raised. There, I visited with some older cousins, children and grandchildren of Grandad's siblings in a tiny village. We enjoyed a special community meal, followed of course by tea. My cousin, with neither telephone nor computer, warms her small home by coal delivered twice a fortnight.

What culture shock to arrive in England! No Hebrew speakers on the streets, no synagogues in plain view, but much Christmas decor and shopping bustle. Pork is popular here in the shops, so finding foods I can eat is a challenge.

On my first day in London, I was touched by the kindness of strangers. It was dark and rainy, and the place I'd just found to make photocopies and internet prints had a broken machine. I asked a woman in the doorway if she knew another place nearby, and she invited me over to her very posh office and promptly provided copies of all I needed. She would accept nothing in return, so I humbly thanked her and blessed her. While waiting comfortably in the lobby, the fashionable front desk clerk referred me to a nearby travellers' hostel. When I thanked him for going this extra mile, he simply replied he could be in my shoes and was glad to help.

Throughout my trip, I was carried by the kindness of strangers. There were passengers who readily gave me directions, including one elderly Jewish woman on a bus who showed me to the library archives. My cousin's neighbours extended hospitality to me. One young gal helped me finally get internet connection on my phone via her phone's Wi-Fi. Hostel staff were especially friendly. A man waiting in the public records office contacted a Chabad rabbi for me, who in turn invited me to his family home for Friday evening Shabbat dinner. These are a few of the most outstanding examples for which I'm very grateful.

Getting around this country was quite frustrating at times. The underground train system (known as the tube) was really phenomenal, the first of its kind 150 years ago, yet in some junctions it's a bit confusing which connection to take next. Once back in London after the holidays, to pick up my new passport, I had to change spots a few times due to availability and cost of accommodation leading up to New Year's Day. Do the local people ever get used to weathering the frequent rain? And though they speak English, I don't always understand what they are saying!

But because I'm here, I decided to see a few of the sites I'd seen in the past: Buckingham and St. James Palaces with the Queen's Guards, Westminster Abbey, Big Ben, Hyde Park, Covent Garden, St. Paul's Cathedral, London Bridge and the Thames River. This time I also took in the British Museum because admission was free. The famous Harrods department store was also free to enter, so I decided to do a bit of research: croc purse cost only 7,500 pounds, some diamond jewellery priced at 5,000, and the most expensive bottle of wine was 27,000 pounds—roughly double those figures for Canadian dollars.

My interest was more in exploring family history. Up in Norfolk with family, I went to Hilgay, Downham Market and King's Lynn. We looked over family albums and stopped by gravesites of up to four generations ago. Later upon returning to London, I went to the old homestead in Brixton where my mother was born. The current tenants invited me in and offered me coffee. There, according to electoral registers dating back to 1945, resided my grandparents, two great aunts and my great-grandparents. They also provided rooming to soldiers. Another day I went to the Camden area where my grandmother was born. I also went to Barking, where my grandmother once worked in a Shabbat candle-making factory. It was destroyed along with many other buildings in East London in the Blitz of 1940.

Last weekend was my first Shabbat in London. It was so good to hear people praying and singing in Hebrew again. Next morn I found one of the oldest running synagogues in a Russian area of West London. There, a little boy led from the front singing Scriptures in Hebrew. A sweet elderly lady welcomed me to partake of a Kiddush meal with her after service. Previous to this weekend, the most connection I had to things Jewish was finding a store in Golders Green after the same name as a major chain in Israel. There, I excitedly waved an Israeli flag and purchased my first siddur (Hebrew-English prayer book).

Last night was my first New Year's Eve in London. Crowds gathered at famous Trafalgar Square awaiting spectacular fireworks, which could be seen on the big screens, as well as live from over the London Eye (Ferris wheel) lit up in the distance by the Thames River. Just before midnight, the rain started again, but I managed a few photos from overtop numerous umbrellas. Today, the first of 2014, the wind is howling wildly, and the rain is gushing down. Soon I pack and fly. A blessed New Year to each one of you!

Between Jerusalem and Judea

Walking through history, the tombs of the prophets en route up the Mount of Olives, this is Jerusalem—where past, present and future meet. My retired military friend from the rabbi's place sounded his large shofar at the Western Wall outside where the Temple once stood.

Some Canadian friends and I gathered in reunion, waving flags in solidarity with this land and people. On re-entry through passport control in January 2014, I told the official how I looked forward to seeing my prime minister arrive in Israel.

One day while walking toward the main bus station in Jerusalem, I found myself travelling the opposite direction of the tide of protestors against the Haredi draft. They represent a strict Orthodox sect. Although I believe there's a role for some to be set apart for Torah study, as the Levites were, I think everyone ought to pull his or her weight in working and contributing toward the healthy function of society—and that includes either army or alternate national service.

Even though single, I connected with the close-knit *yishuv* life, with those pioneering in the Judean Hills. This month, except for a few nights in Old City and Mount of Olives hostels, I've been commuting into Jerusalem from a settlement in the hills of Judea. Not far from here was where the prophet Amos once lived. Bus service is not that frequent, so sometimes I catch a ride along with the locals. The Canadian Israeli rebbetzin invited me to stay at her apartment until I find another suitable place to move within Jerusalem. She liked having someone else around with whom to talk (Hebrew, French, or English), eat, clean and garden. Being here has been a mutual blessing.

One day as I was about to head into Jerusalem to view a prospective rental apartment, I ran into one of my friend's neighbours, who offered me a look at their renovated suite above their home. Being far more spacious and affordable, I decided to take it for a month. While studying Hebrew out on the balcony one eve, in the process of resetting my phone I accidentally dropped the battery into the tall grass below. My landlord set out flood lights and provided me with a weed whacker, with which I prayerfully trimmed back brush as nightfall came. Just when the search seemed in vain, at last there it was: the battery sitting on edge, stuck in some mud! After cleaning it up, my phone still worked.

Another memorable moment at that place was the time I returned from class and discovered soldiers searching the yard. My first thought was fear that something bad had happened to the family. As I hesitated on the sidewalk, I heard my landlord's voice reassure me this whole ordeal was part of a reservists' regular practice drill. Most of the time it is peaceable here in the yishuv. The next-door tenants, as well as my landlord's family, thoughtfully welcomed me to join them for Shabbat meals.

In the interim, an American friend referred me to a nurse living right in Jerusalem who was seeking a short-term tenant. We agreed I would move in the following month. For someone who's undergone as much suffering as she has in life, she turned out to be one of the kindest people I've ever met, and we remain good friends to this day.

During my interlude in the United Kingdom, I revisited my grandmother's birthplace in London, obtaining a copy of her birth certificate. I had hoped to find records pertaining to potential Jewish ancestry. That trip wasn't the same as my first-time excitement visiting England; now it was a form of temporary exile from the Land of Israel.

I applied to renew my passport so it would be valid for the required six months beyond my anticipated stay in Israel. I found the London embassy to be a haven of kindness. From a library computer in another small town where my grandfather once lived, I received the surprising and mightily encouraging news that my passport was ready in record time for pickup! That gave me hope it was God's will for me to return to Israel.

By New Year's Eve, my attitude was, "Maspeak Anglia"

(Enough of England). Seeking enough Wi-Fi and electricity connection between a coffee and fast food shop, I managed to book my return flight to Tel Aviv a couple days hence. I survived the United Kingdom, especially a few close calls where I could have been hit crossing the street with cars driving on the "wrong" side! Recently I extended my overseas health insurance with a new online provider.

Home at last, I boarded a sherut (shared taxi van) straight from the airport to ulpan, where my teacher and classmates welcomed me back. Through limited internet in a nearby small town in England, I had managed to keep up my Hebrew homework, emailing it to my teacher in Jerusalem. She encouraged me to persevere when learning became more difficult. What a source of support she was, as was my original teacher whose parting word to me over my hope to return was simply, "Believe."

Well, I'm back! Along the way, there were other signs of hope. Besides the smiling face of my Hebrew teacher, a couple of Canadian friends (a rebbetzin and an army volunteer) were certain I'd be back. Even my member of parliament showed expectancy I'd return in time for our prime minister's visit this month. The day of my departure from England, one of my cousins expressed confidence I was carrying out my purpose in Israel.

After returning to classes, another sign of hope called out to me from Ben Yehuda Street in Jerusalem. A kohen friend from the rabbi's place spotted me, the one who reminds me to speak "rak Ivrit" (only Hebrew). He offered to coach me to get me ready for my final exam, which was last night. I find out my result in about a week.

Last week I joined in the excitement of our prime minister's first official visit to this land. Big Canadian flags, along with Israeli ones, adorned the streets adjacent to the host hotel and to the federal building. On January 19, after class I headed toward the hotel to meet the arriving delegation. En route, the motorcade passed by. Hotel security allowed me inside the lobby after seeing that a couple of members of parliament readily greeted me; I had assisted on their election campaigns. Along with government officials were various leaders from Canada's Jewish community, several of whom I had met in Toronto. That evening I was honoured to receive an invitation to their special opening dinner reception. I mingled with cabinet ministers, a senator, Canadian and Israeli rabbis, a renowned international lawyer, and leaders of Jewish and Christian organizations. I even met and took photos of our prime minister's chief of staff and his official photographer!

Earlier that morning, I had accompanied a friend as he went to the Government Press Office (GPO) to renew his pass. He wanted to introduce me to a certain journalist, and I met this chief correspondent at the dinner reception that evening. She asked me if I can write and has invited me to her place for Shabbat.

It was from the Mount of Olives that our prime minister viewed the city of Jerusalem on his first day here. Next day, January 20, he made his historic speech inside the Knesset, a first for a Canadian prime minister. I had really hoped to watch from the public gallery, but I learned that only the accompanying Canadian delegates, pre-screened well in advance, were permitted inside at that time. At the grounds outside, I visited with an Israeli diplomatic correspondent, founders of a Christian Zionist organization, and olim (Jewish immigrants) from Canada, including one who gave a personal message of thanks to our prime minister, whom she called a righteous man.

From a nearby hilltop, closely guarded by security, I stood with several from the Orthodox community and watched the red carpet ceremony honouring our Canadian prime minister before he entered the Knesset. As I saw later online, he gave a tremendous message, received with applause and standing ovations. I feel so proud to be a Canadian in Israel. Even after the delegation returned home, a Canadian flag remained beside an Israeli one outside the prime minister's residence here.

The director of the volunteer organization I served with last year welcomes me back and has shown flexibility regarding schedule. For now, while I catch up on Hebrew and am getting a sense of the workload with the media training program, I may be helping out on an occasional basis. The director has a previous media assistant helping out in the meantime. They will be working on shows with a new high-tech camera and lighting system. The additional training I'm receiving will be an asset to this organization as well.

It's so good to be back strolling the familiar streets of Jerusalem. In gratitude for this gift of return, I donated blood at Zion Square. There at the mouth of Ben Yehuda Street, the snow is gone, the flowers again bloom. Many of the leafless trees bear the scars of last month's storm. The street is named after the man who carried out his dream: to see the revival of the ancient Hebrew language.

My first Shabbat back at the rabbi's house in Jerusalem, he and his wife welcomed me "home." This Shabbat at the rebbetzin's in Judea, I plan to take my shoes off and sit outside in this winter warmth.

Shana Achat

It's hard to believe a year ago this month, my father left this earth; that was the last time I was back in Canada. To remember the day of his passing, I took a bus into Tel Aviv–Yafo and walked along the seashore. My brother and I shared thoughts over the phone about how Dad influenced us. I also left voice messages with my sisters. This warm winter still has some cool evenings, when I've worn the sheepskin vest that was Dad's last gift to me. I've read from his Bible, browsed the cards from me he kept, looked at photos of him, and often thought of our times together.

Continuing my next semester of ulpan, I persevere as much as I enjoy learning in the family-like atmosphere. The teachers are so kind and encouraging. To my surprise, I received 86 percent on my exam at the completion of the first level! But now I need my speaking level to reach up to my ability to read, listen and comprehend.

Film production classes provide fascinating insights into Israeli culture and Jewish spirituality. The early stages of my first documentary are coming together; my instructor has approved the story line, and my core character is very enthusiastic about taking part. More extensive filming begins next month.

Though I had missed living in Jerusalem, having ready access to the Old City and the City Center, I did really enjoy being part of a yishuv community. The neighbours' *yeladim* conversed with me only in Ivrit or Français, because they did not speak English. That's how I need to learn: as a little child!

Early mornings, I boarded the bus to travel through the rolling Judean hills. The regular driver would confirm with me in Hebrew, "L'ham-*sheech*?" The verb *to continue* is how one requests a fare transfer to another bus line. After classes I prepared assignments at an outdoor cafe or inside the library, then by evening I returned by bus or local rides. It was quiet there; I could really hear the birds cheerfully sing at sunrise and sunset. The stars shone so brightly in the pitch dark without big city lights.

As beautiful as the land and people of the surrounding area are, Jerusalem is still the place to be. As my Hebrew textbook says, the Messiah is expected here at any moment. He'll appear first to this city, then to the rest of the world. Until that time, the Eastern Gate (*Mercy* in Hebrew) will remain closed. Yesterday I took a visiting Canadian friend hiking up the Mount of Olives. The prophet Zechariah, buried on this mount, spoke of what would transpire there in the last days. Today I had breakfast with another Canadian, who shares a similar posture of humility and desire to learn from the Jewish community in this land. She too has been inspired by the genuine adoration evident toward the King of the universe.

Diversion to Rome

Greetings from Rome. Surprise! As part of my cross-cultural experience, and out of practical necessity, I diverted over to Italy's capital for a few days. It was a low-budget trip on an economy airline, staying at a $15 CAD per night hostel. Each day I hiked around several hours, shooting photos of key parts of this once grand city's history. The Roman Empire—an example of what happens to a nation that runs after idols, engages in all kinds of debauchery and mistreats God's chosen people.

As I went in search of the Jewish neighbourhood yesterday afternoon, all I found was the tiny ghetto where one of the popes once forced the Jewish community of his day. Today there are only a handful of kosher shops or restaurants, as well as a school and a Jewish info centre. Suddenly I spotted a small boy with a kippah playing ball, and I readily greeted him with a smile and "Shabbat Shalom." We exchanged a few words of Hebrew, and he told me he knew little of his language, speaking mostly Italian. Later, I met a few more of the community in the synagogue evening service. Also visiting were some from Uruguay, a couple from Holland and Canada, and some Israelis.

Of course, while in Rome I had to see the two tourist attractions most associated with this city: the Vatican and the Coliseum. When I arrived at the Vatican, it was raining, and few people filled St. Peter's Square. It was too late after my flight to see the Sistine Chapel. I returned just after the American president's visit on March 27; again, it was a good time when there was virtually no line-up. Two things struck me most, besides the immensity of this place and the huge wall surrounding it.

In one of the corridors were antique tapestries. One was supposed to represent the Passover meal Jesus had with the disciples. I was shocked and appalled over what appeared to be on the plate before them. At first it resembled a rag doll. Upon closer inspection, it looked like a whole piglet! Did the artist have no concept of history, of what is kosher?

Later, I saw the famous ceiling painting depicting God giving life to Adam. But what stood out was a wall painting by another artist: it showed a scene of Jesus handing keys of authority to the Apostle Peter. The Catholic Church presents this action as grounds for the authority of the papal succession. Having been in Jerusalem, I observed the background of this painting was set on the Temple Mount. However, the Temple where Jesus and the disciples frequented was missing! Instead, there was a golden dome. Was this artist also ignorant of his own Roman history? The emperor Titus did not destroy the Second Temple until the year AD 70, according to the Gregorian calendar. The mosque wasn't built until over 600 years later. Did the artist not know the difference between a mosque and a temple? Was I the only one to notice such things?

Other sights I stopped to see were the traditional places where the Apostle Paul was imprisoned and later executed for his beliefs, as well as where he was buried. Paul had travelled from Jerusalem to Rome. Thankfully, I'm still alive and back in the Land of Israel as of tonight!

Purim to Pesach

חג פסח שמח (Chag Pesach Sameach)! May this great spring holiday find you happy and able to join in the festivities. This nation has a lot to celebrate over many centuries.

In February, my new housemate took me to a Purim party at shul (Yiddish for synagogue). She came as a clown, and I came as a soldier. She took my photo beside someone dressed as Mordecai. We listened to a reading of the Megillat (scroll of) Esther. This holiday commemorates a victory in ancient Persia, where an official's plot to annihilate the Jews was overturned through the intervention of a courageous woman, backed by her guardian elder cousin. Following a fast, feasting begins. Wow, can the Orthodox whoop it up dancing and having fun!

For Pesach, I joined with other friends at the Great Synagogue in Jerusalem. The leadership there hosted a beautiful Seder meal all in Hebrew. Although it is normally only outside of Israel that people hold a second night of Seder, I enjoyed another in the home of fellow Canadians. This talented musical couple were pioneers when it came to reintroducing Christians to God's Feasts, meant to be remembered through all generations. They recounted the significance of Passover in word and song as we sat around a colourful table, partaking of tasty food and drink. The first eve, a gal from the rabbi's house shared her perspective with non-Jewish guests. "If you say you are grafted in, then show it. When you are adopted into a family, you take on their characteristics. Come learn from us," she invited. "Celebrate Shabbat and the Feasts with us."

The friend beside me responded, "I agree with you 100 percent!"

This month I'm excited that I also get to visit with friends from the original Toronto neighbourhood I moved to from out west. They have family here, and this is the first time we've been in the land at the same time. They treated me to kosher sushi, and I hugged the one I've dubbed my Jewish mama. She and her husband and son have had me over many times in Canada, and we've had such interesting discussions. I've learned so much from them, as well as another neighbour, who recently notified me that she's making aliyah by the end of April.

I feel quite at home in the Orthodox community, even though I was not raised observant. One day as I was leaving the library, a young gal began to talk to me in Hebrew. I let her know I'm still learning the language, and she continued to converse with me, eager to help me with pronunciation. Before we headed in different directions from the bus stop, she offered her number.

As I was returning home from Seder to the row of apartments originally built for new immigrants here, I spotted an Israeli soldier struggling with a load of luggage, along with small children. I offered in Hebrew to help, and we continued to talk up the hill and all the stairs. When we arrived at his family doorstep, he expressed true thanks with all his heart, and I went on my way with deep joy.

On April 17, I went with special busloads of others to the Kotel for the Birkat Kohanim (priestly blessings), which take place midweek during Sukkot and Pesach. The simple blessing, which was given to Aaron and his sons to speak over the nation of Israel, resounded over the loudspeakers. A large group of Ethiopian Jews rejoiced together as they exited the gates toward the City of David.

One day before Pesach, I was heading toward the Old City by Jaffa Gate, and I found myself thinking of John the Immerser. He was regarded as a strong Jewish leader back in his day, a prophet calling people to teshuvah (literally: return, pertaining to repentance). Many came to him at the Jordan River, including the one he termed the Lamb of God, "who takes away the sin of the world" (John 1:29 NASB). Yet some while later, when things didn't turn out as he expected, even he began to question if this was the Messiah, or whether he should keep searching. Word was brought back to him that the blind see, the lame walk, lepers are cleansed, the deaf hear, the dead are raised and "the good news is proclaimed to the poor" (see Matthew 11:4–6 NIV; cf. Isaiah 35:5–6 JPS). The conclusion was left for him to draw.

Much emphasis was placed this year on getting ready for Pesach, doing all the cleaning to ensure no leaven is left in one's home. Out on Ben Yehuda Street, Orthodox men and boys had tables set up with bright yellow signs, signifying here people could sell off their chametz. I took out the last of our household's products, giving some away to people in the park, and the birds enjoyed a pre-Pesach feast of pita pieces. The lady I sublet from appreciated my efforts in helping her to clean and prepare, but she was surprised to come home and find I'd not left even a small amount of yeast to symbolically burn on the last day!

In even stricter traditions, people go far beyond kashering kitchen dishware and cutlery; they will dispose of anything that may have come in contact with this symbol of sin. Is each of us as conscientious about the actual sin in our lives? The day before Pesach, I actually got sick from all the cleaning, but thankfully it's now working its way out of my lungs. The Israelites were promised that if they walked in God's ways, none of the diseases that came on the Egyptians would come upon them. Read Exodus 15:26. The lady I sublet from is a real inspiration as someone who walks closely with her Redeemer. She told me that she knows God is real and that He speaks in her heart.

Lately I've been questioning my purpose here, wondering at what point I return to Canada. What will open up for me there? For now I continue to sojourn in this beautiful land. We have no Hebrew classes during the week of Passover, but I go over audio recordings to practise pronunciation. The midterm exam was hard, yet Baruch Hashem, I received a grade of 83 percent. In the process of filming for my mini-documentary, many things didn't go according to plan, including equipment malfunction. Little time is left this week to have the rough edit ready to review with my instructor after the holidays.

This family-oriented holiday during this spring season stirs up longings, especially as I have gone to the local park to work on projects. There, I watched families enjoying barbecues, playing and laughing together. Is there yet a husband for me? Where is he, and how will I meet him? The Orthodox community puts a premium on helping others find their soul mates. I am thankful for the family I have back in Canada and in

England, and for the sense of mishpacha I have here in Israel, especially in my Hebrew ulpan and with army comrades. Still, I want something more in life …

On the entryway to every Jewish home is a mezuzah containing a Scripture scroll proclaiming Shema Yisrael ("Hear, O Israel"). My Hebrew teacher pointed out the connection between this symbol and Passover. Every time we pass through such a doorway or gate, we are reminded that death passed over us, in the place where the blood covered.

> HEAR, O ISRAEL: THE LORD OUR GOD, THE LORD IS ONE. And thou shalt love the LORD thy God with all thy heart, and with all thy soul, and with all thy might. And these words, which I command thee this day, shall be upon thy heart; and thou shalt teach them diligently unto thy children, and shalt talk of them when thou sittest in thy house, and when thou walkest by the way, and when thou liest down, and when thou risest up. And thou shalt bind them for a sign upon thy hand, and they shall be for frontlets between thine eyes. And thou shalt write them upon the door-posts of thy house, and upon thy gates. (Deuteronomy 6:4–9 JPS).

What a message, what a remembrance! May your remaining days of Pesach bring you great joy!

To Connect to the Roots

Wow, where has the month of May gone? Since Passover, I've been caught up in completing my first documentary and keeping up in Hebrew ulpan. Shavuot begins here in Jerusalem this evening.

Release of "Leheatchaver Leshorashim"

First of all, let me introduce my documentary, which taken from the Hebrew is called "Connecting to Your Roots." The verb has the same root as the word *friend*, and it includes the idea of plugging into the source of power. The film is about my journey of learning from the Jewish community, starting in Toronto and continuing in Jerusalem. It was debuted in the theatre auditorium of the local film school on May 11. Friends in the area came to celebrate this accomplishment.

Just under seven minutes, this creative work took well over 100 hours from brainstorming the topic, to planning scenes, to filming at different locations, to editing it into a flowing story, to fine-tuning colour and audio and finally rendering and encoding it. It was really a gift from God to be able to train for a semester at this highly respected film school.

It's amazing how it all came together, despite several technical difficulties along the way. By the way, it was my instructor's idea for me to be not only the director, scriptwriter, narrator, videographer and editor but also the main character! I wanted to focus on showing the vitality of life here, and he kept insisting there needed to be more appearances of myself in the film, considering it was my journey. Since the premiere screening, I've had requests to show the film at my Hebrew ulpan, at the rabbi's house and amongst several friends. Here is some of the encouraging feedback I've received.

- Fascinated and look forward to a next one.
- Kept my attention all the way through.
- Very authentic, from the heart.
- Beautiful footage.
- Bravo, very professional.
- Moves the emotions.

Classmates applauded, and a couple of them wanted to watch a second and third time! Along with our graduation certificate, we will be receiving a professional DVD of our films.

This week I've determined to speak *rak* Ivrit (*only* Hebrew) in preparation for the big final exam in Level Bet, June 9. But in order for most of you to understand this update to be sent in time for Shavuot, I'm refraining from writing in Hebrew script. Besides, my level of creative expression is not yet so advanced outside of English. Between some frustrations over not being as fluent as I'd like to be by now, I am encouraged by signs of progress.

At the rabbi's house I can now understand more than a few sporadic words. Also, in class and on the streets, I can laugh at Hebrew humour and even make a few quips that make others laugh—and I don't just mean from mispronunciations or confusion with similar words! It's really something to be able to hold conversations that are mutually understood with native Israelis! Recently, one Shabbat I went to read the Haftorah portion from Jeremiah, but I couldn't find this prophetic book. Then I realized I was automatically flipping the pages from right to left in the English version! I'm really going to miss the fun and camaraderie after Hebrew classes are finished. My ulpan has some of the best teachers I've ever had in my life.

Today completes the counting of the Omer, begun during Pesach. On the 33rd day before Shavuot was Lag B'Omer, a celebration with huge bonfires, especially in the north of the country on Mount Meron. One woodpile in Jerusalem was higher than most house ceilings! Not everyone participates in some of the meanings behind the day, which are connected with the death of the famous rabbi Shimon Bar Yochai.

Other holidays of these past few weeks include Yom Hashoah, Holocaust Remembrance Day, when I met a Canadian second-generation survivor at Yad Vashem museum. She was moved to tears as we exchanged a few words, and she let me take her photo by a rock commemorating the six million. Another memorial day is Yom Hazikaron, when my fellow film students and I attended a ceremony at a historic high school in Jerusalem. The crowd showed respect as the names of many fallen soldiers were read from the podiums.

In contrast to the sadness of those days, following was Yom Ha'atzmaut, a time of rejoicing over Israel's independence as a reborn nation from 1948. This historic day is also recounted according to the Gregorian calendar, corresponding to the eve of May 14. Then on May 28 was the Hebrew calendar equivalent of June 7, 1967, now called Jerusalem Day. That's when amazingly Israel won the Six-Day War, fending off attacks from enemies on all fronts, and for the first time in over nineteen centuries, regained access and sovereignty over the Jewish Quarter of the Old City, including the Kotel. I joined in the parade from the City Center to the Western Wall.

One amusing story we learned in Hebrew class took place prior to this era, when parts of Israel were still under Jordanian control. An elderly nun was up on a balcony one day, and her false teeth fell out and landed over the boundary line from Israel. It was quite the ordeal, involving generals from both sides, along with the United Nations, in order to retrieve her chompers! Some people still have issues today over what is termed the green line. Thankfully, there are some friendly and supportive Arab neighbours around here. Not long ago, I observed a Christian Arab brother heartily run up and embrace his Orthodox Jewish brother on the street. They hadn't seen each other in awhile and were obviously very glad for the reunion. Not far from this area, three times this week I've noticed the same dove, the one limping with a scarred foot.

Recently was a historic visit of the new pope. In Hebrew class, we watched live the breaking news as he approached the Western Wall. The following week, the former chief rabbi from the United Kingdom spoke at the Great Synagogue. A less famous but very significant visit was from my former neighbours from Toronto. I had the pleasure of preparing a special meal for them, hosting them in Jerusalem and recounting the times we talked around their table during Shabbat or Pesach. Another Canadian neighbour and friend recently arrived; she's made aliyah!

Another festive occasion coming up is a wedding on June 11. The Orthodox rabbi who regularly hosts me for Shabbat handed me an invitation to join his family in celebrating with one of his many children. His wife has been very ill, so we pray she will be able to enjoy this day with her daughter.

There is so much life, so much beauty in this place called Jerusalem. During Shabbat and holidays, when there is no bus service, to get to the Old City I walk along the boardwalk over the historic tracks leading to the first train station. The city is resplendent with all its greenery, flowers and fruitfulness. As during my first visit to the land, I'm still amazed at the miracle of how things grow and really blossom where there is so little rain.

Now is the time of wheat harvest. This evening people will be wearing white, eating traditional white foods such as cheese and partaking in wine and song. Yet the main feature of Shavuot is all-night Torah learning in different parts of the city, in gratitude for God's great gift of His word to His people back at Mount Sinai. May all of us receive fresh revelation of His heart toward us.

Jewish Renaissance

Last year's campout on Mount Zion with Breslov folk was by far my most memorable experience of Shavuot. These Hasidic followers of the late Rebbe Nachman (nineteenth-century Ukraine) are characterized by a joyful relationship with God. This year the culmination of Shavuot was the night walking tour around the Old City Jewish Quarter, ending up on a rooftop looking over to the Temple Mount.

About a week after intense studying and writing my final exam in Hebrew level Bet, I stopped by the ulpan office to obtain my results. Mistakenly I heard 71 percent and thought, *Well, at least I passed.* But when I repeated this mark in Hebrew, the man behind the desk replied back, "*Lo shiv*-eem v'echad—*tish*-eem v'echad achooz." Wow! Despite this semester being the hardest of all, wondering at one point if I'd even pass, B'ezrat Hashem (with the help of God), I actually pulled off 91 percent! The class before the exam, we enjoyed a party with one of our teachers, each classmate bringing some food to represent his or her country. I made bannock, a cake-like bread of the First Nations, and I bought from a local grocer some Canadian maple syrup.

Around the corner from my ulpan was my favourite coffee shop, a new franchise offering any tasty food or beverage there for only five shekels. Often after class, I would sit outside the cafe to review and to do my Hebrew homework. The regular staff got to know me by name and were only too glad—besides offering excellent customer service—to converse with me in Ivrit and encourage me in my studies. One asked me how I did on the final exam and exuberantly gave me a high-five. Already I miss hanging out on Ben Yehuda Street.

I have such a sense of appreciation for my instructors and the directors of my Hebrew ulpan, and those of film school, who made way for me to learn from them so much of the language and culture. Even the familiar face of a local librarian will be missed. She often extended a smile and readiness to answer questions, knowing I was there many evenings until closing, diligently trying to acquire more Hebrew skills.

Down from King George Street, along Ben Yehuda and opening into Zion Square, is Jaffa Road, the main thoroughfare through the City Center, along which runs the relatively new light rail train, known to locals as the rakevet. After the Jaffa Center stop is City Hall adorned by palm trees, and then Damascus Gate station, one of eight entries into the Old City, lit up at night with a golden glow. During the annual festival of lights, multiple projectors shine additional stunning colours and images onto these walls. Inside the Jewish Quarter, I had the honour to welcome one of my neighbours from Toronto, a recently arrived new olah to the land. Over by King George Street was a regular meeting spot for another of my olah friends, who made aliyah several years ago from New York. Another American, like her, had chosen to convert to Judaism and now lives in the land as a proud citizen. These were amongst my good friends, from whom I continue to learn.

Near the Old City, I visited with some other friends with whom I had volunteered. My media colleague was impressed by my expanded skill level, watching the documentary I had made at film school. Prior to that, I acquired considerable aptitude in video editing through this talented man. I hope to reconnect with the director of this organization upon her soon return; she welcomes me with kindness.

As she puts it, if you really love Israel, here is a way to show it: by educating her enemies in another way, not to hate their cousins. Her heart is to intercept what the terrorists aim to do, to indoctrinate their young in a path of destruction, which glorifies death. For me, convincing evidence of the effectiveness of this organization's efforts came from an Israeli army spokesperson, who reported a regional decrease in violence. The representative even asked the director if she could send more volunteers to help! That got my attention and my respect.

This year, my adventures took me in another direction, and I am grateful for the director's openness for me to pursue additional learning avenues. After spending a couple of months getting a taste of yishuv life, commuting back and forth by bus to Jerusalem for ulpan and film school, I settled into my last residence over by Malha Mall in the south of the city. Upon completing my studies, I decided to spend the rest of the summer serving on army bases, returning some weekends off to this home in Jerusalem.

But before departing to assist the army, I accepted the warm invitation to the Orthodox wedding of my rabbi host's daughter. I recall a story he told at his place one Shabbat. He and his wife knew a couple who were regular guests in the past. They gently inquired why they were not yet married, believing that to be their desire, and the couple admitted they could not afford a wedding. The rebbetzin, moved by their story, together with the rabbi, arranged for the necessities and then announced to them to proceed with wedding plans. The couple were grateful yet concerned they didn't have many guests. The rabbi then began to invite yeshiva students and others they knew in the community. Finally the day arrived, and the bride looked beautiful. But the groom, perhaps unable to afford more for himself, showed up in a stained shirt! What could they do? There was no time to run out and buy a new shirt. The rabbi knew his clothing would not fit the young groom, so he extended the opportunity to his students for a great mitzvah. Who would be willing to offer the groom his shirt? One young man readily came forward, noting he had a new shirt he would be willing to exchange. He took upon himself the stained shirt, and the groom received the clean one.

It's June, and it's the big day for one of the rabbi's daughters. What a spectacular wedding! Not only is the large family there, but included amongst friends are their many Shabbat guests from around the world. Everyone was welcome, everyone an honoured guest, just as we were there at their home. We ate together in a big hall. We were participants alongside, observing the outdoor procession to the chuppah overlooking the Jerusalem skyline. The sun was setting, and what a sight: to see the lanterns, the veiled bride with her mother and father on each side. The men gathered with a tallit covering the couple, an older brother reciting blessings over his sister. How powerful a picture! Back inside, as the new couple enjoyed some private time together, guests continued to visit and eat. Then the bride and groom emerged, and the dancing began. Men on one side, women on the other. Arm in arm, swinging around. Everyone joined in. The bride was lifted high up on a round table. One of my last memories was of mother and bride radiantly rejoicing. What an unforgettable experience!

Now it was transition time again. Before the summer-long stint volunteering on various army bases, there was another place in Europe I'd been wanting to see, and flying from Israel is far more economical than from Canada. Just as Rome left a major mark on Western civilization, so too did Greek culture. I was interested in exploring historic places with biblical significance. How was the Jewish community influenced by these once dominant world empires?

Tel Aviv's airport was especially quiet and sparsely populated. I proceeded to find my check-in counter to present my e-ticket. As it turned out, that was not the right one. I continued over to the other counter. Strangely, I'd been here over five minutes, and no one singled me out this time. I expected security personnel to approach me at any moment and go through routine questioning, but so far nothing! Ahead of me in line were Canadians, and we chatted a bit. Then I booked in and headed over to the screening area with my backpack. A man in a suit cordially asked me if I had additional luggage, to which I replied I had only my carry-on. He indicated I must then go through another gate, but first he had some questions. Here we go. But this time it was brief, and I was on my way.

Upon landing in Athens, I went to access a bank machine to withdraw just enough euros for cash-only needs during my short visit to the country. Request denied! What? Maybe my bank, recognizing I'm not in Israel, put a hold on my card. I went to call, but I cannot use my SIM card here, and I had no cash for a payphone. I went to the information counter and asked for assistance in placing a collect call from their countertop phone. After some consulting, a representative handed me the receiver—with the Canadian embassy on the other end! What a welcome, friendly voice, ready to help. They patched me through to my bank, my card was confirmed and now I had the means to continue my journey.

My Canadian connections continued not only at both airports but also on the train to the city core, where I had my first modern Greek lesson with a kindly older gentleman. Next, at a bus station, I met Greek-born siblings from Toronto. Then in my travellers' hostels, I met in the kitchen a Montreal couple, an Edmonton bunkmate and some other Canadians at reception. Later one evening, I met in the hall a gal from Winnipeg, who'd been part of a heritage trip to Israel.

While going about this metropolis, I couldn't help but keep comparing the two cities, Athens and Jerusalem. Both are famous, ancient and deeply spiritual. Except that here, as one local explained to me, twelve gods are worshipped rather than the one God of Israel. Actually, he described them more as different personality facets of the same being. Upon noticing I wore a Star of David necklace, a gift from my aunt, he expressed his view that Judaism had its origins in Greek mythology. I had my doubts but thanked him for pointing me in the right direction of a public transit station.

Along the way, most people were nice and helpful. My most-used word in Greek was "ef-har-ees-tow," meaning *thanks*. The weather was in the mid-30s Celsius, and I consumed about three litres of water one day. At the central market, the agora, I came across pails and pails of assorted fish (getting splashed as one vendor tossed his livelihood), and I was offered a generous sample of soft white cheese. For a euro I purchased some fruit, and for two I bought a tasty chicken souvlaki pita.

On I went to explore history. The monolithic Acropolis with its former temple Parthenon was a roundabout climb, and I encountered some hassles with my ticket at a certain stopping point. At another, I went to rest and eat some of my Greek cheese while taking in the view, until a historic site guide advised me it was forbidden to eat there. Apparently my dairy intake might offend the gods? The rock seats in the nearby

Odeon were not nearly as comfortable as those in our modern North American theatres.

Initially it's awe-inspiring, walking through thousands of years of history like this, but it's not on the same level as Jerusalem. After awhile it gets somewhat repetitive: ruins of more columns, more monuments dedicated to a myriad of deities. On an innocuous stretch of grass lay an ancient forum for discussing the benefits and shortcomings of modern democracy. Close to sunset, I wanted to make it over to the Areopagus (Mars Hill) and found it with the assistance of a couple of volunteer guides. As a Canadian friend drew to my attention, in the book of Acts, chapter 17:22-31 (NASB), there in the court district the emissary Paul took notice of an altar to an unknown god. He used this Greek cultural bridge to introduce the true God of the universe to the Gentile idol worshippers of his time.

After enjoying the sunset from this elevated vantage point, I headed down to Monastiraki Square, a neighbourhood with restaurants and the old market; then over to Syntagma Square, known for the constitution eventually granted by Greece's first king. Finally finding the economy travellers' hostel I'd booked online, I had a restful night in the red-light district of Athens!

Unlike Athens, the ancient part of Corinth was not so accessible from the main intercity bus station, and so began taxi negotiations. Beforehand, en route I had done some reading, to glean some insights into the culture of the people who lived there centuries ago. In contrast to the holy city of Jerusalem, Corinth had a reputation for licentiousness. Was it that the gods here had different standards? Or was it that, with the rule of people as the political ideal, anything goes … and so it went.

Perhaps not so surprisingly, I discovered some imitations of Judaism throughout the ancient Corinthian ruins. This once grand city, second only to Athens in Greece, had a bema, as every synagogue does. They saw the importance of having an authoritative judicial system and put a premium on worship, investing much time and effort into magnificent temples. But therein the comparison ends. Who or what can compare with the living God?

The Acrocorinth was a hot, winding climb to the fortress on top. Having seen quite a few castles over in England, this one didn't have any more of a draw. But I was here, and this was part of Greece's history which I came to see. I had received a travel tip from a Canadian earlier at a cafe, so before night fell, I walked alongside the Corinth Canal, reading the tributes to the Hungarians who designed and oversaw the building project. Then with the help of a young gal's translation, I made the connecting overnight bus via Athens to Thessaloniki, second-largest city in Greece.

North in this Macedonian region, I had baklava for breakfast in a cafe. Then I freshened up and checked into my hostel. The way to the old part of town was uphill on foot. The city's main Aristotelous Square was a cultural hub with flowers and palm trees leading to the seashore. There was the famous White Tower, formerly known as red (a place of torture under the Turks) and now a symbol of the city. Again around me were signs of idolatry: women placing prayer notes under some saint's coffin, another kissing and paying homage to images on paintings. Later at night, I strolled along the port to the monument of Alexander the Great.

But what stood out to me most was the little Jewish Museum of Thessaloniki. I was excited to hear and converse in Hebrew, and from there I was invited to fish dinner at an outdoor cafe by Israeli lawyers and urban planners. At the museum I learned that Thessaloniki was established by a Macedonian king in 315 BC, named after his wife, sister of Alexander the Great. Following the 1492 expulsion of Jews from Spain, Thessaloniki became a world centre of Sephardic Judaism. Over 50 percent of the city's population was once Jewish. In 1912, Thessaloniki was returned to Greek hands, and in 1917 the accidental Great Fire destroyed two-thirds of the city. By 1943, there was the deportation of the living to Auschwitz-Birkenau, and the desecration of the dead in the destruction of the local Jewish cemetery. Emissary Paul reportedly spoke in an ancient synagogue in Thessaloniki, alluding to the "Tree of Life."

The next morning, I headed to the bus station for the long ride back south to Athens. For much of the trip, I gazed out the window at the flower bushes, fields, olive groves, red cliffs, mountains and lakes. Upon arriving in busy Omonoia Square, I saw streams of yellow taxis. I went by the City Hall and over to the University of Athens, imagining all those students spending their days discussing various popular philosophies. Then there was that beacon of democracy in action, the Hellenic Parliament, with regimental guards out front. Palm trees, waterfalls and turtles were found along the path through the National Garden.

Back out onto the asphalt, I went in search of the restored Panathenaic Stadium, which hosted the first modern Olympics in 1896. To think the worldwide sports extravaganza began here in Greece centuries before, where the human body was worshipped. Amongst the gods, Zeus is most prominent, and like the rest of his associates, a temple was built in his honour. Hadrian's Arch was named after the Roman emperor who was an avid admirer of Greece. Rome and Athens, lead cities of two vast empires, decayed from within and fell.

Shabbat was approaching, and I arrived early at synagogue to light candles. After a small service, I was welcomed at a Chabad house, meeting guests from Gush Katif (that region of Israel where Jews were forced out of their homes), newlyweds and a former student of my Jerusalem rabbi. Connections are worldwide, including Canadian and Jewish! We had Kiddush and enjoyed an evening of good food and conversation.

My last day in Greece, I relaxed on one of the Aegean Islands, jumping into the beautiful greenish blue sea. Then I dried out as I hiked along the hilly dirt roads, noticing pistachio trees in abundance. As the day came to a close, my last stop was the Plaka, the oldest neighbourhood in Athens, where I browsed until I needed to depart for my flight back to Tel Aviv. Oh, to be back in that other more grand ancient city of Jerusalem!

Back to Bases

After returning from Greece, I spent the night in the beit knesset of Israel's international airport, awakening to Rosh Chodesh davening. Men had gathered in their outspread white tallitot for early morning sung prayers at the head of this new month: Tammuz. What a welcome sight and sound, being back in the land!

Later that day, I was due to meet our international coordinator and incoming fellow volunteers for the first in this summer's series of assignments to Israeli army bases. As names were called out and groups formed, I found myself in the middle, between young adults and senior participants. After everyone was accounted for, off we went together in our designated vehicles. For the third time, I would be at the medical base. It would be my first time back since last year, when I received news about my father.

Outside our familiar barracks, we faced another kind of grief this week at a national level, as we watched on TV the funeral of the three Jewish youth who were kidnapped and murdered by terrorists. These yeshiva boys were doing what many locals did in the Gush Etzion region: *tremp*. Bus service isn't always so frequent at certain junctions, and even I was previously encouraged by a rebbetzin to hitch a ride to the yishuv from there. It was considered safe, but now no longer. The army warned soldiers not to take such rides. After the televised funeral, our madricha lit candles beside photos of the three boys, played a song and together observed a minute of silence. That morning at flag raising, additional soldiers joined us, along with officers and a high-ranking official, who went around to each one of us and personally thanked us for coming to help his army.

My former supervisor readily remembered me, but this time I was assigned to work at a different medical warehouse, with a Russian Canadian comrade (on whom I've performed minor first aid twice). When it came to heavier lifting of boxes onto our work table, as the younger one, I naturally expected to do so. But this great-grandmother flexed her muscles to show she too was capable of lifting. Yes, she was sturdy, though she made me nervous when she insisted on using a surgical tool as her case cutter. I steered clear as she wielded that tiny but razor-sharp blade!

Our new supervisors spoke mostly Hebrew, which suited me just fine; we also listened to songs and news on Israeli radio. During one evening activity, an Israeli volunteer and I were barred from participation because our Hebrew knowledge gave us an advantage over the others. I took that as a compliment. We have a large group of friendly volunteers from the United States, Canada, France and Belgium, most of whom are veterans of this program.

Our first weekend off, I was glad to be back in Jerusalem, returning to my former rented room. I'm living on bases all summer, with the invitation to come back for some weekends when I'm missing Jerusalem, leaving additional belongings in storage there. When I offered to contribute, the kind soul from whom I'd rented extended this mitzvah, in appreciation for my service to her new homeland. I am most grateful for her welcome.

This weekend, the area was on high alert: besides the standby security by the Kotel every Friday for when the Muslims finish in the Temple Mount mosques, there was a mass of regular police, riot police, soldiers and border guards stationed throughout and around the Old City. At times, access through one or more gates was blocked, with reported *balagan* (a slang Hebrew term meaning chaos). Everyone is extra attentive to the news these days to see what will unfold with the escalation of violence. Later the same week of the funeral, another body was found murdered, this time an Arab youth, and accusatory fingers were pointed at the Jewish community as the investigation continued. Friday was not only the day before Ramadan (this year, June 28 through July 28), when the Muslims fast food and water from dawn to dusk, but it was also the day of the Arab boy's funeral, so tensions were high.

For one of our volunteers, it was her first time in the land, and I offered to show her around Jerusalem and help her find her way to her hostel. I also hung out with several other friends and did a free walking tour to glean some more history about familiar sites I was revisiting. While en route to the rabbi's for Shabbat lunch, he cordially extended a *bracha* (blessing) of peace toward one of the Arab shopkeepers. The response was an icy-cold retort, "I want no peace with you!" Yet many in the media world still often blame Israel for lack of peace. Arriving at the rabbi's home, I expressed how good it was to see the rebbetzin again; her countenance was looking better. As I was leaving the rabbi's, noting I would not be there as often over the summer while volunteering on army bases, several sang a soldier song and brought a smile to my face. On my way back, I watched Ben Yehuda Street come alive again after Shabbat, and I had an early rising after a late night. I packed up and went to meet at the designated spot for transport back to our base, from where I write from my comfortable bunk.

War is imminent: that's how I interpreted the Hebrew headline of a newspaper. So I was here for such a time. Next day, July 8, Operation Protective Edge began, lasting through to August 26, with air strikes on Gaza in response to the increased barrage of incoming rockets. We were incensed over manipulative, false propaganda spewed via a major American network, calling Israel a killing machine and accusing her of using the deaths of three of her youth as an excuse for war (as per the guest to whom they gave much floor time). Other volunteers were relocated from a high-risk region to our site. That morning we had a drill, and that evening we dove into the trenches for real, we realized as we heard the boom of Iron Dome (Kippat Barzel) intercepting a rocket! And here I expected it to be just another drill, for the sake of the newcomers. It seemed surreal. Strangely, though, as a Canadian never before experiencing such a thing, I felt at peace being there with my people.

Medical and home front commanders personally went around to meet and thank each of us international volunteers for supporting them during this time, when our help is all the more essential. Our madrichot assigned each of us to a buddy system, in case of future red alerts. Later last night, we made two more dashes to designated safe places, then again this morning, and this evening. I was so glad I lost my place in the shower line-up, looking for my toothbrush, as a siren went off. I was not amongst those who had to hastily run out! After supper, when a request for additional help came in, most of us stepped forward to volunteer to prepare shipments of medical aid, for which the one in charge was so appreciative. He called us precious, telling us we had a part in saving lives. Earlier, our regular warehouse supervisors warmly bade us a good weekend off and were eager to have our team continue with them next week.

Between work, meals and trying to sleep these past couple of nights, everyone's been sticking together and keeping up with the latest news reports (the Israeli ones being far more trustworthy sources). Tonight I tried to encourage one of our madrichot, who expressed feeling the weight of responsibility for our protection; I assured her we are all in this together and will do all we can to help. Depending on how things unfold, they still wanted to reward us volunteers with an educational field trip on Thursday to Netanya, to a museum honouring people from Canada, the United States, the United Kingdom,

Argentina and others who stepped forward to assist Israel in the early days, before the IDF became the national army.

For our weekend off, we were taken to a safe place in the Tel Aviv area; by that evening, we heard several rockets explode. The officer in charge advised we not go out at night. Some of us took an afternoon dip in the sea and spent the evening on the phone with family and friends in our native countries. We discussed updates on the situation with soldiers guarding our hostel. We even had the ability to install an app on our phones that was alerted within seconds of every incoming rocket regarding its time and destination. Within half an hour, twelve had been launched from Gaza, and they continued on a regular basis day and night, sometimes seconds apart to different areas of the country.

As I was writing just now, another red alert sounded, and we joined the soldiers in the safe room, listened for the sound of the intercepted rocket boom and waited for the all clear before exiting. This extra time allowance is to prevent injury from falling shrapnel, and to be ready in case another volley of rockets is about to head our way. Again, I just finished typing the above point, and I had to rush back to the safe room as we heard more booms in the sky. Now I'm back to where I left off. Friday morning, we were taking a pre-breakfast swim when lifeguards announced for everyone to stay close to shore. Here you see Israeli resiliency, not bowing to enemy intimidation.

Refreshed by an afternoon nap, I took a brief walk around Old Jaffa. Realizing I would not make it back in time for the start of Shabbat, I improvised and lit candles inside the doorway of St. Peter's historic church. Then I continued on to a tiny Libyan synagogue for evening service before returning to our hostel for Shabbat meal with our comrades. Saturday I visited a Sephardic synagogue with my barracks mate, went for an afternoon walk with other volunteers along Jaffa Port and had another swim in the clear Mediterranean water as helicopters were overhead. Now we've been advised to stay inside, in view of the latest Hamas threat to keep targeting Tel Aviv.

From Underground

The following is my August 23 reply to a Canadian government official.

> Thank you so much, sir, for this reassuring update. I'm proud to represent Canada here amongst the international volunteers with the IDF. Many Israelis are very much aware of our prime minister's strong support, for which I personally have much gratitude and respect. God bless Canada! Shalom from Jerusalem, as I return to my assigned base in the morn.

Earlier that month he had responded via personal email, expressing interest in my writings from Israel. He noted that elsewhere wrong information and criticism abounded, with much media bias. Then he affirmed Israel's right to self-defence when attacked by terrorist entities. He closed his remarks with well wishes for my safety.

Sunday, July 13, was the first day back on base since Thursday's announcement that IDF ground troops entered Gaza. By day's end, thirteen more soldiers died, a total of eighteen, as well as two civilians. Several others were wounded by mortar or shrapnel, or injuries related to responding to red alerts. IAF air strikes continued, in conjunction with attempts to find and destroy terrorist tunnels and rocket launchers that have been steadily and increasingly used to attack the nation of Israel in an unprecedented scope.

By this following Sunday, tonight's British news excerpt seemingly forgot to mention Hamas had anything to do with the devastation, portraying Israel's attempts at self-defence as a massacre. An American network interviewer appeared to try to manipulate and entrap the prime minister of Israel, but he was wise to their tactics and stated the facts, placing responsibility where it belongs. Hamas has refused ceasefire offers, choosing to continue to terrorize, the ultimate objective being to completely destroy the Jewish state. Israeli leadership noted the difference: the enemy in Gaza uses its people to protect rockets (meant to harm Israelis); Israel uses rockets (the Iron Dome missile defence system) to protect our people.

As of this Thursday morning's news at flag raising, thirty-two of our soldiers have now died while fighting against terror. Our madrichot made a memorial comprised of thirty-two stones, around which we gathered in respect. Additional soldiers have been brought to our base to work with us volunteers in packing medical supplies. Last night many of us worked until 2:00 a.m. to help the commander's assistants get an urgent order out to another part of the country.

The media war is intense. Israeli government presented to the United Nations official images of IDF findings, such as tunnels leading into Israeli territory, exposed plots to murder Israelis and use of schools and mosques to store weapons. The relief agency even turned over rockets they found to local police, essentially giving them back into the hands of Hamas!

Headlines of free daily papers show smiling faces of young soldiers who've taken their last breath, contrasted with grieving comrades. From a short distance away, we saw beamed images of some radical Muslims celebrating over claims of abducting an Israeli soldier's body. How sick! Over in local Rabin Square, a small crowd gathered waving blue and white flags, reportedly in support of our soldiers fighting on our behalf. There was an absence of visible protestors, although one clean-cut young man walking by accused the group of being neo-Nazis. Apparently that was his view of Israel supporters!

One of our volunteers was the mother of a Golani infantry unit commander. We watched her as news came in of more deaths, more wounded. One evening a soldier approached me, looking for her; thankfully it was not dreaded news he had to convey. Rather, he was arranging for Kaddish (prayer service of praise and thanksgiving to Hashem) for her other son, who died several years ago. Now her only son had been called into Gaza.

Five younger volunteers of our first group flew home in fear. Some airlines temporarily cancelled flights after a rocket was launched toward the airport area. Five of us from the last group were reassigned to the same base, joined by more Americans, Canadians and volunteers from Italy and Holland. We had a sweet older man, originally from Poland, who reminded me a lot of my late Holocaust survivor friend who was also from there.

One of our American volunteers forgot to pack closed-toe footwear. She asked a local person where the nearest shoe store was, to purchase some before meeting our coordinator at the designated spot. These strangers went above and beyond. They were so grateful she was helping Israel's army that they happily took her out of their way, and they even insisted on buying the shoes for her. What an example of Israeli kindness!

For the weekend, I went to Jerusalem. En route to the Old City, I stopped by Mahane Yehuda market and took a stroll along my favourite Ben Yehuda Street. On approaching the Kotel, in Hebrew I asked a police officer if it was quiet there that Friday morning. Moments after responding that it was, rapid fire was heard from above on the Temple Mount, and a multitude of women fled screaming from the wall while others remained praying there. As a precaution, I ducked behind a side wall, from where I watched young boys diligently davening by their mother as gunshots continued. I spotted what appeared to be an Israeli soldier along the top. Later I asked a news reporter if he knew what had happened. He related some Muslims after their morning prayers were starting to throw rocks on Jews praying below. The sounds we heard were tear gas to disperse those trying to inflict harm. On Friday eve, I enjoyed Shabbat meal with my former housemate and her neighbours. She made homemade challah, and I brought fresh mangos from the shuk. On Saturday she joined me in walking to my regular rabbi host's home.

Another weekend off, we visited a military museum that is free to army volunteers. The staff there was floored that people from around the world were coming to help her country's army. My revisit to the diaspora museum was interrupted by a red alert siren; everyone was directed for a few minutes into the shelter. It turned out it was another rocket heading toward the airport region. Before heading back to our hostel for candle lighting and Shabbat meal with the soldiers, I stopped by Tel Aviv University's botanical gardens and experienced a bit of nature and tranquillity. After a restless night due to someone's extraordinary snoring, I went to a morning service and afterwards crashed in the Mediterranean waves. It's back to the base Sunday morn.

Another Ceasefire

With so many soldiers pouring in, Sunday July 27, we had to meet at another designated area to return to our base. No field trips this program. Supporting the defence operation took priority, of course. We arrived to multiple medical trucks parked outside our barracks; after working the balance of the day, we willingly volunteered to work into the evening in other locations on the base. I helped assemble hospital field kits, including surgeons' vests, as well as special supplies for the soldiers on the frontlines. Box loads of our work were sent out and received within hours. Today, a general came to our base to address all the soldiers and international volunteers, expressing deep gratitude for all the help and moral support.

The most memorable part of Monday's newscast was when an ambassador described the reality of the ceasefire. We cease, and they (Hamas) continue to fire! A highlight of today was writing notes to our soldiers on the frontlines. Our madricha announced a friend of hers was coming in the morning to pick them up and to deliver them. I wrote several in Hebrew. In our work station with my fellow Canadian, we met a soldier who works with the Iron Dome system, ensuring the most effective reallocation for maximal protection of the public. Thank God for this amazing technology He gave someone the wisdom to invent! Without it, there would be even more loss of life and injuries.

We were awakened at 2:30 a.m. by a red alert siren and intercom announcement of an incoming rocket. We headed to the closest safe place: the men's washroom. Just after 10:00 p.m., another siren had sounded; that time we dispersed into comrades' barracks, which have stronger rooftops. The fading siren was followed by a couple of booms, and moments later military aircraft roared through the skies. I checked my phone app, which indicated twelve alerts over a two-hour period, covering south and central Israel.

Daily we gathered to watch the five o'clock news from an Israeli broadcaster. Governing in Gaza, terrorist group Hamas was allegedly open to yet another ceasefire. They've only refused and breached every one of the five which Israel agreed to under international pressure. The latest proposal is understandably met with scepticism, considering the ongoing barrage of rocket fire at us. Yet apparently the United Nations official thinks it is a simple matter of both sides sitting down to talk, having both the humility and will to do so. His televised speech reminded me of someone addressing young children to just get along, and afterwards we could enjoy a nice tea party together.

The facts and evidence are out there: Hamas's ambition is the complete destruction of the Jewish State, to be replaced by an Islamic Caliphate. And much of the world is helping them toward this goal by funding certain causes with taxpayers' dollars, providing supplies to build more weapons and terror tunnels. They are even promoting them at rallies in major cities! We are living in a time when people are calling good evil and evil good (see Isaiah 5:20 KJV).

This Tuesday evening, a fellow volunteer and I brushed up on our Hebrew verb vocabulary. Noon meals are extra crowded these days with busloads of additional soldiers coming to help sort and pack medical equipment and medicine. Outside of our food hall, someone placed a memorial board of news clippings. At last count, 53 of our soldiers have fallen since the start of the operation 22 days ago. Israeli leadership was reported as saying that Israel will continue to root out and remove the terror tunnels (such as those found that led into kibbutzim). Such evil perpetrated by Hamas cannot be allowed to go unchecked, no matter what others in the world think. And others even more extreme are arising: ISIS in Iraq is associated with crucifixions and beheadings. What is the antidote for the poison being fed to young children by these terror groups?

Today, Wednesday, we bid farewell to three of our guys who were transitioning from third-party army volunteers into regular army service; they were all American lone soldiers now, who chose to come alone to Eretz Yisrael and voluntarily enlist in defence of this country. We watched on TV the overwhelming response at the funerals of a couple of other lone soldiers, who fell in the current operation. Thousands came to pay respect at their funerals.

On Thursday morning after flag raising, the general manager of the volunteer organization addressed our group, thanking us for all our additional help during wartime. The evening before, we had a guest speaker who provided resources on getting word out to counteract the false media propaganda against Israel.

We were transported off base and taken to a guarded hostel for the weekend. A fellow volunteer asked a few of us to come along with her up the coast to Netanya. We arrived in time to take a dip under the splendid sunset. Then we strolled along the promenade, where there are French cafes. I had packed some army food to eat there, and we made it back by curfew.

Before Shabbat, I took a walk through another part of Old Jaffa. While I was en route, my sunglasses broke, and I was taken aback by the immediate response of the volunteers with me. I was going to glue them back together, but they insisted on buying me a new pair and seemed delighted to do so. What generous souls I've met here.

Friday evening, several of us went to a Kabbalat Shabbat service, which was normally held on the beach, but because of risk of rockets, it's for the meanwhile held in a community centre. People sang and danced to joyful Hebrew songs. We also had sombre moments as the names of fallen soldiers were read. Afterwards in the courtyard, we each enjoyed a small cup of wine and piece of challah bread together.

Back at our hostel, on Saturday at 6:00 a.m., a red alert siren woke us up, and we headed rapidly to the safe room. Three rockets had been launched into Tel Aviv, and two went toward a neighbouring city. Later that morn, I caught up on sleep before spending the afternoon at the beach with Canadians. For summertime there were not the usual crowds. As of this day, we have lost sixty-two soldiers and three civilians as the fight against terror continues in Gaza.

Today I return to our medical base for my sixth week there. The international coordinator has already advised me I'll be sent to a communications base afterwards.

Komoonikatsya

By Thursday, August 7, we exchanged goodbyes at the medical base, taking one last walk around and recalling memories there of my past four times. Before checking in at our weekend army hostel, another volunteer and I took in a complimentary visit to the Haganah military museum. Has any other country had to defend so much its right to exist?

Over the weekend was a succession of reunions with former volunteers—even one who recognized me from my very first base in 2008—and with former madrichot. For Shabbat I headed into Jerusalem, which at this time does not have the usual amount of summer tourists. Recently there was a terror attack involving a tractor; a young man was killed, and several others were injured. An army volunteer was reportedly struck on the head by a rock one weekend while walking through the Old City market. This I learned from another volunteer as an Arab shopkeeper angrily shooed me from the area, seeing I was wearing a T-shirt that showed support for Israel's defence.

This Friday evening, I was a guest for the meal at the Old City hostel where my friend was staying. From a rooftop in the Jewish Quarter, we enjoyed tasty food (a different variety from army fare), joyful song and interesting conversation amidst the unique ambient sound of frequent gunfire echoing in the distance from Arab neighbourhoods. We heard such is part of their celebratory wedding customs. That night I stayed at the place I used to rent, where my new friend welcomes me for Shabbat between army programs. Later on Saturday, another friend came with me to the rabbi's, and then I shared the last meal of the day with a writer by the Kotel. A comrade and I stopped along Ben Yehuda Street and hung out with a couple of my other friends, before taking the bus back to arrive at our army hostel before curfew.

For the next three weeks, I'm assigned to a communications base. We help repair equipment used on tanks and on soldiers' outfits. So far, no red alerts here, though another kind of siren went off last night as supposedly a bird or cat triggered a building alarm! As of midnight Sunday, another ceasefire came into effect. Just seconds before the last seventy-two-hour one began, Hamas sent multiple simultaneous rockets over our border. Then as soon as the timeframe ended, they resumed firing at us. Even in these talks taking place in Cairo, Hamas has indicated they intend to be part of no further ceasefires unless their unreasonable demands are met. So where does that leave Israel? Does the world expect that civilians' safety and security here be at the whims of terrorists? As one volunteer remarked, can you imagine the allied forces in World War II asking the Nazis what concessions they would like before giving up? No, absolutely not! It was unconditional surrender.

The pace at this new base is much slower. A highlight was meeting a Canadian lone soldier, an officer in training at a search and rescue unit. This Calgary resident joined me for lunch, and we discussed the climate in terms of responses in Canada toward anti-Semitism. Another encouraging point was the conversation with a Swiss volunteer, a Christian, who offered to pray for me. Over supper we met a local volunteer who welcomed us and gave a tasty treat of black licorice candy. Sometimes tiny acts of kindness go a long way.

Though all army-related field trips are cancelled until further notice, some evening activities have resumed, unless urgent work duty supersedes the need. We learned more about the different ranks, played a geography game, and heard a couple of engineering speakers, one of whom served with the navy. Like in our previous location, we are part of a base within a larger base, but this time with longer hikes between our different stations. Flag raising is more formal here, accompanied by dramatic music for the national anthem, "Hatikvah." My latest job assignment is to test the *chashmal* (electricity) on tank radio units and do a final quality control inspection of the refurbished parts our team assembled. Meanwhile, as British news tells us, negotiations go on in Cairo.

Now we are back at our weekend army hostel, experiencing deeper bonding with our new comrades from the Virgin Islands, Mexico, Spain, Poland, the United Kingdom, Belgium and the Czech Republic. Over refreshments we discussed the impact of what's been happening to our friends here, as well as our growing sense of loyalty to this country. Afterwards we jumped into the Mediterranean amidst some of the largest crashing waves I've seen here. The rest of the weekend was low-key, catching up on sleep, taking a couple of walks around the Dizengoff and Florentin neighbourhoods and going to Shabbat services. I met an entire Dutch family who had come together to volunteer; I had worked with one of their sons on a base last year. Later in the evening, I visited with one of our base volunteers and the officer on duty.

During our second week at the communications base, I met a young soldier filmmaker. I had just completed three short videos comprised of some of the best examples of volunteers from our last base. One evening, our madrichot asked everyone to share what brought them here to help the army. We want to be part of the fight against terror, to be spokespersons back in our countries, to represent the good of Israel. I continue to use my Hebrew, especially in communicating with my work supervisor, who knows very little English. Right now in this operation, we feel in limbo: soldiers are hoping friends don't have to re-enter Gaza, yet the situation is far from being resolved. Our enemies present themselves in media as the victors.

Rockets exploded before making it to the safe place during our first *tzeva adom* (literally, colour red) alert siren at this base. Thankfully no shrapnel fell in our area. As we waited out the allotted time before going outside again, I met a commander from a prior base, and he introduced me to his wife, who worked at this base. Again in our final week, the red alert sounded, and we ran from our Hebrew karaoke evening activity to the shelter spot. A fellow volunteer unknowingly left her phone on video and recorded all the chaos.

Last weekend some fellow volunteers and I travelled to Jerusalem together. Thursday, one of them joined a local friend and me for nostalgia night at the historic first train station. We shared lots of laughs with an antique dress-up photo op, an Israeli broadcaster's makeshift studio and other memorabilia. Afterwards we watched a free classic Hebrew movie (about a policeman) from a couch on the sand at the fake beach.

Friday I hung out with other army friends at the shuk; it was a challenge to find each other in the market crowds, even with mobile phones! Later, we enjoyed some Middle Eastern live music, sipping on *limonana* (lemon with fresh mint slush). What a spread we had for Shabbat supper back at my friends' hostel! Then Saturday, after walking about the Old City Armenian Quarter with my barracks mates, I joined my local friends for lunch at the rabbi's. On the way back, I stopped in to visit with the director of the volunteer organization I was with last year.

During our final week, we arrived to find the soldiers having a fun day at the pool. We returned to the standard food fare: tomatoes and cucumbers, boiled eggs, soft white cheese and bread. They also served pudding for breakfast and supper. Occasionally we had home-baked goods and one time even roast beef!

In stark contrast to the food and fun, we encountered the news headline that a four-year-old Jewish boy (who resembled my nephew) was killed by rocket shrapnel on his way to the shelter. In another instance, several children were spared when a father shielded them; he eventually succumbed to shrapnel wounds and died days later. Also honoured in the news were four working dogs, partners to the Israeli army.

Hamas and ISIS now receive frequent mention in the news. While I'm repairing army radio equipment in our warehouse, the army radio station songs are frequently interrupted by announcements of incoming rockets from Gaza.

For one of our evening educational activities, we had a forensic dentist as guest speaker. Other nights we watched films, one about the murder of a leader who sought peace, and another on a children's camp in Gaza, where leaders indoctrinated young children to hate Jews and covet their land. Following a film on the Yom Kippur War, our madricha explained how it changed the Israeli army image; they'd been caught off guard, and the prime minister had a hard time living with their decisions.

Working by day, I had the continued trust of our workstation manager, who had put me on quality control, training others and even locking up the warehouse when finished. I thanked the rest of our team and madricha for willingly pitching in with some heavy lifting and cleanup on our last day on this base. Our last evening together, we had a pizza and sushi night, and we were presented with our volunteer certificates of appreciation. Our madricha's parents were present, and core group members commended her in front of them. My barracks mates and I made a blooper video in English, Spanish and Hebrew addressed to our madrichot, which gave comic relief after these rough weeks. I appreciated the trust of this madricha, who earlier confided in me and expressed thanks for my support. She gave me a special emblem recognizing my genuine heart for her country.

On our second to last day, we went on a field trip to another base as guests at a major ceremony: the transfer of authority from one commander to another. It was accompanied by magnificent music, unit flags, white gloves, pressed uniforms and polished boots. This was the first time we wore our uniforms off our base. At the ceremony, I met and had my photo taken with an army correspondent. Then back at our base, on our last day's flag raising, we witnessed several receive promotions to higher ranks; the commander of the local unit also thanked us international volunteers.

Yesterday we bade farewell as each of us went our separate ways, being dropped off in Tel Aviv. Some are flying back; others are continuing on new bases starting Sunday. I enjoyed a sunset to moonlight dip in the Mediterranean in large white waves. Again I was out just after sunrise to swim in calmer waters and cherish the memories of Tel Aviv–Yafo from various past trips.

This morning at breakfast, I met a Zionist social worker and writer who made aliyah recently from South Africa. She shared the impact she's been making in social media, and she thanked me and a German volunteer for our service to this country. Shortly afterwards, I met a French volunteer by stretching from my chair and accidentally bopping her on the head! She laughed, and we chatted. Last week, we had learned that our army hostel is closed until further notice for repairs, so I am heading out shortly from this bright yellow travellers' hostel to spend Shabbat near Bet Shemesh. Signing off for now from Tel Aviv, Shabbat Shalom.

Post-Op Cleanup

Last Shabbat I spent with a Canadian Israeli friend on her moshav near Bet Shemesh. It is usually a small, quiet community—except when there were red alerts. A rocket even landed just down from her family member's house! We heard a message on the important role of abba. The speaker told a story about elephants who went berserk when separated from their fathers. He related that to what's been happening in Gaza to the group whose name in Hebrew means violence. Imagine what could happen if they caught hold of the heavenly Abba of Israel? While military defence is certainly necessary, what will be the lasting solution to peace? We sang together in Hebrew that God is our *tikvah*, our hope.

My friend's family and I shared a simple Friday evening meal, played with the dogs and relaxed on the comfortable couch. Her daughter also had a friend over, and later Saturday they wanted to try out their new makeup skills on me. We used this image to post on an online dating site. Before this next Shabbat in the Judean Hills, another Canadian Israeli friend eagerly screened with me the potential matches. That's the closest I have right now to a Jewish matchmaker!

This weekend I had quite the scenic trip from the north on successive buses! We left our communications base, having picked up other volunteers from a farther base, and headed along the coast to Tel Aviv. We stopped en route to rest, then again at different drop points in the city, before last of all the

Central Bus Station. From there I caught a bus to Jerusalem, which took much longer than normal with construction and rush hour traffic. I had little time to buy some Montreal-style bagels for my Shabbat host and then catch my connecting bus to the yishuv, only to find they'd moved the bus platform! So now I had to rush outside and catch another city bus to a junction, in hopes of catching up to the other bus. I missed that bus too. Instead, a reserve soldier, who happened to know my friend's neighbours, gave me a lift the rest of the way through the guarded gate into this community.

Seven hours after leaving the base, I arrived at my friend's yishuv, overlooking desert hills and a dry wadi down below. It was here I stayed a few weeks when I re-entered the land in January. From here before Shabbat, I booked my flight back to Canada. Sad as I am at the thought of leaving this beautiful land, I believe it is my time to go. I had hoped to stay until December, and I discovered another media opportunity. But when I put my fleece out to God, asking Him to make clear whether an open or closed door, I got my answer in an SMS. So now I'm left to savour my remaining days until Rosh Hashanah.

This widow of a prominent rabbi has been welcoming me since I first met her in 2010 through a mutual friend who volunteers with the army, making some very substantial contributions with his unique skills. We spoke with him over the phone to Canada before Shabbat. It's so peaceful here, with the sunshine and birds singing in the garden. I really enjoy visiting with this rebbetzin. We have such interesting discussions about what's going on in this country and about various Jewish practices. Yesterday we picked, blessed and ate fresh fruit, figs and pomegranates. Brunch was such a treat after a week of almost the same thing every meal at the base. (Only the lunches were different there.) We enjoyed smoked tuna and kosher caviar with our Montreal-style bagels, and we later had homemade schnitzel. We baked apple and plum cakes together. Then I helped her clean up before we lit candles welcoming in Shabbat.

The weekend's news headlines informed us that the kidnapping mastermind, the one who was behind the deaths of those three young yeshiva boys in July, was indicted. One article spoke of the new normal; currently we're on the twelfth ceasefire, to last for a month ... and then what? The United States is in the midst of airstrikes aimed at major terror targets in Iraq. And this week Joan Rivers died, leaving behind a legacy of humour, as well as her outspoken voice in defence of Israel.

Shabbat morn, I sat out in the garden with my friend, taking turns reading the Torah portion. Meals were served by her children and grandchildren, lawyers and soldiers. We had tasty *marak* (soup) and *ohf* (chicken), followed the next day by eggplant sandwiches filled with melted goat cheese, and grilled salmon with dill sauce. I had restful nights in a regular bed, waking to a spectacular view. Before Shabbat closed, I visited with some of my friend's neighbours. Early Sunday I left on my last ride with my regular bus driver, through the Judean Hills back to Jerusalem.

From there I took the train to the designated meeting spot to find out my last base assignment for the summer. There, I exchanged greetings with a French Canadian madrich soldier, who let me take his photo. Moments afterwards, security approached me and wanted to see my last few shots; I obliged to show him and assured him that I was not taking pictures of anything not permitted. He responded cordially.

My first week at the new base was with a solo madricha, who went the extra mile in working alongside us international volunteers: five men, five women—a fun group. Amongst us are five Americans, one originally from Russia, as well as volunteers from Belgium and Holland.

We have been unloading and sorting items returned from Gaza, breathing in a lot of its dust. As we went to unravel one mesh, we found it partially melted by mortar fire. We piled helmets on shelves, wondering which were on the heads of wounded soldiers. We lifted the heavy bulletproof vests, imagining how soldiers ran in such hot and cumbersome clothing. Amongst the return items were stretchers and body bags. Our supervisors gave us blankets and tools to cover in plastic, and boxes to paint with unit colours.

Our second week at the base, we were hauling and piling huge soldier kit bags. My highlight was a road trip with a soldier driving a big army rig to transfer supplies from another base. We rode with window down, techno music blaring through the Galil region. En route we stopped for cola and ice cream.

My third and final week is approaching. Each day after breakfast begins with flag raising, assembling and standing at ease and then at attention. For evening activities, so far we have had storytelling on family history, describing why we are Zionists, and telling our guest speaker why we volunteer. Our madricha taught us about the special Haredi unit, making provision for those who especially devote themselves to Torah study. We exchanged notes of appreciation with one another, and received an introductory thank-you speech from the unit commander. I have enjoyed hanging out with the soldiers who were here for a week of special training.

Now it's the weekend, and I'm writing from Tiberias. I recalled from my Hebrew ulpan text that the first kibbutz in Israel, circa 1910, was in this area, so I went to explore its original buildings yesterday: the first house, meal room (now a museum archives) and supply warehouse. Outside are colourfully painted farm implements. Inside the grocer's, a friendly neighbour conversed with me, commending me in my Hebrew speaking ability. Afterwards, I hiked alongside the Kinneret to where it meets the Jordan. I watched kayakers and waded in the river. Then I continued along the highway and stopped at a military graveyard, standing by the tomb of an eighteen-year-old.

Last evening, I took the bus back to Tiberias city centre, paused at the old stone watchtower and checked into a guesthouse run by Canadian Israelis. I enjoyed the personal space and drifted off in a white fluffy bed after watching part of a feature on 9/11 subtitled in Hebrew. I rose early to take photos of the sunrise over the Kinneret, jumped in for swim, strolled along the promenade and returned for breakfast, which included yellow dates still on the branch.

For Shabbat, a couple of Canadian musicians warmly welcomed me, and together with other guests we enjoyed a tasty meal outside overlooking the hills. We had homemade challah and Moroccan fish. The yard is full of fruit trees: loquat, grapefruit, persimmon, lemon and pomegranate. It was so peaceful and relaxing there. The music they play is uplifting. Discussions were meaningful, considering the serious times we are in, studying Torah together. I met a Canadian who blogs for the same online news to which I've recently been invited to contribute. This Canadian couple who hosted me are exemplary pioneers here in the Land of Israel. They demonstrate a humble attitude and a willingness to learn from the Jewish community. They have done much to show the non-Jewish world what they are missing out on without an understanding of God in Shabbat and the Feasts of the Lord. I hold this couple in high esteem.

Sunday we returned to the base after bidding our Israeli coordinator farewell, until next time I can return and volunteer in the land. After having volunteered all summer, I have met quite a number of the madrichot. For our final week, a second madricha joined us. Supplies continue to be received back from Gaza, as well as from another base in the north. Yes, there were more of those huge kit bags, each weighing about half my weight! Soldiers tossed them off the long flatbed truck whilst us volunteers wielded them up and over into large metal storage containers. Also, we heaved unit boxes of gas masks into another storage area. Two massive truckloads of military police gear came in as well. Each had to be systematically arranged onto warehouse shelves. We worked under the command of a jovial male officer and the head volunteer supervisor, a tough lady with a big heart of gratitude for all our hard labour.

This morning was my last time to don the khaki uniform and black boots. After flag raising, most of the soldiers were going on a special educational outing. So were we, but to a different place. We went to a nearby community and heard from the relative of one of the early kibbutzim, one who was involved in Israel's early defence system. We met some elderly heroes of those early days, very humble men who boasted not of their own accomplishments but shied away from glory when others lifted them up. The host guides readily welcomed us to come again next time we are in the land. That old kibbutznik spirit of hospitality and readiness to lend a hand is still there. After the local people treated our volunteer group to a special buffet lunch, we returned to our base and had opportunity to relax in the sun before our last supper here. I also took a stroll around the base. Each of us was presented in the evening with another appreciation certificate and pin.

Today, nearing the end of the Hebrew month Elul, I was up to see the last sunrise over the base as I finished reading the book of Daniel. The base commander gave a speech, after which the soldiers gave us volunteers rounds of applause for helping them clean up after the operation in Gaza. Our international volunteer unit major also came by yesterday to personally thank each of us. She recognized my face from different bases over the summer and greeted me with a hug. Our key work supervisors also hugged us, even the tough lady officer, who shed tears over bidding us farewell. Next we turned in our uniforms, packed and boarded the bus to take us to one final educational outing in Zichron Yaakov: a small museum dedicated to an intelligence group operating in Israel's early days. We had a packed army lunch in a park and then continued on to Central Bus Station in Tel Aviv.

This afternoon I returned to Jerusalem, where I'll be spending my remaining week before flying back to Canada after Rosh Hashanah. Yes, my adventure's coming to a close, sad to say. My latest visa is about to expire. But I am thankful for the opportunity I have had to be here this long. I stopped by the shuk to buy enough fresh produce to last until I leave. I bought a smoked fish, olive bread, sweet potatoes and avocados, melon, mango and Jaffa oranges. The city bus ride back was exceptionally long, with all the traffic. But I enjoyed conversing in Hebrew with the elderly lady beside me, whose daughter lives in Toronto. On arrival to the neighbourhood, I purchased milk from the local merchant, who remembered me with a smile. I informed him I'm leaving soon and wished him a happy New Year. While away with the army, the lady I rented from has been kind enough to store my other belongings and to welcome me to stay here until I fly. What a blessing is this new friend!

Leaving Home

Sof sof (literally: end, end), it's September 2014, and the time has come to leave this land, Eretz Yisrael, and to return to Canada, the place of my birth. As much as I love my home nation, I can only imagine the reverse culture shock after living the past eighteen months in the centre of the world. Out of all places in Israel, I will most miss Jerusalem, the City of Gold.

Friday *(Yom Shee-shee)*

Back at the apartment, after living the summer on army bases, I did my usual Shabbat cleaning for my friend while she was at work. Then I prepared myself to welcome in the Sabbath bride, and I headed out while the buses were still running. In the city core, I met up with one of my Canadian Israeli friends to give her a few household items and share a last simple snack of bread and tehina (pronounced "t'chee-nah" in Hebrew). She returned to Bet Shemesh area, and I proceeded to the Kotel to ring in the day of rest with a circle of young women singing, a group from the navy joining in. There's something so special about being there Friday at sunset. From the Old City, I left through Damascus Gate to join my friends at the rabbi's place; we visit outside with other arriving guests until it's time for the door to open, and he personally welcomes each person with honour.

Saturday *(Shabbat)*

That morning near the Old City, I was greeted by an elderly Arab man, who went into an apparent routine of promoting his propaganda. I could see where this was going from the start. I heard others like him, trying to elicit sympathy from tourists by painting a picture of "Palestinians" as victims of Israeli mistreatment. I didn't fall for it and pointed out that if certain Arabs didn't commit acts of terror, then the Israeli army wouldn't need to respond in defence of its civilians.

Consider this: is there anywhere in Israel where the sound of a muezzin cannot be heard? Hardly. Even on an army base, we were subjected to the intrusion of a loudspeaker on the parameter of the grounds, announcing a call to pray to Allah. Similarly, you can be davening at the Kotel and be interrupted by the echoing blast from the Temple Mount above.

On Shabbat I was en route to the Kotel when I noticed a man in Muslim garb (long gown and headpiece) handing out free booklets about Islam. I received one, curious about what the other side was saying. Then another Muslim man began to engage me in conversation. So I took the opportunity to pose a few questions to him.

Why is it that most acts of terrorism worldwide seem to be carried out in the name of Islam? He replied that other religious groups sometimes commit violent acts. I acknowledged such, but reiterated that still, it appeared the majority are fuelled by radical Muslim beliefs. I went on to ask him if the goal of his religion was to take over the world (establish a massive caliphate). He neither confirmed nor denied. I asked if the goal was particularly to destroy the Jews. Another Muslim in the past had calmly and matter-of-factly related that in the end of days, a vast Arab Muslim army would come against the Jews, and even the rocks and trees would expose them to be killed. This man whom I questioned retorted by suggesting that either the other Muslim was lying or I was fabricating this story. I countered with a reference to his Koran, to the portion where it is considered not only acceptable for Muslims to lie to non-Muslims, but that it is like a mitzvah to do so—especially to feign friendship for the purpose of deceiving the infidels. Now what are the implications here for the so-called Palestinian peace process?

I respectfully asked the Muslim man in front of me how I could know that he was not lying to me. Throughout our dialogue, he dodged my main questions. He appealed to an Islamic acceptance of Moses, Jesus and Mohammed, all as prophets. Then he, apparently assuming I was Christian, seemed to try to bring a wedge between his competing religions. He accused all Jews of rejecting Jesus. I replied that some embrace this leader as Messiah and others don't. He suddenly singled out a man walking by in a tallit and point-blank asked him in Hebrew, "Do you believe in Jesus?"

The man with kind eyes stopped, looked at his inquirer, looked at me and did not answer either way. His friend in the kippah quietly questioned how I ended up in this conversation. I admitted I was curious about the Islamic propaganda but was now ready to excuse myself, if I could walk to the Kotel with him and his friend after making one last comment. In front of the Muslim man, I announced that I believed in the God of Israel as the only true God, and that if he chose to follow the prescribed ways of our God, blessings awaited him too.

While insisting his was a religion of peace, that Muslim man's countenance increasingly exuded the contrary. Needless to say, his presentation was not terribly convincing.

During one of my last meals on an army base, a senior official came and sat at the table with a fellow volunteer and me. One of his comrades also joined us. The other volunteer, also honoured they would sit with us, asked why they did not sit at the special table set for commanders. They simply chose to be with us, to show their appreciation for our support. The big man under whose command we had worked now expressed his tender side; unabashedly teary-eyed, he identified with the suffering his people have gone through and continue to endure in the fight for the right to exist.

At the Kotel on Shabbat, I was glad to see a friend was back in the country in time for me to say goodbye. He sang for me one of his tunes of praise to Hashem. Earlier I had read the week's Torah portion from the end of Deuteronomy. I heard the men from the rabbi's house singing heartily. I sure will miss spending Shabbat mornings here in this place of prayer that spans generations.

After Kiddush (blessings spoken over grape juice and biscuits), a group of us walked together to the rabbi's place. Along the way, I took the opportunity to convey farewells to several of the most familiar faces. One handsome man in auburn peyot (sidelocks) responded in a caring tone, "We'll never forgive you for leaving us like this." Wow, I was touched. I hadn't realized I meant so much. Another Haredi guy, to whom I related much respect, jokingly put in an order for some hockey gear when I return from Canada for a future visit.

Over at the humble home of the rabbi, one of his daughters embraced me in a hug. A table full of friends let me know how much I'm loved. In good humour they told me it was up to the rabbi, and if he did not permit, I could not leave. I replied I really didn't want to leave either, but my visa was about to expire. I let them know we didn't have to say goodbye quite yet, because I was planning to come for Rosh Hashanah. As much as I don't like goodbyes, it can be occasions like these where we find out just how much we mean to one another.

After Shabbat sundown at the Kotel, I joined the women watching the men perform the Havdalah ceremony (separation between light and darkness). A braided candle is lit, and fragrant herbs or spices are passed around, wishing a sweet week ahead. The simple ceremony ends with a blessing of Scripture spoken over an overflowing cup of wine.

> Behold, God is my salvation; I will trust, and will not be afraid; For GOD the LORD is my strength and song; And He is become my salvation. Therefore with joy shall ye draw water out of the wells of salvation. (Isaiah 12:2–3 JPS).

From the Western Wall, I walked to my favourite Ben Yehuda Street to meet up with an American friend who lives nearby. Remembering that one of my Canadian friends was due to arrive also this day, I tried her mobile number. We simultaneously asked each other, "Where are you?" It turned out that she was already on the street where I was heading, so the three of us hung out together. Along the way, I ran into five other friends, two of whom served with the army. Here on the midrachov is where local Israelis and tourists come to celebrate the start of a new week. A group of Koreans regularly sing here Saturday nights. Restaurants and shops reopen and the vibrancy of life returns to the street.

Sunday *(Yom Ree-shon)*
From midnight until 4:00 a.m., many gathered at the Kotel for Selichot penitential prayers, in preparation for Yom Kippur, the Day of Atonement, which this year falls on Friday eve to Saturday, October 3–4. I joined my people as shofars sounded at different intervals and voices cried aloud. Rather than walk the long way home, I stayed with a friend inside the Kotel tunnels until sunrise.

With little sleep, I went ahead with plans to take a bus into

Sderot, the city that has been hardest hit with rockets since Hamas took over the Gaza Strip in 2007. Today, while this month-long ceasefire is still in effect, it was quiet. It seemed a normal place with modern amenities, shoppers at the outdoor market. I stopped in a community centre, and a worker there talked with me at length about her experiences since becoming a resident close to Gaza. Here, one has only 15 seconds to find safety when a siren sounds. With strong grounding in Torah, she had boldness in the face of terror. Afterwards, I met a couple of young men attending a tefillin (phylacteries) table and commended them for their courage, letting them know they are not forgotten as rockets also flew into other parts of the country this time. They readily received the encouragement. My last stop was the police station, to witness the piles of fallen and mangled rockets stored out back. The newest one was marked July 2014.

Monday (*Yom She-nee*)

Today was beach day. A visiting Canadian friend picked me up in her rental car, and we headed to Ein Gedi, to relax in the Salt Sea. Some parts of this Dead Sea are known for mud baths; others are known for the unusual salt pillar formations. Here were deeper waters, with a few salt rocks along the shore. They looked like glazed jelly doughnuts. My friend and I chatted and prayed, recalling our first time visiting the land. By the time we left the beach, the temperature had dropped—from forty to thirty-nine degrees Celsius.

On the way back, we swung by ancient Jericho, dipped our feet in cool Elisha's stream and sampled local bananas. Then in Jerusalem we had a simple bread and hummus meal with wine, in anticipation of a sweet New Year ahead.

Tuesday (*Yom Shlee-shee*)

The next day would be the eve before Rosh Hashanah, so I had some errands to take care of before everything closed.

I had to turn in my Jerusalem post box keys and cancel my local phone plan. That felt final. As it happened, the post office computer went down, so they weren't able to close out my account. From there I aim to have it redirected to a postal box in Canada. The smiling guard at this post office wished me well on my journey.

Now mid-afternoon, I went to pay my respects to this country at Mount Herzl. There was the grave of Zion's visionary, as well as other national leaders. The only other visitors this day were combat soldiers, going to the fresh graves of their fallen comrades. I nodded as I made eye contact. One sat smiling by a tomb, apparently recalling the good times with his friend or family member. Nearby I found the decorated gravesite belonging to Michael Levin, a lone soldier who voluntarily left his home country of America to fight for Israel. Wounded and killed by terror group Hezbollah in 2006, he was regarded as a hero. People such as these are what make this country great. I rode the train back the full length of the line, making goodbye calls while my phone service was still active.

Wednesday (*Yom Re-vee-ee*)

In preparation for erev Rosh Hashanah, I cleaned my friend's apartment one last time while she was at work, and then I waited for my laundry to dry on the line. I had already given away some more belongings, so now I did a preliminary sort of the remaining items to ensure I did not go over my luggage limit at the airlines. There were yet buses to catch downtown, but I left for a last walk around my favourite places to take any final pictures. I continued by train to City Hall, and from there I hiked into the Old City, where I put on new sandals as a symbol of walking in new ways.

By the Kotel, I read the last portion of the fifth book of Moses, as well as the traditional reading of Nehemiah 8. The New Year rang in at sunset, just after 6:00 p.m. To special High Holy Days prayers, I heard Breslov Jews exuberantly rejoicing over in the men's section. I sure will miss this mystical atmosphere. Accompanied by guests from America, Poland and Israel, I walked to the rabbi's house for a festive meal. En route, a Jewish convert told me how the impact of Zohar writings had discouraged the Jewish community from readily sharing their faith with the Gentile world. I had thought it was a pendulum swing reaction to others trying to force their beliefs on the Jews. There is so much to be learned.

On arrival at the rabbi's, his children and small grandchildren happily welcomed each guest. We enjoyed a feast of salads, sautéed fish, roasted chicken, sliced beef and sweet noodle kugel, and together we blessed each symbolic food on the *"see-man-eem"* plate. The rabbi kissed the forehead of a young man, whom he regarded like a son, and continued to teach us in English and in Hebrew until midnight.

Thursday (*Yom Cha-mee-shee*): Rosh Hashanah 5775

Up at sunrise, I had stayed on a friend's couch in a neighbourhood near Mea Shearim. I read from sefer Tehillim (book of Praises) and enjoyed a coffee and cookie on her balcony. From there I headed to the Kotel to hear the blowing of the shofar, and to read from the special holiday siddur called a machzor. The preface described the shofar sound as a homing signal confusing the enemy. That reminded me of the story someone told me of what happened when soldiers entered a house in Gaza. They found a woman strapped with explosives. One soldier felt prompted to cry out, "Shema Yisrael" (שמע ישראל) and the woman in Muslim garb suddenly melted in tears. They learned she was really a Jew who'd been forced to convert to Islam. The signal called her home, the soldiers were able to disarm her and the whole disaster was averted. Baruch Hashem! The machzor also spoke of a collective longing, culminating in the anticipated Messiah's shofar on that great day.

After placing my hands on that ancient waxy stone wall

one more time, I backed away and proceeded on my last trek over to the rabbi's house. This day we enjoyed salmon and turkey, then brownie and pareve glida (non-dairy ice cream substitute) for dessert. The woman who had received her new name (meaning light) sat with us. She helped coach another of the guests, who evidently had a fear of lack, to share the food platters around the table. The rabbi sounded the shofar to the various types of tunes. He publicly blessed me after I expressed gratitude to his family for hosting me all these times, and I bade farewell to all my friends there. Amongst them was the younger man, with whom we walked from the Kotel to the rabbi's on Friday nights. There was also the older man, who patiently conversed with me in Hebrew while walking back from the rabbi's many Saturday afternoons. This day I had entered the Old City via Shar Shechem (Damascus Gate) and exited via Shar Yafo (Jaffa Gate).

Before dark, I returned to my friend's apartment by way of the original train tracks, now a historic promenade. I was able to enjoy (with some sadness) my remaining days in Jerusalem. The timing seems right. Besides touching base with those for whom I had phone numbers, I was able to connect with others whom I ran into along the way. These were like divinely orchestrated appointments to provide closure.

Friday (*Yom Shee-shee*)

The remainder of Thursday night, I consolidated and repacked my luggage, ready for the anticipated scrutiny of airport authorities. My housemate returned from work, and we visited for a bit. I thanked her for all her kindness. By 2:00 a.m. I was off to the airport.

To my complete surprise, I was hardly asked any questions this time, nor was I searched extensively as I have been in the past. What they were most concerned about was knowing whether I'd received any gifts, and from whom. I was prepared with an itemized list, including what I'd received from volunteering with the army. They respectfully and apologetically advised they needed to open my worn guitar case, held together with tape and rope. The suspicious item was a jar of honey I was bringing to my neighbours, my Shabbat hosts in Canada. Once satisfied the gift would cause no harm on the flight, they carefully helped me to secure the guitar case, and I was on my way to the boarding area by sunrise. I was so tired that I could barely stay awake until we took off the runway, but I didn't want to miss my last view of this precious land.

Feeling numb, I sign off one more time from Eretz Yisrael. Shalom, Shalom, Carrie of Canada.

Postscript

On landing, I did not feel at home like I have previously, at least not until I touched our maple leaf flag hanging at the airport. An army buddy whom I'd last seen in Israel picked me up in his classic car, and we stopped for coffee before arriving at my neighbours' for a Shabbat meal and engaging discussions around the table. Here in this community was where my journey of Jewish learning began.

I don't want my great adventure to be over. It meant more to be a Canadian in Israel. Strangely, I feel a bit in exile here. Conversations and customs once familiar to me now seem foreign. So where do I go from here? The learning journey I began in Toronto went even deeper in Jerusalem, and now it continues on another level again in Canada's largest Jewish community.

Though nothing compares with being in Israel, here along the Bathurst corridor, I have a sense of home, of being amongst my people. Here I can hear Hebrew spoken not only in synagogues but also occasionally in coffee shops and kosher grocery aisles.

Have you ever found yourself along a path you never imagined yourself to be? You headed some direction for what you thought was one reason, but in retrospect you see a guiding hand that let you go there but for another (or additional, bigger) reason? That's how it began with me.

While growing up, I recall no awareness, no distinction between groups of people known as Jew or Gentile. Neither do I recall being exposed to anti-Semitism. My introduction to a faraway place called Jerusalem was in a children's storybook, a tale of a duck who travelled there. Why that stuck with me, I don't know. During university, I enrolled in a course in Judaism. Before that, I remember wondering whether there was really a God up there in whom I could reasonably believe. It wasn't enough for me to believe in something that was just the figment of someone's imagination. What would be the point? As a child, I was told there was a tooth fairy and a Santa, only to be informed later they were not real. Would an adult someday also tell me the same about God? Yet somehow I sensed there was only one God, that He was the God of Israel. I searched further, turning to the Bible as the measuring stick for truth.

During those early adult years, I examined what many others believed, learning about the history of various religions and cults. But none compared with the God who revealed Himself to and through the nation of Israel.

Fast-forward to the new millennium era. That's when unknowingly, I was about to move into the largest Jewish community in Canada. Stirred by a sense of needing to return to my roots, I moved from Edmonton to Toronto. I scoped out a job and a place to live ahead of time while out for a cousin's wedding. Not until I noticed a menorah on my new landlady's calendar did I realize I was in a Jewish home. When I told my father over the phone I'd found an apartment, and he asked where, that was when he informed me I was in a largely Jewish area. The time of year I moved was during the Fall Feasts; in fact, my window looked out into a sukkah. My learning continued as I experienced the change in seasons and met other neighbours who observed the holidays. Seeing that I was interested, they invited me over for Shabbat, Passover and Rosh Hashanah. That's one of the many things I like about Judaism: it's very hands-on, full of symbols and meaning. And the food's very tasty too.

The next turning point was my first dream trip to Israel. Between official tour stops, some new friends and I made the most of every opportunity to experience as much we could. When it approached time to go, I felt utterly homesick at the thought of having to leave Jerusalem, and I didn't know why.

Back in Canada, I read an article in a magazine about a family who made aliyah, and they had the same surname as my maternal grandmother. I told my nana, and she noted another surname on her side that sounded like a Jewish connection. Suddenly I wondered about my identity. Could I actually be Jewish by ancestry? Was our family identity lost (or hidden) due to persecution? Bit by bit, Nana shared about her earlier years, including the anti-Semitic remarks made against her and her sister by other schoolchildren in England, who'd pegged them as Jews. They weren't raised with an awareness of being Jewish, although throughout much of my grandparents' lives, they had numerous Jewish acquaintances (employers, co-workers, landlords, neighbours and friends). I learned from an Israeli who'd made aliyah from the East End of London that it was a big Jewish community back in the day. The clue that made me wonder the most was my grandmother telling me how her mother commonly referred to her neighbours as Gentiles.

Since this discovery, I have tried finding more definitive proof either way of my identity. I am okay with however I was born. But when occasionally asked the question, "You're Jewish, right?" I was left with responding maybe or probably. Several people, after having met me, concluded I have a "Jewish soul." Even my nana before she died referred to me lovingly as her Jewish granddaughter.

Over in Israel, I was known as Carrie of Canada. Once back in Canada, friends were introducing me as Carrie from Israel! Outside of Hebrew classes and army bases, another main connection for me was the family who regularly hosted hundreds for Shabbat. What an example of chesed (lovingkindness). My last Shabbat before I was due to fly back to Canada, I was overwhelmed by the response of a table of the regular guests there. They begged me not to leave them like that, insisting I belonged there with them. Even my friends in Canada have been asking the question, expecting that I will return to Israel—it's not a question of if but when. I was in the land with the people; now both are an integral part of me, and evidently I with them.

Section V: Shavuot (2016)

Week One

It's time to return to the Land of Israel, but this time it's different. As the plane gets ready to land, excitement builds. I think of Bereshit (Genesis) 12, God's promise to Abraham before he set out for his new home.

During the flight, I prepared by immersing myself in Hebrew: the traveller's prayer, the Amidah (three times daily standing prayer), my mini vocabulary text, as well as listening to local radio available on the airlines. Before taking off, I was subjected to the expected type of security questions. I told the airline representative that previously I thought I may be; now I know I am Jewish.

At first glimpse of land, behind me I see a cloud-covered sea as I watch the flapping plane wing. I switch my phone on to the current time, 13:18 (both significant numbers, one symbolic of God, the other of life). There is this sense of re-entering my ancestral homeland. While en route to Jerusalem by sherut, I read the Hallel Psalms 113–118.

Outside a cafe on Jaffa Road, a close friend welcomed me back with a hug. She was the last one I saw before flying back in 2014, and now she's the first to see on arrival. This evening's meal and drink toasting, "Lechaim!—To life!" began my series of congratulatory mazel tov responses, my belated bat mitzvah experience.

After our visit, I chatted by phone with a friend and mentor in Canada, giving her a virtual tour from City Center Jerusalem until I reached Jaffa Gate of the Old City. She recognized in my voice a joy over a sense of belonging. At the Western Wall, I spoke a Hebrew bracha (blessing) with an elderly woman who left me with a gift of fragrant leaves. Then I settled into my hostel, from where I awoke to a power outage and therefore a cold, dark shower. But I didn't mind. I was here.

Next day, after a large Israeli breakfast consisting of tomatoes, cucumbers, yoghurt, cheese, bread and fruit, I boarded a bus for Efrat. This developed community was the place where the biblical Ruth passed through on her journey with Naomi. Nearby runs Derech Avot, the path of our fathers Abraham, Isaac and Jacob. Now it has special connection for me, Rebecca Ruth (my Hebrew name). My friend, a rebbetzin from Montreal who took me under wing several years ago, treated me to a tasty lamb burger lunch, and later she prepared an evening tea with decorative cheese and fruit tray. Like another friend, she also topped off the food with tiny Israeli flags.

On Friday, out on the rebbetzin's patio overlooking the hills, we savoured a breakfast of sunny scrambled eggs, cottage (Israeli term for those cheese curds), baba ganoush (eggplant dip) and cucumber tomato salad. Last night I read the book of Ruth; this morning together we recited in Hebrew a key phrase from 1:16. Yesterday I enjoyed helping her with gardening, as Ruth serving Naomi, declaring to her, "Your God is my God, and your people are my people." Then today I accompanied her on local errands to a pharmacy (beit merkachat), the post office (ladoar), then to buy a bottle of Judean Hills wine (yayin) for Shabbat. After watching this rebbetzin wave farewell to me from her balcony, I received a ride into Jerusalem in time to meet two young new Israeli citizens at the shuk. Following an enthusiastic iron-grip embrace and photo updates, we visited over iced coffee. They eagerly asked if I'd also made aliyah. As they caught their bus home for Shabbat, I saw them off with flowers for their adoptive parents.

On my way back to the hostel, I passed by Damascus Gate, remembered a fallen young female border guard and blessed those on duty. A friend from 2010 met me at our hostel lounge for a wine lechaim and hamotzi (blessing over bread) for his birthday yesterday, and for my recently joining the Jewish community. I lit candles, my first as a Jewish woman in Jerusalem, before heading out for Kabbalat Shabbat (receiving the Sabbath) at the Kotel, where circles of singers gathered.

Later outside the rabbi's place, I was welcomed back by various friends. Greeting guests at the door, the rabbi's face lit up on seeing me back. He announced my special arrival from Canada, extending a public mazel tov to Rivka Rut. He also extended to me a bracha: gates open to the highest blessings. He invited me to speak, so I alternated in Hebrew and English, relating that before I thought, but now I know I'm Jewish. I attributed this change with thanks to the large influence of this rabbi and his late wife of blessed memory. The house full of guests formally welcomed me to the community with songs of peace over me, and of rejoicing over sons and daughters coming home.

During last night's meal, I met a young pharmacist who offered to speak with her boss about future work opportunities if I make aliyah. I used to work with the same retail chain in Canada. After the late walk back to my hostel along Rehov HaNevi'im (Street of the Prophets), I arose early and said the Amidah while listening to doves, having spotted my first one outside the window my first morning here. We had a lengthy breakfast with a friend and other guests eager to learn Jewish perspectives from us. He gave a *d'var* Torah on how we saw the sounds at Sinai, based on the literal Hebrew in Exodus 20:18. What did God's revelation of His core commandments look like?

Over at the Kotel, I read the parsha for both Israel and Canada, as the Torah portion cycle varies occasionally in the diaspora. One verse stood out to me regarding overlapping provision from the shemitah (meaning release), referring to the seventh year leaving the ground to rest into the eighth year while new crops grow. The rabbi conducting a service took names for healing prayer, including some of my family and friends. During Kiddush afterwards, the rabbi spoke on second Pesach, second chance. One month later from 14 Nisan, on 14 Iyar, some who missed out got to partake (see Numbers 9:1–14 NIV). A friend and I walked together with the rabbi via Shar Shechem, extending shalom en route to his house. Some Arab shopkeepers received it positively. Morning and evening, I observed what the rabbi punned "birds of pray" circling above people davening at the Kotel, like they were drawn again and again to this atmosphere of life! The late rebbetzin's paintings surrounded guests seated for lunch, reminding us of her lovingkindness while with us. As I walked with a British friend back to the Kotel for Havdalah, I learned the location of the rebbetzin's gravesite. There, I planned to visit before Tuesday's shi'ur (lesson), still on the book of Yeshayahu (Isaiah)!

By the Kotel, we saw the tiny spunky lady from the rabbi's daughter's wedding. She told us she once served as medic in the Canadian military. Guests on Friday night had shared in mazel tov for the rabbi's new granddaughter, named after his wife. Close to Havdalah, I received from another woman at the Kotel a written bracha for finding a good husband. Motzi Shabbat, I waited awhile for a bus to a suburb, for a visit with the adoptive parents of the new immigrants. We spoke Hebrew over late-night bread, soup and tea. A difference I noted since last time here were the protective posts surrounding the bus shelters, preventing vehicular attacks against pedestrians.

Most mornings I arise naturally with the sun at about 6:00 a.m., and today, Sunday, I went for Shacharit (morning prayers) at a Conservative synagogue. There, I updated the older rabbi of my status and was offered the honour of an aliyah. I was invited up front to read the Hebrew blessing over the Torah reading. At this shul, I met a woman who'd come upon the scene of a bus bombing, stating she was determined not to live in fear.

While waiting for my friend to return from a class, I napped on my old bed at my former residence. Then together with her and another American Israeli friend, we headed for Yam HaMelach (the Salt Sea) to a unique old beach. Arab boys and a woman in full black attire shared the sparsely populated shore, along with a mud-coated young Jewish couple. We refreshed ourselves with watermelon, and on an upper deck table shaded by palm and pomegranate trees, my friend and I did a blessing over bread. We floated and chatted in the sea, followed by laps in a large pool surrounded by Moroccan decor. The way driving home took us in and out of the territory of Binyamin. Back at the hostel, I ate fish on the rooftop after making trip plans for Monday. That evening in the lobby, I met a Bergen-Belsen survivor who worked as a licensed tour guide. We took photos and engaged in interesting dialogue with an exuberant tourist woman from Ireland and two Jewish gals who'd just had their first experience exploring Israel.

I woke after a short sleep, long before my alarm, and made it to Jerusalem's main bus station on time, and still I missed the first two buses trying to find the stop! Finally after asking bus and security staff, soldiers and passengers, I found it on Jeremiah Street, but it was too late for any morning departure. Yet a kind female soldier waiting there found for me another way—back over to the main station!

En route to Kedumim, I noticed signs of blessing on one's coming and going from each city. On arrival at this pioneer town, a security check was done on me to determine who I was, where I was from and why I was here. Who did I know, and what was the nature of the photos I was taking? From there I contacted a former government official, who invited me to her home, and I received a ride to her door by a kind local resident. In this neighbourhood, this leader explained, was the birthplace of Kedumim, the first Jewish community in the

Shomron after many years. Beginning in 1975 they dwelt in tents, later in trailers and houses. A blue sign hangs, denoting the agreement with the government, their eventual approval that Jews could remain here.

This pioneering woman spoke with me in her interview room and then asked me to stay for lunch with her family. I was humbled by her servant heart, insisting on waiting on us with such pleasure. We enjoyed tasty chicken soup, mushroom rice and grape leaf rolls. We parted with my leaving her a symbolic gift for the continued building up of this well-established community.

From south to north, I walked along the main road, taking video footage to complement my Canadian Israeli rebbetzin's story, told to me as I filmed her. Her family was the eighth to settle in this neighbourhood. By nightfall, I called security to let them know I was heading back on a direct bus to Jerusalem.

I was very tired and hungry, so I had a burger from my hostel rooftop barbecue and a glass of locally brewed beer in the lounge with a couple of elderly ladies from England, who were eager to learn about my Jewish connection. The eighty-six-year-old had climbed the rampart walk around the Old City walls that day!

At morning minyan (gathering of 10 for public prayer), I met another friend and was amazed at her level of Hebrew cantorial ability. There, the main rabbi enthusiastically gave me a high-five and offered me an aliyah of Haftorah (blessing over the prophetic reading). I thanked him for the honour, expressing hope that my level of public reading may be up to par by Simchat Torah. Afterwards in the lobby, my friend and I visited with others in the congregation before we headed out to have brunch on Emek Refa'im. This friend was visibly touched as I shared my Jewish experience.

Following our visit, I strolled along this quaint main street and happened on an incident where an Orthodox woman exiting a bus fell out on top of her baby stroller. She rapidly got up to check that her crying baby was not harmed. Those in closest proximity rallied to her aid. Baruch Hashem, the strapped-in child was protected by the covered frame of the stroller.

From there I went on to find the house of someone who'd shown me kindness last time I was here, inviting me over after a community centre film night. She and her son welcomed me in for a visit over lunch. Her mother had been a volunteer on army bases many years ago, and the sweet elderly lady greeted me with a smile.

Through Rehavia neighbourhood, I continued by way of Mount Zion Gate into the Old City Jewish Quarter, where the rebuilt Hurva synagogue stands. In a nearby shop, I related to one of the Canadian proprietors news of my new name. He wished me mazel tov, and I left fitted with a new ring with the Hebrew inscription of "I am my Beloved's."

Next, I davened at the Kotel before heading to find the rebbetzin's grave. There, I thanked God for memories of her impact on myself and others. Ironically, on my way to a lesson at the rabbi's, an old acquaintance spotted me and wanted to talk. I wished him *kol tov* (all good). The shi'ur was on the last couple of verses of Isaiah 27, speaking of threshing and ingathering, and the sounding of the great shofar. A common theme with friends has been the question of if or when I'm making aliyah. The rabbi's youngest daughter came over and put an arm around me, and her sister wished me mazel tov. I related I'd just visited their mother's grave and would have liked to have been able to tell her my news as well.

Week Two

After three hours of bus transfers via Tiberias and Safed, today I arrived in the far northern city of Meron for Lag b'Omer. This 33rd day of counting the Omer between Pesach and Shavuot occurs during the Hebrew month of Iyar, this year in May. In line at the Jerusalem bus station, I met a Jewish convert, who invited me to come sometime to her place in Shiloh. I had a front seat, good for photos on the road, but the driver's taste in music "lo kol kach tov" (not so good). I called a Canadian co-worker, describing the shimmering turquoise Kinneret ahead, and she wished now that she'd come along. In Safed I arrived in time for the Sefer Torah procession down the street into the bus station. As people rejoiced, I spoke with the locals and was wished success on a prospective aliyah.

I made it to Meron by sunset and joined the crowds making the pilgrimage to the kever of Rav Shimon Bar Yochai, who was from the second century. Along the path were beggars and vendors selling wares of candles, books and anise-flavoured liquor. I prayed to God outside the tomb area. From the bandstand view of men enthusiastically davening below, with the mountain silhouette in the background, I called my Canadian neighbour. We awaited the lighting of the torch, viewed on a big screen. There were thousands singing and dancing, bopping up and down in unison. I recalled from my Hebrew ulpan text the story of three-year-old boys' initiation rite in Meron, their first haircut, making their connection to abba.

When crowds became pushy and loud, I was ready to go, pausing briefly in the food tent for kugel and a kosher hotdog. Then I took a direct bus to Jerusalem, sitting and conversing alternately in Hebrew and English with a Yemenite Jew, who shared with me on her phone a popular song about Ben Yehuda. Stopping by the shuk, I had a shot of that licorice-tasting drink with two good-looking guys, toasting a lechaim from Canada to Israelis. One responded that because I'm here, I'm also an honorary Israeli.

By 1:00 a.m., I was comfortably asleep in my hostel bunk. I had breakfast with the Brits, bidding them farewell, and then was off to Bet Shemesh to meet my olah chadasha (new immigrant) Canadian friend. Her daughter there recently gave birth to twins. Her son-in-law welcomed me as part of the community, and he treated us out to Asian food at a local mall.

My friend and I then caught a bus via Bnei Brak (a suburb of Tel Aviv, comparable to Mea Shearim in Jerusalem) to see her new abode in Safed. It's a quaint little place overlooking the Kinneret. She and her newlywed husband make a cute couple. Friday I awoke to the soothing sound of cooing doves on the balcony. For breakfast we had homemade challah, a little round loaf, served with fresh apricot jam and coffee. My friend's husband's daughter was thrilled to prepare a Shabbat meal for everyone.

So to give her kitchen space, I went with my friend and her husband to the traditional tomb associated with Hushai, loyal confidant of King David, a man who didn't go along with Absalom's rebellion, as recounted in 2 Samuel 15–17 (JPS). My friends said they sensed something spiritual there. We continued by car into Biryia Forest, to the site of a blue dome, where I joined with a busload of young *banot* (daughters) each circling and asking God for a righteous husband. As we headed back to the parking lot, an ice cream truck rang out the wordless tune of a popular Christmas jingle.

We drove to the old city of Safed and later walked back from the beit knesset, where we had participated in a welcoming of Shabbat service set to lively melodies. I've never seen a women's section so packed, and I joked with my friend about needing protective wear—goggles, hard hat and steel toes. (We used to work together in Canada at a safety organization.) The service was hard to follow with the strong Ashkenazi pronunciations, so I read in English at my own pace, the light being obscured by surrounding standing participants. As I waited outside for my friend and her husband, I watched Haredi pouring out into the narrow cobblestone alley, children dressed alike by families, boys with shaved heads and peyot.

Hungry, we rapidly walked back to my friends' apartment and enjoyed squash soup, nutty brown challah, purple basil salad, various spreads and dips, chickpeas and chick wings, meatballs and then elephant ear cookies and cherries for dessert. As guest I contributed a couple of bottles of Galil wine.

Shabbat morn, I read the parsha by the balcony door, the wind howling at this high altitude. There was a reminder to remember covenant with people and land. I recalled last night's mitzvah of a man beside the shul who invited us to light Shabbat candles, because we'd missed out while rushing out the door.

We arrived at my friends' home shul in time for musaf, the additional prayer service. There were windows looking out to the lake. Afterwards my friend walked with me to see the mikvah (natural immersion pool) in the forest by raspberry patches. We watched birds soar and then returned for lunch, again prepared by her husband's daughter. She topped it off with gourmet ice cream.

While others rested, I hiked to the old part of the city, receiving mixed directions from passersby: *lemala, lemata, lemala* (up, down, up)? There were so many *madregot* (stairs) to get to the tombs of ancient sages Isaac Luria (known for the mystical teachings of Kabbalah) and Joseph Karo (known for the code of law *Shulchan Aruch*). Along the way, I took notice of synagogues which dated back to the sixteenth century. Composer of the famous hymn "Lecha Dodi" ("Come My Beloved"), Solomon Alkabetz, used to join with his contemporaries outdoors in welcoming in the Sabbath as a bride. It rained again en route back, and children stared as I donned a blue poncho, keeping with the predominant colour scheme of Safed.

Back at the apartment, I browsed a children's book of 39 Shabbat "no work" stipulations and explanations. Key to understanding is the Hebrew word *melacha*, which encompasses creative endeavours. For our third meal, we partook of fish tacos. I expressed gratitude for all the scrumptious meals, as well as my hosts' delight in preparing them for us. I bade farewell to my friend and her husband, thanked them for the special Shabbat in Safed and took a direct bus to Jerusalem.

On Sunday, over breakfast at the hostel, I met a French-speaking Swiss man who greeted me with, "Shalom aleichem" ("Peace be upon you"). This day I went to see friends in a suburb of Jerusalem called Pisgat Ze'ev. However, the bus driver told me my card was not valid in Jerusalem. "Lama rak bachutz?" ("Why only outside?") With the assistance of a young female passenger, I went to the transit office to inquire. Take a ticket. Wait half an hour. Same response. Therefore I had to buy more local rides. Then I continued on my way to visit friends, who had a big spread prepared with other guests, mostly Ukrainian, including an eighty-four-year-old who looked in her forties! We listened to a Holocaust survivor play accordion and observed such a giving, kind family serving us around the table with pleasure. Later, I chatted with my friend by the balcony, and she spoke of trusting God to provide and guide. We hugged until we meet again.

An American friend who had also moved to that neighbourhood met me by my centrally located hostel, and we went for muffins and shakes on Ben Yehuda Street. We greeted local shopkeepers who welcomed me back with a big smile. I reconnected with a Ukrainian friend at Zion Square and saw some of the spectacular light show on Jaffa Road. My young friend broke into a dance with some youth and then waved to me with a smile from the back of her bus. Back at the hostel, I contacted a Canadian friend's son. He sounded kind and was open to meet in Jerusalem the following evening to see the rest of the festival of lights.

Late to bed and early to rise, I bade farewell to my Filipino roommates, then I headed off to find the bus stop at the main station. This one was easy: I got off at the centre of Neve Daniel and met a New York woman, who assured me there's a way things all work out. From the local store, I received a lift to the start of the trail of Derech Avot (Way of the Patriarchs).

The guard at the security gate gave me a contact number if there were any problems but did not anticipate any. Along the way were two Jews on bikes, one in a car, soldiers stationed by the ancient mikvah and in a military vehicle. It was a sunny day and peaceful, with birds singing. I saw vineyards, fig and olive trees atop a ridge with gardens below. I had a sense of personal contact with history—part of the original route between Hebron and Jerusalem, with a Roman road marker. The trail ended at Alon Shvut, with a lone oak tree up the road, a significant symbol for Gush Etzion in 1948.

Afterwards I rode to the parameter of nearby Kever Rachel. Outside the protective barrier along Bethlehem were male and female soldiers who talked with me in Hebrew, trying to find a driver who would take me to the tomb area. Rachel, who was initially childless, had her longing fulfilled—only to die in childbirth on the way, giving Jacob his twelfth of the tribe, the favourite Benjamin.

I caught a ride to the Har Homa junction and from there I took a bus back to Jerusalem via Hebron Road to the corner of King George and Ben Yehuda. My ulpan had moved to a new location; its director and administrator wished me mazel tov. My core teacher would not be back until later in the week. I relished walking along my favourite street, where I had an iced coffee from my favourite shop. Then I went by my old apartment on Shammai and along Hillel.

A journalist acquaintance was expecting me at his office, and he welcomed me home with a hug and some fatherly advice. He showed me his latest documentary, which shows what goes on behind the scenes. It counters false propaganda about Israel promoted by some mainstream media. After our meeting, I called my former film teacher, who readily remembered me. I shared my news of being Jewish, to which she readily responded, "Eze yoffi!" Maybe there will be a sequel to my documentary?

On a stone bench outside Jaffa Gate by sunset, blocked

in by bread vendors, I waited to meet my Canadian friend's son. We toured around the light displays, stopping by the colourful waterfall. We discussed a mutual interest in writing and photography. After stopping to pray at the Kotel, we had a bite to eat, and then he ensured I got back safely to my hostel. Before parting, he invited me to spend Shabbat on his yishuv, where he found a sweet elderly couple to host me. He also lined up various host families for meals.

The next day over breakfast, the elderly Swiss man was back and insisted on giving me a goodbye gift of a Hebrew-French text so I could better retain both languages. I thanked him and blessed his journey home. Then I caught a bus to another yishuv, where I visited with a Canadian friend recuperating at her daughter's place. Along the way, my bus passed by the traditional grave spot of the prophet Samuel. On arrival, my friend and I went outside in the fragrant yard. We shared another lechaim with grape juice and an appetizer of crackers and cheese. I met her little grandson, as well as his other grandmother from France. I picked some pitango berries from the tree out back. We said the bracha over new fruit together.

We went through Kedumim and Derech Avot pictures and highlights. She spoke tearfully of her love for her late husband and her love for the land. She did not blame God for bad things that happen. I blessed her to receive full healing restoration and sweet dreams. As she recommended, upon night return to Jerusalem, I walked through the shuk and looked at caricatures of famous Jewish figures, murals painted by the son of an artist she knows.

Week Three

In view of the spree of stabbings, this time for safety, I decided to revisit Hebron as part of an organized tour group. I was both curious and a bit sceptical of how overall the guide would present, in conjunction with the local counterpart.

Our Jewish guide, wearing peyot and tzitzit (knotted fringes as reminders of commandments), led us on public transit to the ancient city, and gave an introduction. Hebron comes from the root word for friend: chaver. He noted that Abraham was considered a friend of God, both in Jewish and Islamic cultures. Our guide's objective was to find a way to work together, despite the different narratives.

He explained that 80 percent of Hebron is under Palestinian Authority control (H1), and 20 percent is under the Israel Defense Forces; the majority of the tour would be in H2 region. The four holy cities are associated as follows: Hebron, earth; Tiberias, water; Safed, air; and Jerusalem, fire. The visionary Gush Emunin movement was instrumental during the 1970s in the return of Jewish community to historic Hebron.

Then in 1987, an intifada began with a tax revolt and stone throwing. Israel was forced to negotiate with her enemy, the Palestine Liberation Organization (PLO), which had been kicked out of Jordan, moved to Lebanon and later to Tunisia. Following the 1993 Oslo Accords, the name was changed to Palestinian Authority (PA), and they settled into the West Bank and Gaza. The Judea and Samaria region was broken into administrative areas: A, all PA; B, military IDF, civilian PA; C, all IDF. Hebron is under a separate agreement, designated H1 and H2.

What follows is a narrative according to our Muslim tour guide.

This handsome, well-dressed man told us he was friends with some Israelis but that it was not possible for him to have friendship with settlers. He took us inside the mosque section of the Cave of the Patriarchs, the place where Isaac and Rebecca were buried. There, an imam throne-like seat towered above two red and white striped huts. Our guide told us how grievously a Jewish settler in 1994 entered and killed twenty-nine Muslims while in their vulnerable prayer position. Dozens of others were wounded. Since that time, he resentfully related, soldiers could enter with boots on, watch them via camera access and even have the larger area and better view of the caves. In order for us non-Muslims to see the tombs, mosque personnel required us to wear pointed hood ponchos and to remove our shoes. When I asked the guide why Isaac was in this section since Ishmael is the one they uphold, he replied they also revere Isaac as a prophet. Ishmael by Islamic tradition is buried in Saudi Arabia.

This guide repeatedly conveyed the sentiment, "This is what we're always suffering," referring to security measures such as the gate turnstile. Concerning Israeli law, he said there's only to listen, because one can't say no. He lamented the inability to renovate old buildings, because they are required to be empty when military is stationed atop. Again and again was the "us versus them" mentality, fostering bitterness.

He introduced us to a shopkeeper who spoke with what sounded a mix of Arabic and British accent, and even thicker propaganda. Claiming the Israelis toss garbage and urine on them, he appealed, "Give us a chance to live in peace." He said, "They ignore us." But then he added, "We are strong. We are tough. This is our homeland." He questioned, "Are we animals?" He solicited the group's support, urging us to take pictures to show back home.

Inside the house of an Arab man who proudly refused to sell at any price his house to Jews, they served us Turkish coffee as we sat in a circle. The guide explained that in 3500 BC, Canaanites went from Gaza to Hebron, and he identified his people as such. Apparently he did not realize the implications according to the Torah! He did acknowledge that under the British Mandate, everyone was considered Palestinian. The new Israeli shekel (NIS) was introduced in 1985, replacing the earlier version. He correlated the term *Palestine* with Philistines, who had occupied Canaan centuries ago.

The Muslim guide admitted sixty-seven Jews were killed in the 1929 massacre, saying no one was proud of it but alluding to a story behind it, that the assailants were reacting to news of a purported threat. Though many Jews returned to Hebron in 1931, most were evacuated by the British between 1936 and 1939 during the time of the Arab revolts. Our guide related that Islam was against racism and killing. He called his grandfather a refugee from 1948, claiming a right of return. He showed us a map with Jewish settlements in the Hebron area, including Kiryat Arba. Over 700 settlers reside in Hebron. Yet he emphasized in a mocking tone that, despite an overwhelming Palestinian majority, there is a three to one ratio of soldiers to settlers for their protection. He went on to accuse settlers of not working but depending on government support, permitted to be armed. He contrasted a potential 10-year sentence for a Palestinian who throws one stone.

The familiar narrative continued, noting the first "settlement" and subsequent "occupation" as alleged proof that Israelis are not serious about wanting peace. The guide viewed the PA as helping Israel more than the Palestinians. This guide admitted to being anti-Zionist and proposed a one-state solution, under one government. It was a question of who rules, conveying it's a matter of time until Palestinians will have the larger population. When the American professor in our midst asked if he believed Jews have a right to exist, the guide conveniently dodged the question. In front of everyone, I brought it back, even summarizing for clarification what was his ideal scenario: rather than being under what he resented as Israeli control, he wanted an Islamic caliphate established. With a nervous grin, he also dodged my question and headed out the door.

At the kosher restaurant by the main entrance, I waited for our Jewish guide. There, another guide commended what our guide was doing, observing that many tours only present the other side. This way, tourists could also hear a Jewish perspective.

What follows is a narrative according to our Jewish tour guide.

The Cave of the Patriarchs is the oldest gravesite in continued use. Abraham purchased this burial place for his wife Sarah. Together here, Isaac and Ishmael buried their father. Under Muslim control, for 700 years Jews were allowed only outside up to the seventh step. Chief Rabbi with the IDF Shlomo Goren came and entered the cave in 1967, when those who call themselves Palestinians had already surrendered in fear of retribution for the 1929 massacre. Then in 1994, Dr. Baruch Goldstein's actions, condemned by the majority, led to separation between synagogue and mosque. A compromise was struck: for ten days each per year, during key Jewish and Muslim holidays, the area is accessible exclusively to that observant group.

Throughout Hebron, our Jewish guide pointed out memorial sites of slain babies and rabbis. Groupings of heavily armed and protected IDF soldiers were stationed at intervals. The Avraham Avinu Synagogue of 1540 was rebuilt decades after its desecration in 1948 under Jordanian control. We listened to the story from post 1967 of how a girl was lowered down through a narrow hole to explore, and tombs were discovered beneath the mosque section of the Cave of the Patriarchs. Year 1981 was the last the actual graves below the ancient caves were accessible, for when Muslim authorities realized the passageway up to the mosque, they sealed it off. In contrast, our guide opened up an ark containing reclaimed Torah scrolls in a reconstructed Sephardic shul, telling the story of a tearful man who was present for their dedication, being a Jew indigenous to the area. We paused at the yeshiva where studied one of the boys who were abducted and subsequently murdered the summer of 2014.

We walked along King David Street, named after the monarch who, prior to reigning from Jerusalem, had ruled from Hebron. We entered the historic Beit Hadassah, which now housed a museum dedicated to the memory of those whose lives were brutally taken in the 1929 massacre. For hundreds of years, Jews and Arabs had close bonds in Hebron under Ottoman rule. During the British Mandate, the Grand Mufti incited against the Jews, claiming a threat to Al-Aqsa mosque in Jerusalem. In reality, the Orthodox merely wanted to install a *mechitsah* (partition between men and women prayer sections) at the Kotel. Arabs heading for Jerusalem turned back at Gush Etzion and went after Hebron, slaying men, women and children. The museum displayed some of the weapons, along with graphic photos of the severely wounded. Some Jews were saved by Arabs, like the man attacked in the doorway stating, "Over my dead body." One British officer reportedly fired a shot in the air to disperse the crowd. In 1968, the first neighbourhood of Kiryat Arba was re-established in Judea and Samaria, on the outskirts of Hebron.

Inside Beit Hadassah, a local woman shared with our tour group gathered in a circle. She told of how her grandmother's life was spared thanks to the intervention by a courageous Arab man. She conveyed the sense of shock and betrayal by friends, noting that in 1929, there was no "excuse" of occupation. Her own father was heinously murdered. Our guide later pointed out the house where it happened. This local woman emphasized the long-standing Jewish presence in Hebron, citing archaeological evidence: a seal "to the King of Hebron." Recently there have been about fifty stabbing attacks on this street. Even she herself experienced a near miss, where a soldier intercepted her attacker. We were taken to the stairwell where other acts of terrorism occurred. Since the road has been closed off, stabbings have decreased. She concluded her talk, saying she welcomes those who want peaceable living, but if not, restrictions are needed.

As our Jewish guide was taking us around, another guide was obviously speaking exceptionally loud, as if to convey that what he had to say was of greater importance. Sadly, the couple he took around seemed to be lapping up his propaganda. Despite evidence, still our enemies deny proof.

We again paused at another spot at the top of a road: here took place an event for which a young Israeli soldier was to stand trial. Along our way, I made a point of encouraging, expressing thanks and respect to the Israeli soldiers. I also conveyed to our female speaker gratitude for her courage, and I let her know I had joined with her people. Hopefully on this trip, I too could be of some influence against the negative narrative.

That evening on return to Jerusalem, I paid another visit to my ulpan. There, I surprised my former teacher, conversing with her in Hebrew. She was encouraged over what I'd retained and affirmed my commitment to the Jewish community. I went on to Ben Yehuda Street, which featured some Jerusalem artists. Back at my hostel, I relaxed on a hammock, listening to a song on the radio. The words spoke of being time for a change, a new way to live. Is the next step aliyah?

The following morning, I ran into a British friend en route to a teaching centre, where some rabbis remembered me. The rabbi of Canadian origin smiled and said to me in Hebrew, "Pleased to meet you, Rivka Rut." His lesson was on Genesis 11, the Tower of Babel. Languages were confused, and the people dispersed because in arrogance, they tried to make a name for themselves. The rabbi noted the connection between the Hebrew word for *man* and for *fire*, both containing the same letters alef and shin, but with different vowel markings. Fire is associated with a creative act. The American rabbi noted that like it or not, you can't stop being who you are—Jewish. The matter, consequently, is what quality of life you want.

In between classes, I went through Hezekiah's Tunnels, immersing in the ancient underground waterway that flowed through the City of David. Earlier that morning, I tried to ascend the Temple Mount, to connect with that ancient part of history where Abraham offered up Isaac, but the officer at the security point, after establishing that I was Jewish, told me to come back later. At first I thought he was looking out for my safety. That afternoon I returned, but this time I was denied seemingly because of my uneaten lunch in my backpack. Even after I removed the food, the officer refused to let me up. I felt shocked and betrayed over this response. In contrast, earlier this morning a group of about ten women in Muslim garb were freely roaming around the Kotel, video recording bar mitzvah boys and women davening.

Elsewhere in the Jewish Quarter, I shared with a Canadian acquaintance the role his teaching had in the formation of my Jewish journey. In appreciation, I bought his book on the biblical Ruth. Then in view of what happened at the mount, I decided to tour an updated facility which houses reproduced instruments, garments and furnishings, ready for the advent of the Third Temple. The human and supernatural elements they saw as working together: we do our part in preparing components according to blueprints, and Hashem does His part when the time is right. There was a longing for the return of glory, God's manifest presence. A voice exclaimed from the male youth tour group, "We want Moshiach now!" I could not help but think of the contrast, of how I was denied access to the place which one day would be recognized as the place of prayer for all nations!

After chatting briefly with a friend in the Jewish Quarter's food court, I proceeded through the Kotel plaza and happened on a *tekes* (ceremony) about to begin: a Golani infantry induction. Earlier, I'd expressed respect toward a South African lone soldier I'd met from this unit. Still hearing the tune of their theme song, I walked to meet a retired army friend for cappuccino on Ben Yehuda Street. Like old times, we conversed in Hebrew, he using surroundings as a teaching tool. He was impressed I'd kept up the language, walked me back to my hostel, visited further in the lobby and wished me mazel tov over a cup of cola.

This weekend I felt sad I'd be booking out of my home base hostel. I walked via Shar Shechem to Lion's Gate, to a lookout point from the Mount of Olives, from where I could see more of the Temple Mount. I browsed the Old City shops en route Jaffa Road, stopping again at the Kotel. There appeared that same group of apparently Muslim women, again shooting video footage of Jewish women praying! I found this behaviour more suspicious, so I began obviously zooming in and snapping multiple photos of them. With that they left. (These pictures were subsequently submitted for security to review.) I went on to the post office, where the friendly guard remembered me. Then I did banking and more shopping in preparation for Shabbat.

A Beersheva-bound bus took me to the entrance of the yishuv, where my Canadian friend's son picked me up and brought me to my hosts, who had matching smiles. With them I felt very accepted. They even offered their phone number and welcomed me back. One of the meals this weekend was with a couple who, amongst other things, taught Christians about Jewish perspectives. After shul, we ate in the home of a new immigrant American couple, who also hosted a South African Canadian couple. I appreciated their gracious generosity. The third meal of Shabbat began at my hosts' home and progressed to a Sheva Brachot at a community hall, celebrating blessings with a newlywed Persian couple. Afterwards I was given a ride to a train station, from where I travelled to Tel Aviv. I appreciated the kindness of an Orthodox family who guided me to a bus stop that took me to my next hostel.

Sunday morning, upon exiting the hostel elevator, there was mutual recognition of a fellow volunteer from my first army base. This fellow from Italy and I travelled together to meet our coordinator at the designated spot. It was a reunion with some other familiar faces, one of whom was assigned the same medical base where we had served together during a previous operation. Our coordinator congratulated me on how far I've come since my first time volunteering. With that, we were off on another bus to home base. Here served our original "dream team" (as one Swiss volunteer called us), and here my dad had affirmed me as his lovely daughter over the phone. I proudly put on the uniform, this time having even more meaning as a Jew. I was disappointed my usual warehouse supervisor was not there this time, being on holiday, but I was glad to help out in another familiar supervisor's warehouse, where we also had much fun and a variety of tasks. Upon meeting an oleh from Australia, I was encouraged to learn I could still be an army volunteer if I made aliyah.

At Monday morning flag raising, we sang the national anthem. As a five-time veteran here, others sought my advice, and I showed them around, telling them about trenches and rockets. Our madricha took us to the canteen to buy cold, creamy glida. We walked past the huge wall mural painted by former volunteers. In Hebrew script it says, "We are with you" above the image of internationals standing hand to hand and spanning the width of the building. In today's news was a young fellow caught crossing a border, and intelligence uncovered from him information on another tunnel plot. The new commanding officer spoke with us at length during evening activity, telling of his background as a medic. He praised our important role in saving lives, ensuring supplies are in order. It was good to greet other military and civilian staff I knew from prior stays. Before retiring to my bunk, I enjoyed some warm quiet evening air, punctuated by chirping crickets.

Today we assembled field surgeon kits and paramedic bags, after the past couple of days of emptying packs of outdated supplies. Our supervisor's precision and pet names of products made work lively and interesting. We had a positive team spirit, working together with kindness, patience and humour. The evening activity was on berets and ranks. Today began a new month: Rosh Chodesh Sivan. Under sliver moon and stars at the barracks, the atmosphere was so soothing that it was hard to go inside to sleep, but then, 6:00 a.m. comes early.

Week Four

My barracks mates and I have bonded quickly, sharing similar views on Israel. Today I chatted with a newly observant Jewish friend. She offered to pray for me for a husband. After this evening's presentation on kibbutz life, we received our volunteer appreciation certificates. I thanked our leaders for all they do and are. They encouraged me to keep in touch.

Tonight, June 8, outside our barracks our madrichot conveyed breaking news of a terror attack in a Tel Aviv chocolate cafe. Four were gunned down by assailants in suits, and several others were left badly injured. This past weekend I had walked by this area. From our base we could hear sirens of ambulances.

This next day is Thursday, already our last on the base, so I took in my surroundings, recalling the memories as I walked around. I davened by the ditches, pausing again to reflect by the eucalyptus trees. This morning I raised the flag for my first time as a Jew. We presented appreciation papers to our madrichot, and I gave them little Canadian flag pins. Our team cleaned up, packed and then turned in our uniforms. We had one last meal together, boarded the bus and dispersed at the train station.

From there I had a long ride to Rothschild, with the driver initially not understanding my pronunciation: he corrected me to say, "Rot Cheeld." We went via Dizengoff, past Herzl and Allenby Streets in Tel Aviv. After checking into my hostel, I walked to the beach and enjoyed splashing in the waves until the sun began to set. Then I strolled the shore into Old Town Jaffa, enjoying an ice cream bar. The historic clock tower was covered up for renovations. Ramadan has started. I reached the port by sunset, the sliver moon under cloud.

I dipped my feet in the sea one more time before proceeding to my former army hostel. This time I paused outside, pondering hopeful memories, recalling my last conversations with Dad. I also remembered my first time here around a fountain with international comrades. En route back to my travellers' hostel for the night, I called and thanked our Israeli coordinator for her role, providing positive feedback of our group experience.

Friday morning, I took a short bus ride north to one of my favourite museums, the Palmach, where we received a soldier-guided tour. He told us this unit began in 1941, functioned as a striking force (against strategic places, not people), and disbanded after seven years. It was a self-sustaining army, training and working 50-50 on kibbutzim. Many lost their very young lives for their ideals. The room to room film series depicted real characters who served this country. The whole museum is interactive, addressing us as recruits and simulating forest, camp and rocky hiking ridge. The comrades were a close family, knowing all about one another. The Palmach helped during the siege by forging an alternative road, known as Burma, and bringing in crucial supplies. I had spotted remnants of this convoy displayed along the highway to Jerusalem. I tried to follow the Hebrew conversations while also listening to the English audio guide. Before leaving, I signed the guestbook, noting usually I am not so fond of museums, but this one's outstanding. The reception staff was visibly moved by our conversation, because I'd shared about Grandad being here with the British, and now I was here as part of the Jewish nation, serving on army bases.

Next stop was Independence Hall, which took on new meaning for me, especially as I looked at the microphones where the *kol* (voice) made the declaration, and I stood for the singing of "Hatikvah." Herzl Street was the original main thoroughfare of Tel Aviv, and I paused there to imagine how it looked back then. Upon returning to my travellers' hostel, I took a few minutes to write out a postcard. At checkout, I was pleasantly surprised to find my former ulpan classmate working at front desk. We exchanged greetings, then I walked to the station to catch an express bus back to Jerusalem.

Initially being aware of pre-Shabbat time constraints, I

rushed to buy some wine and challah, as well as cheese buns for Shavuot. But after a local fellow insisted I had more time, I made a last stop at the shuk, where I also bought some cherries and flowers for my hosting friend. By then caught up in the environment, I lost track of time—and missed the last bus! In the process of trying to find out if another route 18 was coming, I had a near miss of a car rushing by on the one-way street. In Hebrew, the number 18 represents life, and I was thankful I still had mine to celebrate this last Shabbat in Jerusalem. I had to take a taxi to arrive in time for candle lighting.

My host friend and I shared for breakfast a coffee, some fruit and a cheese bun, and then I headed along the shorter route she suggested into the city core. En route I noticed a pillbox from the British era and wondered whether Grandad had helped build or guard this tower. I arrived at shul, where I was given the honour of holding the Torah scroll up front, returning it to the ark. The rabbi's message exhorted us to be the change we want to see in others, noting everyone has a part to play. Before saying goodbye upon service ending, I expressed heartfelt thanks to the rabbi, for here in Jerusalem was my first time ever holding a Torah scroll. I mentioned I was considering making aliyah. He replied with a quote from Herzl, "If you will it, it is no dream." "Destiny is in your hands," he told me with a smile. With that, I pondered as I continued to walk into the Old City.

At the Kotel, I read the Torah portion and then joined with another rabbi and friends for Kiddush. En route his place for lunch, a friend from northern Israel emphasized it's Hashem's favour that opens the way to move here. A couple of other guests gave impacting messages: one that we were there and heard at Sinai, and another that we are made in His image; therefore no one is to kill—His presence is in us! A kohen friend heartily welcomed me back to Jerusalem, reminding me again to speak rak Ivrit (only Hebrew). I also received a warm greeting and hug from one of the rabbi's daughters, who is so much like her late mother. After the meal, I walked back to the Kotel for another Kiddush with a British friend.

There at the Kotel ended Shabbat and ushered in Shavuot. Crowds gathered. Our attention was briefly diverted as we heard and saw water falling from the Temple Mount pedway above. I continued reading the remaining Shabbat Psalms from 95 to100, and then I proceeded with Shavuot readings. They spoke of firstfruits offering, what to give and attention to the poor. I began my final counting of the Omer at the wall, today reaching the forty-ninth day.

As the sun was setting, a friend from the rabbi's walked with me. We stepped onto the rampart to catch a better view of the hillside of houses known as the City of David. Despite knowing the extra pretty lights were for the occasion of Ramadan, I took in the beauty. Then we continued to Mount Zion, where I anticipated an amazing time like I had back in Shavuot 5773.

Yet I wondered whether I'd be disappointed. My friend encouraged me to view each experience in its own right, without comparing it with others. Still, I held tonight up to the memories from before. Up on the mount, few campfires burned amongst the many tents. This time there were fewer people, and the tone was more subdued. Plain-clothes security roamed about with rifles. Nevertheless, a woman sweetly went about serving a tray of snacks. I met two older ladies seated waiting for the meal. Eventually a women's group gathered, and a white-garbed rebbetzin led a lesson speaking Hebrew, followed by a few wordless songs known as niguns. A man from Montreal came over and led us in Kiddush. I shared my bottle of sweet wine. There we ate matzah, in this atmosphere that welcomed newcomers. I recalled the angelic-faced young gal who taught me about the various food blessings my first Shavuot on Mount Zion.

Awhile later, I was beckoned by name by a familiar voice telling me that others from the rabbi's house had arrived, inviting me to join their table. We sat and listened to a young Israeli teach us on character traits, paraphrasing in fresh English from the Hebrew book in front of him. He urged us to focus on the task at hand, paying attention to the *how*, not just the *what*. He referenced the head, the heart and the liver. I recognized the lingual connection between the Hebrew root of the latter body part, and the words for heavy, glory and honour. I saw in this young man a sincere humility. We thanked our teacher and then walked as a group over to the synagogue named after Eliyahu haNavi (Elijah the Prophet). Here in this old Sephardic shul, a seasoned rabbi taught a series lasting until four in the morning. I barely lasted until 1:00 a.m., a friend nudging me a couple of times as I dozed off. What stood out were the titles of his books, calling Judaism a religion of love, and inviting one to let God in.

After about four hours of sleep at my hostel, I made the hike to my friend's neighbourhood, planning to accompany her for a reading of the scroll of Ruth. But I arrived to find no one home! As it turned out, she was called upon to assist in the saving of life. Under such circumstances, work is permitted on a Sabbath or Yom Tov. I turned around and aimed to make it to the Great Synagogue in time to hear the traditional Scriptures read. I arrived to hear the Ten Commandments, so fitting in this regal place. In walked a woman in a wide-brimmed hat, and I was happy to see the friend I'd been trying to reach by email. She responded to me by name and sat beside me. After service we walked to her place. What a case of mistaken identity, the material for a sitcom! Though not who at first I thought she was, she invited me into her quaint studio apartment for refreshments.

I walked back to the Kotel before heading to the rabbi's for my last time this trip. At this festive meal was a lesson on honour those present will never forget. Someone who was less than an ideal guest showed up. She invaded personal space. Her behaviour was loud and disruptive. Her appearance: unkempt hair, filthy attire and dirty bare feet. Other guests appeared uncomfortable at her presence, especially those whom she flicked with her fingers! Someone amongst the serving crew saw fit to escort her out. When someone announced how she was carrying on outside the door, the rabbi got up and proceeded to the door. I heard him comment, "No wonder," and then remarking, "She does not belong out there but inside with us." He invited her back in and showed her to a seat of honour by him at the head table! She did not carry a pleasant odour. The rabbi seemed only to notice she was a fellow human being with dignity, and he publicly affirmed her worth in front of us all. I looked over and noticed one of my friends choking up with tears. He realized that I noticed and commented, "Isn't this beautiful?"

When our host invited others to speak, I stood and thanked everyone for how much they have taught me, and told them how much I'd miss my mishpacha here. Upon receiving further rabbinic blessing, I headed past the table of three of my friends, who nodded as they finished thanking God for this meal together. Back at the Kotel where Breslov followers were rejoicing in dance the evening before, I read the rest of the book of Ruth, our model for Shavuot.

After sunset on this festival, Ben Yehuda Street again sprang to life, and I took in its night life before catching a bus back to my friend's place where I'd been staying. There with her housemate, I quickly prepared a birthday surprise. Shaped like a slice of cake, I stuck a candle in a piece of cheese. We sang to her and gave gifts. It was a girls' last late night for me there.

Ready and packed, we drove and parked to catch a shuttle to the Kotel, where we arrived just in time for her friends' son's bar mitzvah. How fitting this day after Shavuot! In reference to my being denied access to the Temple Mount, my friend by the ramp entry exclaimed between us that when Moshiach comes, we'll have the grand tour. Back at the historic train station, I treated my friend to a birthday brunch of shakshuka (pan of spiced tomato and egg), served with a basket of bread. We eagerly discussed aliyah. Back at her apartment, we had a few more laughs. I took one last look around where I used to live, and then I headed off as my friend left for work, waving with a smile from her car. The local grocer and his family sent me off with smiles and blessings. Again I caught bus 18 to the centre of town.

My last hours were spent on Ben Yehuda Street, having mango passion ice cream with friends, one of whom called herself a born-again Jew. We exchanged hugs goodbye. I lingered on, reviewing some Hebrew as I sat where I used to sit after ulpan. I didn't want to leave again, but sadly I made my way, leaving a last gift with an elderly woman playing music she said was for God's glory.

From the top of Ben Yehuda at King George Street, I boarded a bus to the train station, luggage in tow. The journey was longer than expected due to construction. They took cash only for the ticket. I got off at Lod, and a kind man led me to the taxi depot outside the station. It turned out the remaining ride to the airport would cost more than I had in cash, and they did not accept credit cards. Seeing that I was stuck, that kind man readily handed me the shekels needed. Hand over heart, I deeply thanked him, and I arrived on time for my flight.

After checking in through the express machine, still I had to join others in a long, winding line. Someone commented that with such post-Shavuot crowds, the flights would likely be delayed. They would not leave without us. While waiting, I conversed with others in line and chatted over the phone with an army buddy. I had to discontinue our talk when security came to me in line. For the first time since my first time in Israel, I had the least amount of questioning and searching ever! They respectfully inspected and returned the rolled gift painting from a friend. At the boarding area, we waited in another line, and by then I was really tired. I fought to stay awake until we were off the runway, to watch the last of the visible night lights over Tel Aviv's shore.

Postscript

Judaism takes the commandments of our Creator so seriously that over the centuries, fence laws were set in place to prevent even going near that which God forbids. Now in some instances, I personally find some have gone unnecessarily too far, perhaps even losing sight of the original intent of the law. However, consider the prohibition against adultery. Most other people would hopefully agree such behaviour is detrimental to families and society. Is it enough to merely avoid outright blatant sin? Or is it not wise to not even put oneself in a position where he or she may be tempted along the slippery slope? Do we trust our Commander of the heavenly armies that He truly has our best interest at heart?

None of us has the full picture, the capital on truth, whether Jewish or from amongst the nations. That's why we benefit from being humble enough to learn from one another. Personally, I have gained much insight and growth through friendships built across the full spectrum of Jewish expressions. We may not agree on all points, but there is something of value in each one. I'd like to include here a couple of quotations from a well-known and respected rabbi, Zalman Schachter-Shalomi (z"l), of Orthodox background, who recognized and embraced the larger Jewish community.

> The words of Yeshua of Nazareth, after all, are the teachings of a rebbe to his Hasidim, all of whom lived and died as Jews. He meant them as a midrash, or commentary, on Torah. (*Jewish with Feeling*, 206)

> We have some Jews today whose souls have been touched by the gospels [good news],

wonderful searching spirits who have felt the need to become Hasidim of the Nazarene Rebbe and to follow the midrash of the Gospels. These Jews, too, are God-wrestling. I believe that we should regard them with an expanded sense of *ahavat Yisrael*, love of Israel, and that ostracizing them is wrong. (*Jewish with Feeling*, 213)

Yes, Israel and the diaspora Jewish community fall short of being the light to the nations we were intended to be. Yet I have this inexplicable drawing—for better or for worse—like a wedding pledge. As Ruth of the Bible, I am now joined in covenant with God and with the Jewish nation. Your God is my God, and your people are my people.

Conclusion: Honeymoon (2017)

Goldbergs' Mazel Tov

A fortieth anniversary reunified Jerusalem commemorative keychain became our link. Following my 2016 trip to Israel, now officially as a Jew, I sought God for a husband with whom to build a Jewish home. Shortly thereafter, a mutual Israeli friend offered to introduce me to an American man who shared the qualities I desired in a spouse. We began corresponding through email, and by Sukkot he drove up to Canada to meet me for the first time. I showed him around my home turf and received positive feedback from my inner circle. We connected as soul mates; our friend became our matchmaker. By Pesach we were engaged to be married before Sukkot 2017.

In the heart of Toronto's Jewish community, we had a beautiful wedding under a chuppah. Our ceremony carried, by our design, significant meaning. Similarly to my rabbi's place in Jerusalem, guests represented a wide array of both Christian and Jewish expressions. Everyone respected one another and exuberantly entered into the simcha of our occasion.

Later that night, we departed for our honeymoon in Israel. That keychain, that I had earlier discovered, was hanging in what would become our new home together in South Dakota. I recognized it was the same one I had received during my first trip to Israel. My future husband and I were actually at the same event, the Jerusalem March, yet we did not knowingly cross paths! It took a matchmaker from Israel to bring together this American and Canadian marriage.

In the early hours of September 18, we boarded our flight, still wearing our wedding attire, and were warmly received by fellow passengers frequently greeting us with, "Mazel tov!" At different intervals, we had people davening all around us. I enjoyed having Hebrew conversations with others aboard.

Our route was rather circuitous, so we had to rush to make our tight connections. We sat bolt upright in the last row and so did not get much sleep. Nevertheless, I was too excited. Now I was Mrs. Goldberg, and we were spending our first days of married life in Israel! We landed in Tel Aviv and, before settling into our reserved hotel, posed as bride and groom in the Mediterranean. I found a Russian woman in a yellow bikini who gladly took our pictures on my mobile phone. My wedding dress gained an extra train comprised of surrounding white waves.

Later on our honeymoon, we enjoyed wading in the ocean and a romantic promenade through Jaffa by sunset. We toured a diamond factory, looking at refined natural wonders. We passed along Rothschild Boulevard, taking notice of the building where Israel was declared reborn as a nation. We spent the last night of our honeymoon in Tel Aviv, sharing a sweet bottle of pomegranate wine.

But let's go back to Efrat, where on our first day in the land, a Canadian Israeli friend hosted us to a special Sheva Brachot (literally: seven blessings) dinner. Jewish tradition invites family and friends to celebrate a full week with bride and groom, taking care of meals, so the couple can focus on getting to know each other. For us, it was a joy to include in this way friends who were unable to attend our wedding abroad in Canada.

The next day, an American Israeli friend hosted us for brunch at her place in Jerusalem. In advance of our trip, she had offered for us to stay there over Rosh Hashanah. We walked from her abode and were able to share in another New Year feast with additional friends hosted by a local rabbi.

There, we received a kohen's blessings, surrounded by guests shouting with smiles, "Amen!" While pausing in the Jewish Quarter and looking toward the Mount of Olives, my husband blew his new shofar.

Our first Shabbat as husband and wife, we drank from our new Kiddush cup. For that weekend, we had booked a private room at a historic post office turned hostel. Saturday morn at synagogue, we received our first aliyah as a married couple called to the front, saying blessings over the Torah reading.

Later on in Jerusalem, while staying at another centrally located hostel, we fasted for Yom Kippur. Afterwards we headed over to our American Israeli friend's place to help her set up her sukkah. In preparation for Sukkot, the week-long festival of commanded joy, we went shopping for our lulav and etrog near the shuk. We stayed at another quaint hotel, this time off Ben Yehuda Street, and built our own sukkah on our balcony. Hearing jazzy saxophone and exquisite violin playing outside our window added to our honeymoon ambience. Earlier one evening, we went downstairs into the street, joining dancers who were heartily singing, "Chag sameach!" wishing everyone a joyful holiday. Another highlight in Jerusalem was wading with my newlywed husband in the Gihon Spring, which flows into the Pool of Siloam in the City of David.

North and west of Jerusalem is Haifa, where my husband had picked out another place online for us to stay by the beach. We were surprised to find no one swimming as we approached the shore. We went ahead—and found ourselves laughing as we were tossed ashore like ragdolls. Next day, we learned the beach to go to was on the other side; there, we joined with many Russian-speaking swimmers. Fish began nipping at our heels in these much calmer waters. Our time in Haifa included ascending Mount Carmel, entering what is known as the prophet Elijah's cave.

Back east, and a bit farther north, is the mystical city of Safed, where the colour blue abounds. A Canadian friend who had recently made aliyah was living there with her newlywed husband. These new olim were delighted to host us for a weekend at their place overlooking the Kinneret. We walked to synagogue together, took delight in the Sabbath and entered our first post-marital mikvah in the land here.

An even more ancient city is Jericho, heading in the direction of the Dead Sea. As a couple we rode a cable car for a view over the archaeological ruins adjacent to the more modern buildings. Nearby, we took a dip in what is called the prophet Elisha's Spring.

Over at the Dead Sea, we looked forward to a relaxing float in the silky salt water. But right after disembarking from the public bus, I suddenly realized my mobile phone was not amongst our belongings. Oh, no! I had taken it out to look up something online, and I realized it must have fallen between the seats. All our contacts were in this device. Now what? What chance did we have of recovering it? Before we even made our way over to a nearby hotel lobby to make a call to the bus company, there it was—our bus! It had circled back on its route, so I flagged it down. The driver stopped and let me aboard to search, and sure enough, there it was embedded between two seats. Baruch Hashem! Now we could truly relax at peace on the shallow, warm sea.

My husband had arranged a couple more special places for us to enjoy our honeymoon. One was a camel ranch in the Negev. We took a two-hour caravan trek through dry valleys and over desert mountains. In the common kitchen, we prepared our first cooked meal together as newlyweds. We ate on a mat in the sand, and we slept in a tiny hut.

Way down through the Negev, at the southern tip of Israel, is Eilat. There by the Red Sea, my husband eagerly anticipated our extended stay in a romantic guesthouse, where our room had an en suite hot tub. From our balcony, we had a view of the night lights over the sea. By day we went snorkelling near the shore, catching glimpses of an array of yellow, purple and blue tropical fish. By the time we emerged, I had a burning rash along my belly, which was soothed by natural aloe plant. Farther along the shore, another day we experienced up close diving dolphins.

These were the highlights, by geographical region, of the last time I set foot in the Land of Israel. Not only have I previously had a taste of Israeli life as a single woman, walking into deeper identity with the Jewish nation, but now I am married to a Jewish believer and am learning how to live in a pioneering tiny Jewish community in the United States. I remain a Canadian citizen and look forward to future visits with my Toronto home community—and of course with our larger mishpacha in the biblical land of promise.

Afterword

Early on in life, I caught the travel bug. It was partly inherited by my maternal grandmother, who, despite not being wealthy, worked hard and saved up so she could go explore faraway places. She would give me a taste of where she'd been, showing me slides through the handheld viewfinder. That was quite impressive back then, giving me a window into virtual reality.

My father also taught me to appreciate hands-on learning. He was a schoolteacher from my first ability to remember until my mid-teens, and he had summers off to take the family travelling. We camped across much of Canada and the United States, especially favouring the west. Dad kept a record of his observations, talking into a tape recorder as we went along. One could say I was unconsciously mentored to become an adept storyteller. His father also captivated our attention during visits as he recounted interesting tidbits of life. Therefore it's in me to paint pictures through words.

As a young adult living on my own, I adopted a simple lifestyle. Instead of spending money on home furnishings and gadgets, I put greater value on saving up to go places in the world. And four- or five-star hotels aren't really my style. Yes, I like to do some of the main tourist attractions, but I like to go beyond, off the beaten track, to find out about how the local people live.

If I have only a short time to explore, here's my strategy for capturing the cultural essence. I check out websites to see what the options are. Then I narrow down what are the most famous sites, which ones most interest me. I rise early from a trustworthy travellers' hostel and venture out to the spots that are open only during business hours. Some buildings I'm satisfied to see from the outside and shoot a few pictures, so these I leave until later (unless en route). To keep nourished on my low-budget trek, I eat the usual hostel complimentary breakfast, and I stop by a grocer's for lunch items to go. By nightfall, once I've covered enough territory, I may stop into a local pub or cafe for a simple hot meal. Before retiring for the night back at the hostel, I do a daily photo review, deleting duds and keeping the best expressions or exposures of duplicates. That way I can recharge batteries while I jot down several of the day's highlights—adventures that were not depicted in pictures.

The key to enjoyable travel, in my opinion, is travelling light. Mix and match a few interchangeable, multipurpose outfits. A knapsack works best for varied terrain and keeps your back in good shape, evenly redistributing and making the weight feel lighter. It also keeps your hands free, which is necessary for focusing with a DSLR camera—and holding on when climbing or riding public transit! Although luggage on wheels with pull handles are a handy invention, not only do they pose a danger to people walking behind their owners, but their wheels don't fare so well bumping over ancient cobblestone and stone steps or schlepping through desert sand! You've got to be practical to really enjoy exploring new adventures on foot.

Having travelled fairly extensively outside of North America, as of 2020, I can say I've been to England, Scotland, Wales, France, Germany, the Czech Republic, Poland, Italy, Greece, Cuba, Brazil, Jordan (Petra), Egypt (Mount Sinai) and Israel. By far my favourite country outside of Canada is Israel, where I have returned several times since my first visit in 2007.

Decorated Beach Camel

Shofar Silhouette, Mount of Olives

Western Wall Blocks

Fig Tree Branch

Six-Point Pomegranate

Rudimentary Rusted Rockets

Watchful Perched Dove

Aromatic Incense Bowls

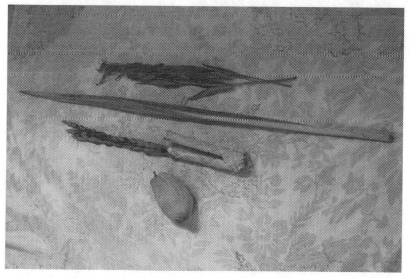

Lulav Ensemble, Four Species

Tallit Duo Walking

References

Books

Chayat, Shlomit; Israeli, Sarah; and Kobliner, Hila. *Hebrew from Scratch*, parts I and II (Alef + Bet level ulpan texts). Jerusalem: Academon (Hebrew University), 2012 and 2013.

Jungreis, Rebbetzin Esther (z"l). *The Committed Marriage: A Guide to Finding a Soul Mate and Building a Relationship Through Timeless Biblical Wisdom.* New York: HarperOne, 2002.

Olivestone, David, ed. *The NCSY Bencher: A Book of Prayer and Song.* New York: Rothman Foundation, 2012.

Schachter-Shalomi, Rabbi Zalman (z"l), and Segel, Joel. *Jewish with Feeling: A Guide to Meaningful Jewish Practice.* New York: Riverhead, 2006.

Websites

alittlehebrew.com/transliterate: Applied prevalent Sephardi spelling, or occasional personal phonetic rendering. For example: כ chaf / chet ח (sounds like blowing air over tonsils without using vocal cords), tsade צ (pronounced like zz in *pizza*).

biblehub.com: JPS (Jewish Publication Society), KJV (King James Version), NASB (New American Standard Bible) and NIV (New International Version).

Tanakh: Acronym for Torah (first five books: Bereshit, Shemot, Vayikra, Bamidbar, Devarim), Nevi'im (prophets) and Ketuvim (writings) comprising the Hebrew Bible; cf. Brit Chadashah (New Covenant).

Hashem: Literally, the Name (a reverential third-party reference to God).

Hebrew (lunar) or Gregorian (solar) calendar: The year 5770 corresponds roughly to 2010, although Jewish Rosh Hashanah occurs in the fall, whereas the Catholic New Year begins January 1. Also, BCE/CE ("common era") refers to the same timeframe as BC/AD (pivotal around the arrival of Christ in world history). A Jewish day begins the evening before at sunset. The Hebrew calendar is believed to start at creation.

merriam-webster.com: First mention of Israeli terms in italics (if not listed in dictionary). Unique Canadian spellings retained to reflect author's heritage (e.g. honour, traveller, centre).

translate.google.com: Employed as aid with transliteration tool.

wikipedia.org: Used for comparison during editing process. Most knowledge learned via tour guides, museums, or local people.

Printed in the United States
by Baker & Taylor Publisher Services